MW00389915

THE ULTIMATE
SLOW COOKER
COOKBOOK

THE ULTIMATE SLOW COOKER COOKBOOK

NO-FUSS RECIPES FOR CLASSIC DISHES & NEW FAVORITES

EDITED BY LINDA LARSEN

ROCKRIDGE
PRESS

Copyright © 2020 by Rockridge Press, Emeryville, California

No part of this publication may be reproduced, stored in a retrieval system, or transmitted in any form or by any means, electronic, mechanical, photocopying, recording, scanning, or otherwise, except as permitted under Sections 107 or 108 of the 1976 United States Copyright Act, without the prior written permission of the Publisher. Requests to the Publisher for permission should be addressed to the Permissions Department, Rockridge Press, 6005 Shellmound Street, Suite 175, Emeryville, CA 94608.

Limit of Liability/Disclaimer of Warranty: The Publisher and the author make no representations or warranties with respect to the accuracy or completeness of the contents of this work and specifically disclaim all warranties, including without limitation warranties of fitness for a particular purpose. No warranty may be created or extended by sales or promotional materials. The advice and strategies contained herein may not be suitable for every situation. This work is sold with the understanding that the Publisher is not engaged in rendering medical, legal, or other professional advice or services. If professional assistance is required, the services of a competent professional person should be sought. Neither the Publisher nor the author shall be liable for damages arising herefrom. The fact that an individual, organization, or website is referred to in this work as a citation and/or potential source of further information does not mean that the author or the Publisher endorses the information the individual, organization, or website may provide or recommendations they/it may make. Further, readers should be aware that websites listed in this work may have changed or disappeared between when this work was written and when it is read.

For general information on our other products and services or to obtain technical support, please contact our Customer Care Department within the United States at (866) 744-2665, or outside the United States at (510) 253-0500.

Rockridge Press publishes its books in a variety of electronic and print formats. Some content that appears in print may not be available in electronic books, and vice versa.

TRADEMARKS: Rockridge Press and the Rockridge Press logo are trademarks or registered trademarks of Callisto Media Inc. and/or its affiliates, in the United States and other countries, and may not be used without written permission. All other trademarks are the property of their respective owners. Rockridge Press is not associated with any product or vendor mentioned in this book.

Interior & Cover Designer: Karmen Lizzul
Art Producer: Hannah Dickerson
Editor: Cecily McAndrews
Production Editor: Matthew Burnett

Photography © 2020 Annie Martin; food styling by Craig Murli, pp. ii, vi, 32, 72, 110, 124, 144, 148, 152, 188, 216, 290, 294; © Marija Vidal, pp. x, 52, 116, 184, 270, 272, 274; © Monica Buck, p. 10; © Darren Muir, pp. 24, 48, 59, 90, 248, 254; © Antonis Achilleos, p. 47; © Elysa Weitala, p. 71; © Hélène Dujardin, pp. 76, 198; © Andrew Purcell, p. 220; © Evi Abeler, p. 260. Author photograph courtesy of Picture This Northfield

ISBN: Print 978-1-64611-741-3
eBook 978-1-64611-742-0

R0

I dedicate this book to my dear husband,
Doug, who happily eats anything I cook,
and to my mom and dad for supporting me
in every endeavor.

CONTENTS

INTRODUCTION

I bought my first slow cooker more than 30 years ago. It was a very simple model with a three-quart capacity and a dial on the front that read "High," "Low," and "Off." I used that slow cooker for years, happily experimenting with stews, roasts, casseroles, rice puddings, and side dishes. As the slow cooker market expanded and manufacturers started adding new features, I branched out. I bought a bigger slow cooker in an oval shape to handle roasts. I was intrigued by programmable cooking functions and bought a fancy variety to use when entertaining. That led me to slow cookers that could link together for serving at buffets. And I admit that I have fallen for some beautiful slow cookers with fancy designs and colors on the casing.

But they all work the same despite the difference in sophistication and cost. The low and slow cooking method really produces great food with very little effort. The types of recipes I prefer have very little prep time, can be prepared ahead, use inexpensive ingredients, and have just a few shortcuts. In fact, the cheaper the cut of meat, the better the result in the slow cooker! Chopping an onion and peeling a couple of carrots is the work of minutes. You just put everything into the slow cooker, give it a stir, and turn it on.

Let's face it: We seem to have less and less time to relax with our families these days. We're working longer hours, have longer commutes, and are usually exhausted when we get home. The last thing anyone wants to do is spend an hour or two cooking dinner in the evening. That's where the slow cooker saves the day. It's so nice to come home to a house that smells amazing because you cooked your grandmother's famous beef stew in the slow cooker. All you have to do is dish it up and dig in.

This is the eighth book I have written about slow cookers. And I could easily write a dozen more! This versatile appliance turns hefty, inexpensive cuts of meat into tender and succulent roasts. Large, tough carrots become meltingly soft with incredible flavor. Did you know you can bake a cake or even bread in a slow cooker? With the exception of adding grill marks or making French fries, there's very little that a slow cooker can't do.

And the food you make in your slow cooker doesn't have to be boring despite what some critics claim. Why not make a Spicy Coconut and Shrimp Chowder (page 93)? Or how about delicious Pulled Pork (page 186) you can use in enchiladas? Tangy Beef Short Ribs (page 230) make for an excellent warming dinner for a cold winter night. Chicken Saltimbocca from Italy (page 173) is a satisfying chicken dish. Cuban Picadillo (page 253), Chili Verde (page 95), and even Crème Brûlée (page 291) can also be made in this wonderful appliance.

So, now that I have your attention, let's learn a bit about the slow cooker and get advice for using it to its full capacity. An adventure awaits!

Almond Berry Coconut Granola,
page 12

CHAPTER 1

SLOW-COOKING BASICS

The slow cooker has long been an indispensable part of kitchens around the world. This appliance can turn a handful of ingredients into a delicious and healthy meal. It cooks all day by itself, so you can come home to dinner that is ready when you are. The best part about the slow cooker is it does all the work!

This book will cover just about every recipe you can think of and offers tips and tricks to get the most out of this appliance. You'll learn how the appliance works, the best foods to cook in it, and how to make sure that everything you cook turns out tender and flavorful. Let's get started!

Get to Know Your Slow Cooker

The slow cooker is a pretty simple appliance. The outer casing holds the heating element, which evenly transfers heat to the thick ceramic insert (or crock) that gently heats the food. The food simmers, steams, and cooks slowly for hours. One of the most important parts of a slow cooker is the lid. The lid sits in a small trough in the ceramic insert, which forms a seal. The seal keeps steam and moisture in the ceramic insert, so the heat stays constant and the flavor compounds don't escape. There are many brands, sizes, and types of slow cookers on the market. Here's what you'll need to know when selecting the slow cooker that is right for you.

The Many Sizes and Shapes of Slow Cookers

Slow cookers on the market range from one to eight quarts. The one you'll want to buy will depend on the size of your family and the quantity you like to cook. This book will offer recipes for all sizes of slow cookers with just a few adjustments in ingredient amounts.

Slow cookers also vary in the type of controls they have. The simplest has a dial with "High," "Low," and "Off" settings. Some slow cookers also have a "Keep Warm" function that will keep food warm for up to two hours after it's done cooking. The most complicated slow cookers have programmable functions that let you delay cooking time, preset cooking modes, and customizable time and temperature settings.

Slow cookers also come in different shapes. Most are round, but some are oval, which makes it easier to cook a whole chicken or beef roast. If you want to cook large chunks of meat, think about buying an oval slow cooker.

Whatever size and shape you buy, it's important to know that, for best results, every slow cooker should be filled one-half to two-thirds full. If there isn't enough food in the slow cooker, it will burn; if the appliance is overfilled, the food may not cook through, or the slow cooker may actually overflow since liquid doesn't evaporate as the food cooks.

Making Slow Cooker Recipes in a Multicooker

A multicooker (the Instant Pot is the best-known brand) is a completely different appliance than a slow cooker. Not only does it perform the function of a slow cooker, but it can also pressure cook and even act as a rice cooker, steamer, and yogurt maker.

The sizes of a multicooker compare to slow cooker sizes on the market, although the smallest are usually around three quarts. They are also comparable in cost. Think about what foods you cook in the kitchen. If you like to make yogurt and pressure cook, consider buying a multicooker. If all you want is food that cooks all day and is ready to eat when you get home, a slow cooker is just fine.

5 THINGS YOU DIDN'T KNOW ABOUT YOUR SLOW COOKER

1. Slow cookers have been around since 1940. The inventor of this wonder appliance, Irving Nachumsohn, developed it so his family could eat hot food on the Jewish Sabbath, when doing any type of work, including cooking, is forbidden.

2. Did you know that you can use the slow cooker ceramic insert in the oven? Some models even say it's microwave safe (read your instruction manual!). But don't use it on the stovetop because it will crack and you'll have a potentially dangerous mess on your hands.

3. Have you ever had candy made in the slow cooker? **The low and slow heat is ideal for melting chocolate.** Melt some milk or dark chocolate for about an hour, add ingredients like nuts or coconut, and drop the mixture onto wax paper to cool. You can also roast nuts or make candied nuts in the slow cooker. And use your slow cooker to make dessert! With just a little adjustment, you can make fabulous cakes, brownies, and cheesecake in this appliance. There's a whole chapter of desserts in this book (see page 273).

4. Cleaning the slow cooker is a breeze. If any food is stuck on the insert, add water and turn the slow cooker to high for an hour or two, and the stuck food should lift right off.

5. The slow cooker really became popular in the 1970s when women entered the workforce and didn't want to have to cook a full meal after work. In fact, the first marketing campaign for this appliance was aimed at working women.

Using Your Slow Cooker Safely

The slow cooker is a very safe appliance. However, since it heats up and uses electricity, there are some rules you must follow.

If your machine is older or if you bought it at a garage or estate sale, have it checked by an electrician to make sure the cord is still in good shape. If the cord is frayed, do not use it; get it repaired first.

The slow cooker should be placed on a heatproof surface (I once ruined a Formica countertop by using a slow cooker on it). I like to use the smooth cooktop on my stove, or you can put it on a sturdy, large trivet. Don't put the slow cooker under low cabinets, and keep it away from anything flammable, like cooking oils or cooking sprays.

TO BROWN OR NOT TO BROWN?

Browning meat isn't necessary when you're using a slow cooker, with one exception.

Ground meats need to be browned in a saucepan before you add them to the slow cooker. If you don't do this, the recipe will be too fatty, and the ground meat will be unpleasantly mushy. Thoroughly brown ground beef, lamb, sausage, pork, chicken, and turkey in a pan on the stovetop, stirring it with a fork while it cooks to break it up. Drain the meat and add it to the slow cooker. You can do this the night before if the ground meat is completely cooked. Store it in the refrigerator until you're ready to slow cook.

Browning adds great flavor and color to the food. If you want to brown meat before you slow cook it, sprinkle it with a bit of salt, pepper, and flour, and brown it in a pan on the stovetop with some butter or oil. Do not do this ahead of time; if you do, the meat will go through the danger zone of rapid bacterial growth (40°F to 140°F) too many times.

You could also try a reverse sear. If you're cooking a roast, just pop it into the slow cooker on top of veggies, add seasonings, and cook it. When it's done, carefully remove the roast and broil it in the oven or sear it in a pan on the stovetop to add that great browned crust.

Keep kids and curious pets away from the slow cooker. Although it does cook at lower temperatures, the outer metal casing gets very hot and can cause burns. Also, don't use an extension cord with this appliance. The cord on the slow cooker is short for a reason; you don't want to trip over the cord and spill hot food everywhere.

Food safety is an issue anytime you cook meats, poultry, eggs, and sea-food. Foods should be heated to the right temperature (140°F) as quickly as possible since, at room temperature, pathogenic bacteria can double in volume every 20 minutes. The danger zone for food poisoning is 40°F to 140°F. Food should get over 140°F ASAP, so avoid putting a big chunk of frozen beef in the slow cooker; instead, thaw it in the refrigerator overnight before you start cooking. And don't leave cooked food in a turned-off slow cooker for more than two hours. After that point, it must be refrigerated.

When you're cooking, avoid cross-contamination. In other words, keep raw beef, pork, lamb, poultry, fish, and eggs away from foods that are eaten uncooked because dangerous bacteria can transfer to the raw foods. Use sep-arate cutting boards for meats, veggies, and fruits, and wash your hands with soap and water after you prepare meats.

Low Versus High Temperatures

Most slow cookers have two settings: high and low. In older models, the low setting cooked the food at about 185°F. That seems low until you learn that chicken must reach 165°F before it's safe to eat. In today's slow cookers, the low setting is about 200°F. The high setting used to be just above 200°F, but now it is set at 300°F. That means that older recipes need to cook for a shorter time period. Please note that newer recipes, like the ones in this book, are developed for the new hotter slow cookers.

The difference in temperature between low and high means that you can extend the cooking time of some recipes. The general rule is for every hour you cook a recipe on high, you can cook it for two hours on low. But if you have a new hotter slow cooker, stay at home the first time you use it to see how it works. If the food starts overcooking or burning before the time is up, you'll need to adjust the cooking time.

8 WAYS TO COOK SLOW LIKE A PRO

Slow-cooked food tastes so good because the long cooking time allows flavors to develop and blend. Vegetables become sweeter, fruits caramelize, and meats become tender and succulent. As a bonus, flavor compounds that would otherwise escape in steam are held inside the appliance and flavor the food. As easy as it is to use a slow cooker, here are some special strategies that will make your food taste even better and make cooking easier.

1. Prep your ingredients in advance. If you're making a stew, start prepping the ingredients the night before. You can peel and chop onions and carrots and mince garlic. Don't brown the meat ahead of time, however, because it can be dangerous unless it's fully cooked. But you can precut your meat so it's ready to cook the next morning. Measure out seasonings and put them into a baggie. Make sure you have broth or stock on hand. Refrigerate everything until morning.

2. Layer food as called for in the recipe. Root vegetables generally take more time to cook than meats, so they're usually put in the bottom of the slow cooker, while meats go on top. And that is another bonus: Meat juices will drip onto the veggies as the food cooks, adding even more flavor!

3. Let the slow cooker do its job. For the best results, don't lift the lid at all while the food is cooking. Every time you lift the lid to check on the food, you'll need to add another 20 minutes to the total cooking time. Also, lifting the lid releases those valuable flavor compounds into the air! You can twirl or gently shake the lid while it's seated on the slow cooker insert to remove condensation and see inside, but avoid breaking the seal.

4. Understand doneness. Different foods have different doneness tests. Keep cooking until the appropriate temperatures and conditions are reached. Meats are done when they reach a safe temperature: 145°F for cuts of beef, lamb, and pork; 165°F for chicken and turkey, including ground poultry; and 160°F for all other ground meats. Eggs should be cooked to 160°F and fish and shellfish to 145°F. Vegetables and fruits should be tender when you test them with a fork. If the food isn't done, cover the slow cooker, cook for another 20 to 30 minutes and then test it again.

5. Season food correctly. The flavor of herbs and spices tends to become muted after long cooking times. Refresh the food before you eat it by adding a bit more of the seasonings you used at the start of cooking. Or chop some fresh herbs and sprinkle them over the food before you serve it. Foods should be salted before cooking to bring out the flavor.

6. Use the slow cooker to make a fabulous sauce. All of the flavor from cooking will be in the liquid remaining in the slow cooker when you remove the food. All you have to do is thicken it. The easiest way to do this is to make a slurry of flour or cornstarch and a bit of water. Use one tablespoon of flour for each cup of liquid. Remove the food, put it in a serving dish, and cover it. Put the liquid and the slurry in a saucepan on the stove and cook, stirring with a whisk, until the sauce boils and

thickens. Taste for seasoning and adjust if necessary (salt is the secret to great sauce) and serve.

7. Think safety. Take all necessary precautions when you bring your slow cooker to a party or a tailgate session before the big game. Cook the food completely before you go and leave while the food is still hot. Make sure the lid is secure and wrap the slow cooker in big towels or blankets to avoid burning anyone with hot food if the lid comes off. If you transport your slow cooker often, think about buying a slow cooker that is made for transporting food with a locking lid for safety and cool-touch housing.

8. Garnish your food when it's ready to serve. Any chopped fresh herb, such as basil or chives, will add great flavor and make the food look appetizing. You can also sprinkle the food with some freshly grated cheese, such as Parmesan or Cheddar, or toast some buttered bread crumbs and add those for some crunch.

About the Recipes

All of the recipes in this book were developed to be easy, interesting, nutritious, and delicious. You'll be proud to serve any of these dishes to family and friends. Here are some particulars you'll need to know before you start cooking.

The Labels

Most of these recipes have one or more labels: Gluten-Free, Low-Calorie Vegan, Vegetarian, and Weeknight Hero. Gluten-Free recipes don't use any ingredients that contain gluten. Low-Calorie recipes are 400 calories or less per serving. Vegan recipes contain no animal products at all. Vegetarian recipes contain no meat, poultry, or seafood but may contain cheese, dairy, or eggs. And Weeknight Heroes are the special recipes; they contain just a few easily accessible ingredients that require 15 minutes or less preparation and cook for at least seven hours. Think dump and cook!

The Ingredients

The ingredient lists for these recipes are as short as possible while still making recipes that are delicious and good for you. You can buy all of the ingredients at the grocery store. I don't call for offbeat or unfamiliar ingredients, just plain wholesome food. And the recipes use as few processed ingredients as possible. You'll find recipes that call for canned tomatoes or mustard or ketchup; that's as processed as they get.

Cooking Ranges

Many of these recipes have a doneness time range simply because no two slow cookers are exactly alike. Your slow cooker may cook a little hotter or cooler than others. I recommend that you check for doneness at the minimum time listed on the recipe. After all, it's easy to cook food for a longer period of time, but you can't undo overcooked food.

The Tips

About half of the recipes have tips. These are meant to give you options and help you organize your kitchen to make slow cooking easier and more fun.

INGREDIENT TIP: This tip will give you extra information on the origin, health benefits, preparation, or other interesting tidbits on an ingredient used in the recipe.

A LITTLE LIGHTER: This tip will give you an idea on how to make the recipe healthier, such as using half-and-half or whole milk instead of cream.

IF YOU HAVE A MINUTE: This tip will make the recipe even more delicious with just a little extra work, such as browning meat or stirring in more spices.

EXTRA EASY: This tip will help you make the recipe even easier, such as using frozen or precut veggies instead of fresh whole veggies.

GAME PLAN: This tip will give you ideas for turning leftovers into another meal, prepping a recipe ahead of time, or saving you some time.

Oatmeal with Blueberries and Cardamom, page 14

CHAPTER 2

BREAKFAST AND BRUNCH

Almond Berry Coconut Granola

GLUTEN-FREE, LOW-CALORIE, VEGAN

PREP TIME:
10 MINUTES

COOK TIME:
6 HOURS ON LOW
OR
3 HOURS ON HIGH

SERVES 8

PER SERVING:
Calories: 382; Fat: 32g;
Saturated Fat: 9g;
Cholesterol: 0mg;
Carbohydrates: 19g;
Fiber: 9g; Protein: 11g;
Sodium: 146mg

Granola is one recipe most people don't think of when they think "slow cooker." But this delicious dish is a natural for this appliance. One of the best things about making your own granola is that you control what goes into it. A lot of store-bought granola is loaded with preservatives and sugar. This easy-to-make recipe will become a staple in your kitchen.

Nonstick cooking spray
2½ cups unsalted almonds
¼ cup unsweetened coconut flakes
½ cup dried berries
¼ cup chia seeds

1 teaspoon ground cinnamon
½ teaspoon sea salt
¼ teaspoon ground nutmeg
¼ cup coconut oil
1 teaspoon pure vanilla extract

INGREDIENT TIP:
You can substitute a liquid oil for the coconut oil if you'd like. Choose an unflavored oil such as peanut, safflower, or sunflower oil. Olive oil will add too much peppery flavor and isn't appropriate for a granola recipe.

1. Grease a 3-quart slow cooker generously with nonstick cooking spray.
2. Place the almonds, coconut flakes, dried berries, chia seeds, cinnamon, salt, and nutmeg in the slow cooker.
3. Place a medium saucepan over medium-low heat and melt the coconut oil. Whisk in the vanilla.
4. Pour the oil mixture into the slow cooker, stirring to make sure all the ingredients are moistened.
5. Lay a small towel or 2 paper towels in between the slow cooker and the lid to create a barrier. This will prevent the condensation from dripping on the granola while it cooks. It's important to catch the condensation, or you will end up with soggy granola.
6. Cover and cook on low for 6 hours or on high for 3 hours.
7. Transfer the granola in an even layer to a baking sheet to cool. Store in an airtight container at room temperature for up to 2 weeks.

Whole-Grain Porridge

LOW-CALORIE, VEGETARIAN, WEEKNIGHT HERO

Orange juice provides a fresh flavor in this satisfying and healthy multigrain hot cereal recipe. Add a drizzle of some cold cream on top for a wonderful contrast. Drizzle or not, a breakfast chock-full of fiber, potassium, and iron is a perfect way to start your day and keep you energized.

½ cup wild rice

½ cup wheat berries

¾ cup hulled barley

¾ cup steel-cut oats

⅔ cup dried cranberries

3 tablespoons honey, plus more to serve

2 tablespoons vegetarian brown sugar

1 cup freshly squeezed orange juice

7 cups water

½ teaspoon sea salt

PREP TIME:
15 MINUTES

COOK TIME:
8 HOURS ON LOW

SERVES 8

PER SERVING:
Calories: 273; Fat: 2g;
Saturated Fat: <1g;
Cholesterol: 0mg;
Carbohydrates: 62g;
Fiber: 6g; Protein: 7g;
Sodium: 147mg

1. Place the wild rice, wheat berries, barley, oats, cranberries, 3 tablespoons of honey, brown sugar, orange juice, water, and salt in a 4- to 5-quart slow cooker. Stir well to combine.
2. Cover and cook on low for 8 hours, or until the grains are tender.
3. Stir gently and serve warm with more honey drizzled on top.

EXTRA EASY: If you like this recipe and make it a lot, combine equal amounts of wild rice, wheat berries, hulled barley, and steel-cut oats and store it in an airtight container at room temperature. When ready to make, just measure out 2½ cups and use in the recipe.

Oatmeal with Blueberries and Cardamom

GLUTEN-FREE, VEGAN, WEEKNIGHT HERO

PREP TIME:
5 MINUTES

COOK TIME:
8 HOURS ON LOW

SERVES 4

PER SERVING:
Calories: 414; Fat: 6g;
Saturated Fat: 2g;
Cholesterol: 6mg;
Carbohydrates: 84g;
Fiber: 10g;
Protein: 15g;
Sodium: 54mg

Is there anything as comforting as waking up to the heavenly aroma of a luscious breakfast? You won't even need to bribe a family member to prepare it. Simply put everything in your slow cooker, set it to low, and wake up to a healthy, gluten-free breakfast treat. You can use rolled oats in this recipe; just reduce the cooking time to 3 to 4 hours.

2 cups steel-cut oats

1 cup coconut milk

⅓ cup granulated sugar

¼ teaspoon ground cardamom

Pinch sea salt

7 cups water

2 cups fresh or frozen blueberries

Toasted almonds or pecans, for serving

1. Place the oats, milk, sugar, cardamom, salt, and water in a 4-quart slow cooker.
2. Cover and cook on low overnight (for up to 8 hours). Stir in the blueberries and let cook for 15 to 20 minutes longer while you get the rest of breakfast ready.
3. Spoon the oatmeal into serving dishes and top with toasted almonds or pecans.

INGREDIENT TIP: Steel-cut oats are the whole groat that is sliced into pieces. It is a very sturdy version of oatmeal and cooks very well in the slow cooker.

Quinoa with Apricots and Pumpkin Seeds

GLUTEN-FREE, LOW-CALORIE, VEGAN, WEEKNIGHT HERO

Brighten up the flavor and color of quinoa with a burst of juicy apricots and the crunch of pepitas (pumpkin seeds). Quinoa is an ancient grain that is a complete source of protein. It's high in fiber and has a nutty taste. Eating it as a hot cereal is an excellent way to start your day.

1 cup quinoa, rinsed
  and drained
3 cups vanilla almond milk
1 cup roughly chopped
  dried apricots
Pinch sea salt
4 tablespoons hulled
  unsalted pumpkin seeds

1. Place the quinoa, almond milk, apricots, and salt in a 3-quart slow cooker. Stir gently.
2. Cover and cook on low for 8 hours, or until the quinoa is tender.
3. To serve, spoon it into 4 bowls and top each portion with 1 tablespoon of the pumpkin seeds.

INGREDIENT TIP: Quinoa is coated with a phytochemical called saponin, which has a very bitter taste. It evolved to protect the grain from birds. Unless the package states that the quinoa has been prewashed, you must rinse it with cool running water for a few minutes before you cook it to remove the saponin.

PREP TIME:
10 MINUTES

COOK TIME:
8 HOURS ON LOW

SERVES 4

PER SERVING:
Calories: 353; Fat: 9g;
Saturated Fat: 1g;
Cholesterol: 0mg;
Carbohydrates: 63g;
Fiber: 7g; Protein: 10g;
Sodium: 136mg

Pumpkin-Apple Breakfast Bars

GLUTEN-FREE, LOW-CALORIE, VEGETARIAN

PREP TIME:
25 MINUTES

COOK TIME:
7 HOURS ON LOW

SERVES 6

PER SERVING:
Calories: 386; Fat: 21g;
Saturated Fat: 3g;
Cholesterol: 66mg;
Carbohydrates: 43g;
Fiber: 8g; Protein: 12g;
Sodium: 228mg

Yes, you can make breakfast bars in the slow cooker! These bars are very moist and tender because of the temperature and environment created by the slow cooker. This recipe is full of texture and flavor, and these bars are a great way to start your day full of energy.

1 cup solid-pack pumpkin purée (not pumpkin pie filling)

2 large eggs

2 teaspoons pure vanilla extract

1 cup 2% milk

½ cup apple juice

2 cups old-fashioned oats

1 Granny Smith apple, peeled, cored, and finely chopped

½ cup raisins

⅓ cup almond flour

1 teaspoon ground cinnamon

1 teaspoon baking powder

¼ teaspoon sea salt

Nonstick cooking spray

1 cup chopped walnuts

1. In a large bowl, mix together the pumpkin purée and eggs. Stir in the vanilla extract, milk, and apple juice, and then stir in the oats, apple, raisins, almond flour, cinnamon, baking powder, and salt.

2. Tear off two long strips of aluminum foil, fold them in half lengthwise, and place them into a 6-quart slow cooker in a cross shape. This makes a sling so it will be easy to remove the bars when they're done. Then put a layer of parchment paper, cut to fit the slow cooker, on top of the foil. Spray the parchment paper with nonstick cooking spray.

3. Spread the batter evenly in the slow cooker, and sprinkle with the chopped walnuts.

4. Cover and cook on low for 7 hours, or until the bars are almost firm when touched.

5. Turn off the slow cooker and remove the lid. Let cool for 1 hour.

6. Using the foil sling, lift the bars out of the slow cooker and cool them completely on a wire rack. Cut into bars and serve.

Potato and Sausage Frittata

GLUTEN-FREE, LOW-CALORIE, WEEKNIGHT HERO

This is a pretty basic frittata, but it's really delicious. The breakfast sausage adds great flavor, while the potato adds earthiness and texture. Finishing with a quick gremolata (classically made of lemon zest, garlic, and parsley) boosts the flavor even more, adding a bright and fresh herbal essence to the breakfast that you'll enjoy.

PREP TIME:
15 MINUTES

COOK TIME:
8 HOURS ON LOW

SERVES 6

PER SERVING:
Calories: 254; Fat: 18g;
Saturated Fat: 7g;
Cholesterol: 273mg;
Carbohydrates: 10g;
Fiber: 1g; Protein: 13g;
Sodium: 495mg

8 large eggs

¼ cup 2% milk

½ teaspoon sea salt, divided

½ teaspoon garlic powder

¼ teaspoon freshly ground black pepper

2 cups frozen diced potatoes

1 cup sliced button or cremini mushrooms

8 fully cooked breakfast sausage links, sliced

2 tablespoons unsalted butter, at room temperature

½ cup chopped fresh parsley

2 garlic cloves, minced

Grated zest of 1 orange

1. In a large bowl, whisk together the eggs, milk, ¼ teaspoon of salt, garlic powder, and pepper.
2. Fold in the frozen diced potatoes, mushrooms, and sausage.
3. Grease the bottom and a few inches up the sides of a 3- to 4-quart slow cooker with the butter. Pour in the egg mixture.
4. Cover and cook on low for 8 hours, or until a food thermometer reads 160°F.
5. When you're ready to eat, in a small bowl, stir together the parsley, remaining ¼ teaspoon of salt, garlic, and orange zest.
6. To serve, slice the frittata and sprinkle the parsley mixture over each serving.

A LITTLE LIGHTER: For 6 fewer grams of fat per serving, use 5 eggs and 5 egg whites in place of the 8 eggs. Reduce the amount of butter to 1 tablespoon. And use only 6 breakfast sausages instead of 8.

Mushroom, Bacon, and Cheese Frittata

GLUTEN-FREE, LOW-CALORIE, WEEKNIGHT HERO

PREP TIME:
5 MINUTES

COOK TIME:
6 TO 8 HOURS
ON LOW OR
3 TO 4 HOURS
ON HIGH

SERVES 8

PER SERVING:
Calories: 349; Fat: 28g;
Saturated Fat: 8g;
Cholesterol: 216mg;
Carbohydrates: 5g;
Fiber: <1g;
Protein: 20g;
Sodium: 499mg

This is a hearty and satisfying breakfast to send everyone off to school or work and a great one for weekends when everyone is on the go from one activity to another. If you're vegetarian, omit the bacon and load this up with your favorite vegetables—some of mine include zucchini, onions, and broccoli.

Nonstick cooking spray

8 large eggs

2 cups reduced-fat 2% milk

½ cup grated Parmesan cheese

½ teaspoon sea salt

3 (6-ounce) jars sliced mushrooms, well drained

8 ounces bacon, cooked and crumbled

1½ cups shredded medium Cheddar cheese, divided

1. Grease a 3- to 4-quart slow cooker generously with nonstick cooking spray.
2. In a medium bowl, whisk together the eggs, milk, Parmesan cheese, and salt.
3. Place the mushrooms, bacon, and ¾ cup of Cheddar cheese in the slow cooker. Pour in the egg mixture, covering the ingredients. Top with the remaining ¾ cup of Cheddar cheese.
4. Cover and cook on low for 6 to 8 hours or on high for 3 to 4 hours, or until the eggs are set and a food thermometer registers 160°F.

INGREDIENT TIP: You can substitute two 8-ounce packages fresh mushrooms that you have sliced and sautéed in a bit of butter until they give up their liquid and it evaporates. Don't just plunk fresh mushrooms into a recipe like this because they will give off too much moisture as they cook and the frittata will be runny.

Savory Brunch Casserole

GLUTEN-FREE, LOW-CALORIE

This hearty casserole covers all the bases while boasting of one of the most powerful anti-inflammatory ingredients available to us—broccoli! As a cruciferous vegetable, broccoli has been shown to decrease the risk of both heart disease and cancer. It's delicious in this filling casserole that also uses sweet potato and chicken or turkey sausage.

PREP TIME:
15 MINUTES

COOK TIME:
4 TO 5 HOURS
ON LOW

SERVES 4

PER SERVING:
Calories: 316; Fat: 18g;
Saturated Fat: 7g;
Cholesterol: 340mg;
Carbohydrates: 15g;
Fiber: 2g; Protein: 20g;
Sodium: 928mg

- 8 ounces bulk chicken or turkey sausage
- 1 tablespoon unsalted butter, at room temperature
- 6 large eggs
- ½ cup 2% milk
- 2 teaspoons Dijon mustard
- ½ teaspoon sea salt
- 1 teaspoon garlic powder
- ⅛ teaspoon freshly ground black pepper
- 2 cups broccoli florets
- 1 medium onion, diced
- 1 cup diced canned, drained sweet potato

1. Place a medium skillet over medium heat. Add the sausage and cook, stirring with a wooden spoon to break up the meat, for 7 to 8 minutes, until cooked through. Drain if necessary.
2. Grease a 3½-quart slow cooker with the butter.
3. In a medium bowl, whisk together the eggs, milk, mustard, salt, garlic powder, and pepper.
4. Place the broccoli, onion, sweet potato, and cooked and drained sausage in the slow cooker. Pour the egg mixture on top, making sure the other ingredients are covered.
5. Cover and cook on low for 4 to 5 hours, until the eggs are set and the vegetables are tender, or until a food thermometer registers 160°F. Serve.

Cinnamon-Raisin French Toast

LOW-CALORIE, VEGETARIAN

PREP TIME:
10 MINUTES

COOK TIME:
2 HOURS ON HIGH

SERVES 6

PER SERVING:
Calories: 299; Fat: 11g;
Saturated Fat: 3g;
Cholesterol: 195mg;
Carbohydrates: 38g;
Fiber: 3g; Protein: 12g;
Sodium: 325mg

Making French toast for the whole family can be time-consuming—not to mention impractical on a busy morning—especially if you have a small griddle. A slow cooker, however, does the work for you while you enjoy a hot cup of coffee and prepare for the day.

1 tablespoon unsalted butter, at room temperature

1 loaf cinnamon-raisin bread, cut into 1-inch cubes

6 large eggs

1 cup 2% milk

1 tablespoon pure vanilla extract

1 teaspoon ground cinnamon

1. Grease a 4-quart slow cooker with the butter. Place the bread cubes in the slow cooker.
2. In a medium bowl, whisk together the eggs, milk, vanilla extract, and cinnamon. Pour the egg mixture over the bread, making sure all the bread is soaked in the mixture.
3. Cover and cook on high for 2 hours, or until the mixture is puffed and a food thermometer inserted into the center registers 165°F.

GAME PLAN: Perform the first two steps the night before you plan to serve the French toast and place the prepared slow cooker insert, covered, in the refrigerator. Then set the insert in the base first thing in the morning and cook, adding 20 minutes more of cooking time.

Italian Sausage Strata

LOW-CALORIE

This delicious breakfast casserole is full of healthy vegetables, fragrant herbs, and savory sausage. Serve with a small bowl of fresh fruit and a steaming cup of coffee for a meal that's also perfect for kiddos (minus the coffee!) on the way out the door to school; it'll keep them brimming with energy until the lunch bell rings.

1 tablespoon unsalted butter, at room temperature

1 tablespoon extra-virgin olive oil

1 yellow onion, halved and sliced

2 spicy Italian sausage links, casings removed

1 red bell pepper, seeded and diced

2 cups roughly chopped fresh spinach

2 tablespoons minced fresh chives

2 cups cubed French bread

6 large eggs, whisked

½ cup 2% milk

½ teaspoon sea salt

⅛ teaspoon freshly ground black pepper

1. Grease a 4-quart slow cooker with the butter.
2. Place a large skillet over medium heat and add the oil. Once hot, add the onion and cook for about 8 minutes, until soft and translucent. Transfer the onion to the slow cooker.
3. In the same skillet, brown the sausage for 8 to 9 minutes, breaking the meat up with a spatula or wooden spoon as it cooks, until the sausage is cooked through. Use a slotted spoon to transfer it to the slow cooker.
4. Add the bell pepper, spinach, chives, and bread cubes to the slow cooker.
5. In a medium bowl, whisk together the eggs, milk, salt, and pepper. Pour the egg mixture into the slow cooker and stir gently to combine.
6. Cover and cook on low for 8 hours or until the mixture is puffed and a food thermometer reads 160°F.

PREP TIME:
20 MINUTES

COOK TIME:
8 HOURS ON LOW

SERVES 6

PER SERVING:
Calories: 268; Fat: 13g; Saturated Fat: 4g; Cholesterol: 212mg; Carbohydrates: 22g; Fiber: 2g; Protein: 16g; Sodium: 676mg

INGREDIENT TIP:
Italian sausages come in two flavors: mild (also called sweet) and hot. You can choose either one for this flavorful and delicious breakfast strata.

Denver Strata

VEGETARIAN

PREP TIME:
25 MINUTES

COOK TIME:
8 HOURS ON LOW

SERVES 6 TO 8

PER SERVING:
Calories: 623; Fat: 38g;
Saturated Fat: 21g;
Cholesterol: 342mg;
Carbohydrates: 39g;
Fiber: 5g; Protein: 32g;
Sodium: 1,473mg

A Denver omelet is made with ham or bacon, bell peppers, onion, and cheese. We'll turn that recipe into a vegetarian slow cooker strata using mushrooms instead of ham and whole-wheat English muffins. This is a great weekend brunch. Let it cook overnight and wake up to a delicious meal.

1 cup sliced cremini mushrooms

1 onion, chopped

1 red bell pepper, seeded and chopped

1 yellow bell pepper, seeded and chopped

8 whole-wheat English muffins, split, toasted, and cubed

2 cups shredded provolone cheese

1 cup shredded Cheddar cheese

8 large eggs

1 cup light cream

3 tablespoons Dijon mustard

1 teaspoon sea salt

1 teaspoon dried oregano

⅛ teaspoon freshly ground black pepper

½ cup grated Parmesan cheese

1. Layer the mushrooms, onion, red and yellow bell peppers, cubed English muffins, and provolone and Cheddar cheeses in a 4- to 5-quart slow cooker.
2. In a large bowl, whisk together the eggs, cream, mustard, salt, oregano, and pepper until smooth.
3. Pour the egg mixture into the slow cooker, making sure the other ingredients are covered. Top with the Parmesan cheese.
4. Cover and cook on low for 7 to 8 hours, or until a food thermometer reads 160°F.
5. Uncover and let stand for 10 minutes. Slice and serve.

Artichoke and Sun-Dried Tomato Breakfast Casserole

LOW-CALORIE, VEGETARIAN, WEEKNIGHT HERO

The flavors of the Mediterranean shine through in this simple vegetarian breakfast casserole. If you prefer, you can substitute other Mediterranean vegetables for the sun-dried tomatoes and artichoke hearts, such as olives, scallions, or roasted red peppers, for endless flavor combinations.

PREP TIME:
15 MINUTES

COOK TIME:
8 HOURS ON LOW

SERVES 4

PER SERVING:
Calories: 314; Fat: 13g; Saturated Fat: 4g; Cholesterol: 282mg; Carbohydrates: 33g; Fiber: 4g; Protein: 16g; Sodium: 572mg

1 tablespoon extra-virgin olive oil

½ cup chopped sun-dried tomatoes

1 cup chopped drained jarred artichoke hearts

1 tablespoon minced fresh oregano

2 cups cubed French bread

6 large eggs

½ cup 2% milk

Sea salt

Freshly ground black pepper

1. Grease a 3-quart slow cooker with the olive oil.
2. Place the sun-dried tomatoes, artichoke hearts, oregano, and bread cubes in the slow cooker.
3. In a medium bowl, whisk together the eggs and milk and season with salt and pepper. Pour the egg mixture into the slow cooker and stir gently to combine.
4. Cover and cook on low for 8 hours, or until the mixture is puffed and set and a food thermometer reads 160°F.

Better Buffalo Wings, page 38

CHAPTER 3

APPETIZERS, SNACKS, AND DRINKS

Five-Spice Glazed Nuts

GLUTEN-FREE, VEGETARIAN

PREP TIME:
10 MINUTES

COOK TIME:
3 HOURS ON LOW

SERVES 10

PER SERVING:
Calories: 501; Fat: 46g;
Saturated Fat: 6g;
Cholesterol: 9mg;
Carbohydrates: 19g;
Fiber: 7g; Protein: 11g;
Sodium: 118mg

Chinese five-spice powder adds zip to these sweet nuts with its combination of spices and Sichuan pepper. Maple syrup adds a smoky sweetness. Although the recipe calls for a combination of pecans, walnuts, and almonds, you can use any unsalted nuts and seeds you choose.

2 cups shelled unsalted whole pecans

2 cups shelled unsalted whole almonds

2 cups shelled unsalted whole walnuts

⅓ cup pure maple syrup

3 tablespoons unsalted butter, melted

1½ teaspoons Chinese five-spice powder

½ teaspoon sea salt

Grated zest of 1 orange

1. Place all of the ingredients in a 3-quart slow cooker. Stir well to combine.
2. Cover and cook on low for 3 hours, or until the nuts are glazed. Remove the nuts and spread on a parchment paper–lined cookie sheet to cool. Store in an airtight container at room temperature.

Party Snack Mix

LOW-CALORIE, VEGETARIAN

Though it seems counterintuitive, the even heat of a slow cooker makes it the perfect tool for crispy snack mix. When you're entertaining guests, be sure this savory and satisfying snack mix is on the menu. It's flavored with paprika, onion, and garlic and is quite addictive. If there's any left, store it at room temperature in an airtight container.

4 cups rice Chex cereal

1 cup corn Chex cereal

2 cups small pretzels

1 cup shelled peanuts

2 tablespoons unsalted butter, melted, or extra-virgin olive oil

1 teaspoon smoked paprika

1 teaspoon garlic powder

1 teaspoon onion powder

1 teaspoon minced fresh rosemary (optional)

1 tablespoon vegetarian Worcestershire sauce

1. Place the rice cereal, corn cereal, pretzels, and peanuts in a 3-quart slow cooker. Stir to combine.
2. In a small measuring cup, whisk together the butter, paprika, garlic powder, onion powder, rosemary (if using), and Worcestershire sauce. Pour this mixture into the slow cooker on top of the cereal mixture and stir gently to thoroughly coat.
3. Cook on low, uncovered, for 2 hours. Stir several times to ensure that the mixture cooks evenly and does not stick to the slow cooker. The mix is done when the cereal is glazed.
4. Remove the mix from the slow cooker, spread it onto a parchment paper–lined baking sheet, and let cool for 2 hours before serving or storing.

PREP TIME:
10 MINUTES

COOK TIME:
2 HOURS ON LOW

MAKES 8 CUPS

PER ½-CUP SERVING:
Calories: 121; Fat: 6g; Saturated Fat: 2g; Cholesterol: 4mg; Carbohydrates: 14g; Fiber: 1g; Protein: 3g; Sodium: 164mg

Marinated Mushrooms

GLUTEN-FREE, LOW-CALORIE, VEGETARIAN

PREP TIME:
15 MINUTES

COOK TIME:
2 TO 3 HOURS
ON LOW

SERVES 8

PER SERVING:
Calories: 64; Fat: 3g;
Saturated Fat: 2g;
Cholesterol: 8mg;
Carbohydrates: 6g;
Fiber: 1g; Protein: 2g;
Sodium: 78mg

These marinated mushrooms are a delicious and healthy alternative to stuffed mushrooms, which are often filled with bread crumbs and a hefty amount of cheese. Serve these as part of an appetizer platter alongside fresh, crisp vegetables.

2 ounces dried mushrooms

2 (8-ounce) packages button mushrooms

2 tablespoons unsalted butter, plus more as needed

2 shallots, minced

¼ cup dry sherry (not cooking sherry)

1 tablespoon herbes de Provence

¼ teaspoon sea salt

¼ teaspoon freshly ground black pepper

1. Place the dried mushrooms in a small bowl and cover with hot water. Let stand for 10 minutes to rehydrate. Drain; then remove the tough ends of the stems and discard. Coarsely chop the mushrooms and set aside.

2. Slice the larger fresh mushrooms in half, leaving the smaller ones whole.

3. Place a large skillet over high heat and melt the butter. Add half the button mushrooms and cook until browned; then push the first batch to the sides and add the remaining button mushrooms, adding more butter as needed to brown them. Transfer the browned mushrooms to a 3-quart slow cooker along with the chopped rehydrated dried mushrooms.

4. In the same skillet, cook the shallots for about 3 minutes, or until slightly softened. Transfer the shallots to the slow cooker and add the sherry, herbes de Provence, salt, and pepper.

5. Cover and cook on low for 2 to 3 hours, or until the button mushrooms are tender and brown.

Jalapeño Poppers

GLUTEN-FREE, LOW-CALORIE

Jalapeño poppers are not an authentic Mexican food, but they do have authentic Mexican flavors, and they are a cinch to make, if a bit fiddly. A mixture of cream cheese and Cheddar cheese is spooned into jalapeño halves, which are then wrapped in partially cooked bacon. While they cook, the juices from the spicy jalapeños and the smoky bacon infuse the cheese with flavor. Because this is a moist-heat type of cooking, the bacon won't get really crispy. If you want, you can remove the bacon after cooking or just make these without it. Another option is to cook the bacon until it is crisp and then mix it in with the cheese.

PREP TIME:
30 MINUTES

COOK TIME:
4 HOURS ON LOW
OR
2 HOURS ON HIGH

SERVES 24

PER SERVING:
Calories: 89; Fat: 7g;
Saturated Fat: 4g;
Cholesterol: 23mg;
Carbohydrates: 1g;
Fiber: <1g; Protein: 5g;
Sodium: 205mg

24 slices bacon

1 (8-ounce) package cream cheese, at room temperature

¼ cup sour cream

¼ cup grated Cheddar cheese

12 jalapeños, seeded and halved lengthwise

⅓ cup Chicken Stock (page 263 or store-bought) or water

1. Place the bacon in a large skillet over medium heat and cook, turning frequently, until partially cooked but still bendable. Drain the bacon on paper towels and let cool.
2. In a medium bowl, mix together the cream cheese, sour cream, and Cheddar cheese until well blended.
3. Divide the cheese mixture evenly among the jalapeño halves. Wrap each stuffed jalapeño half with a slice of bacon; secure the bacon with a toothpick.
4. Pour the chicken stock into a 3- to 4-quart slow cooker and add the stuffed jalapeños.
5. Cover and cook on low for 4 hours or on high for 2 hours.
6. Using a slotted spoon, remove the stuffed jalapeños from the slow cooker. Serve hot or at room temperature.

Spicy Cocktail Meatballs

GLUTEN-FREE

PREP TIME:
15 MINUTES

COOK TIME:
6 HOURS ON LOW

SERVES 10

PER SERVING:
Calories: 404; Fat: 13g;
Saturated Fat: 4g;
Cholesterol: 75mg;
Carbohydrates: 50g;
Fiber: <1g; Protein: 19g;
Sodium: 570mg

Cocktail meatballs are always a hit at any party. Serve with fancy toothpicks right in the slow cooker set to low or "keep warm."

1 large egg

¼ cup 2% milk

1 cup crisp rice cereal, finely crushed

2 tablespoons honey mustard

1 teaspoon sea salt

¼ teaspoon cayenne pepper

1 teaspoon dried thyme

2 pounds lean ground beef

2 tablespoons extra-virgin olive oil

1 (18-ounce) jar apple jelly

⅓ cup Dijon mustard

⅓ cup grainy mustard

1. In a large bowl, mix the egg, milk, cereal, honey mustard, salt, cayenne pepper, and thyme. Let stand for 5 minutes so the cereal softens.
2. Add the ground beef and mix gently but thoroughly with your hands. Form into 32 (1-inch) meatballs. (The meatballs can be prepared up to this point and stored in a covered container in the refrigerator for up to 2 days.)
3. Place a large skillet over medium-high heat and add the olive oil. Once hot, add the meatballs, in two or three batches, and brown them for 3 to 4 minutes per batch. Once browned, place the meatballs in a 4-quart slow cooker.
4. In the same skillet over medium-high heat, add the apple jelly, Dijon mustard, and grainy mustard, stirring occasionally to scrape up any browned bits from the bottom of the pan, until the jelly melts and the mixture is smooth.
5. Pour the jelly mixture over the meatballs.
6. Cover and cook on low for 6 hours, stirring gently once if you are home, or until the meatballs read at least 160°F on a food thermometer. Serve with toothpicks.

Artichoke and Spinach Dip

GLUTEN-FREE, LOW-CALORIE, VEGETARIAN

The combination of artichokes and spinach in a cheesy and creamy dip is classic. And it cooks beautifully in the slow cooker. Serve this delicious appetizer with corn chips, breadsticks, crackers, or toasted bread rounds.

1 (14-ounce) can artichoke hearts, drained and chopped

2 cups frozen chopped spinach, thawed and squeezed dry

1 tablespoon minced garlic

½ cup 2% milk

1 (8-ounce) package cream cheese, at room temperature

1 cup grated Parmesan cheese

¼ teaspoon sea salt

⅛ teaspoon freshly ground black pepper

1. Place the artichoke hearts, spinach, garlic, milk, cream cheese, Parmesan, salt, and pepper in a 2-quart slow cooker. Stir well to combine.
2. Cover and cook on low for 2 hours, or until the cheese is melted and the dip is hot.
3. Serve the dip in the slow cooker with the heat on low or "keep warm."

INGREDIENT TIP: The frozen spinach in this recipe really does have to be squeezed dry before you add it to the slow cooker, or the dip will be runny. Squeeze moisture out with your hands; then put the thawed spinach between paper towels and press out any additional excess moisture.

PREP TIME:
10 MINUTES

COOK TIME:
2 HOURS ON LOW

SERVES 16

PER SERVING:
Calories: 96; Fat: 7g; Saturated Fat: 4g; Cholesterol: 21mg; Carbohydrates: 4g; Fiber: 1g; Protein: 5g; Sodium: 278mg

Spicy Chicken Nachos

GLUTEN-FREE, WEEKNIGHT HERO

This recipe makes amazing traditional nachos, or you can simply melt the cheese in the slow cooker and use it as a dip (see the Game Plan tip).

2 pounds boneless, skinless chicken breast

2 large tomatoes, diced

1 medium yellow onion, chopped

3 medium jalapeños, seeded and chopped

1 (15-ounce) can black beans, drained and rinsed

1 tablespoon chili power

½ teaspoon garlic powder

½ teaspoon sea salt

½ teaspoon freshly ground black pepper

1 packed tablespoon brown sugar

½ cup Chicken Stock (page 263 or store-bought)

1 (13-ounce) bag tortilla chips

2 cups grated pepper Jack cheese

2 cups grated Colby or Cheddar cheese

Sliced jalapeños and black olives, for topping

Guacamole and/or sour cream, for serving (optional)

PREP TIME:
15 MINUTES

COOK TIME:
8 HOURS ON LOW
OR
4 HOURS ON HIGH

SERVES 8

PER SERVING:
Calories: 636; Fat: 24g;
Saturated Fat: 8g;
Cholesterol: 95mg;
Carbohydrates: 44g;
Fiber: 7g; Protein: 37g;
Sodium: 791mg

1. Place the chicken, tomatoes, onion, and jalapeños in a 4-quart slow cooker. Stir to combine. Spoon the black beans over the chicken and vegetables.
2. In a bowl, whisk the chili powder, garlic powder, salt, black pepper, brown sugar, and stock. Pour the mixture over the chicken, vegetables, and beans.
3. Cover and cook on low for 8 hours or on high for 4 hours.
4. Using two forks, shred the chicken; then mix it back in with the other ingredients.

CONTINUED

5. Preheat the oven to 400°F. Pile the tortilla chips on a baking sheet. Remove the chicken mixture from the slow cooker with a slotted spoon and put it on the tortilla chips. Top with the pepper Jack and Colby cheeses, and bake for 10 to 15 minutes, or until the cheese is melted and beginning to brown. Top with sliced jalapeños and black olives, and serve with guacamole and sour cream if you like.

GAME PLAN: To serve this as a dip, top the chicken mixture in the slow cooker with the pepper Jack and Colby cheeses and then cover the slow cooker and cook on high for 10 minutes, or until the cheeses melt. Top with sliced jalapeños, black olives, and your other favorite toppings and serve hot with tortilla chips.

Cheesy Caramelized Onion Dip

GLUTEN-FREE, VEGETARIAN, WEEKNIGHT HERO

This recipe takes the ubiquitous dip made with powdered onion soup mix to the next level. There's nothing as good as caramelized onions enveloped in a creamy, cheesy, thick, and rich sauce. Serve this at a party with breadsticks, crackers, crudités, and toasted bread slices, and everyone will cluster around the bowl. Trust me, it goes fast.

PREP TIME:
15 MINUTES

COOK TIME:
9 TO 12 HOURS
ON LOW

SERVES 8 TO 10

PER SERVING:
Calories: 418; Fat: 36g;
Saturated Fat: 20g;
Cholesterol: 98mg;
Carbohydrates: 10g;
Fiber: 1g; Protein: 15g;
Sodium: 574mg

4 yellow onions,
  2 chopped and 2 sliced

5 garlic cloves, sliced

2 tablespoons extra-
  virgin olive oil

½ teaspoon sea salt

⅛ teaspoon freshly
  ground black pepper

1 teaspoon dried thyme

2 (8-ounce) packages
  cream cheese, cubed

½ cup sour cream

1 cup shredded Swiss cheese

1 cup shredded
  provolone cheese

½ cup grated Parmesan cheese

1. Place the onions, garlic, olive oil, salt, and pepper in a 3-quart slow cooker. Stir well to combine.
2. Cover and cook on low for 8 to 10 hours, or until the onions are deep golden brown. If you are at home during cooking time, stir the onions once or twice.
3. Stir in the thyme, cream cheese, sour cream, Swiss cheese, provolone cheese, and Parmesan cheese.
4. Cover and cook on low for another 1 to 2 hours, or until the dip is creamy and smooth.
5. Stir gently and serve.

INGREDIENT TIP: If you want to make this dip vegan, use two (8-ounce) packages vegan cream cheese and one (12-ounce) package silken tofu in place of all the dairy cheeses.

French Onion Dip

GLUTEN-FREE, LOW-CALORIE, VEGETARIAN, WEEKNIGHT HERO

PREP TIME:
15 MINUTES,
PLUS 3 HOURS
CHILLING TIME

COOK TIME:
6 TO 8 HOURS
ON LOW

SERVES 16

PER SERVING:
Calories: 95; Fat: 9g;
Saturated Fat: 3g;
Cholesterol: 7mg;
Carbohydrates: 3g;
Fiber: 1g; Protein: 1g;
Sodium: 112mg

This recipe is perfect for a Super Bowl or tailgate party. Skip the French onion dressing packets with all those artificial ingredients, additives, and sodium, and make your own French onion dip from caramelized onions using your slow cooker. This recipe works best when the onions are cooked overnight, cooled, and then blended into the final dip.

4 yellow onions, thinly sliced

2 tablespoons extra-virgin olive oil

1 tablespoon unsalted butter

½ teaspoon sea salt

Pinch granulated sugar

½ cup sour cream

½ cup mayonnaise

⅛ teaspoon freshly ground black pepper

1. Place the onions, olive oil, and butter in a 3-quart slow cooker. Season with the salt and sugar and stir to combine.
2. Cover and cook on high for 6 to 8 hours, or until the onions are a rich, dark brown. If you're around during the day, stir the onions every 2 to 3 hours to prevent burning.
3. Transfer the cooked onions to a food processor using a slotted spoon. Process until still slightly chunky.
4. Add the sour cream, mayonnaise, and pepper and pulse until thoroughly combined.
5. Cover the dip and chill for 3 to 4 hours before serving. Refrigerate leftovers in an airtight container up to 4 days. This recipe does not freeze well.

Two-Chile Queso

LOW-CALORIE, VEGETARIAN

This is a classic Tex-Mex dip. My smooth and creamy version adds jalapeño and poblano chiles to give it a kick. Queso is traditionally served with tortilla chips, but there are endless possibilities—consider boiled or roasted fingerling potatoes for a unique, nontraditional dipper or any type of raw veggie.

PREP TIME:
20 MINUTES

COOK TIME:
2 HOURS ON LOW

SERVES 16

PER SERVING:
Calories: 118; Fat: 10g;
Saturated Fat: 6g;
Cholesterol: 31mg;
Carbohydrates: 3g;
Fiber: <1g; Protein: 5g;
Sodium: 254mg

Nonstick cooking spray

1 medium yellow onion, chopped

1 large tomato, seeded and chopped

3 medium jalapeños, seeded and chopped

1 medium poblano chile, seeded and chopped

1 garlic clove, minced

1 cup whole milk

1 (8-ounce) package cream cheese, cut into 1-inch cubes

8 ounces American cheese, chopped

1. Grease a 3-quart slow cooker with nonstick cooking spray.
2. Add the onion, tomato, jalapeños, poblano chile, garlic, milk, cream cheese, and American cheese to the slow cooker. Give everything a quick stir with a wooden spoon.
3. Cover and cook on low for 2 hours. Stir the dip and serve.

INGREDIENT TIP: To seed a tomato, cut it in half. Squeeze out the seeds over the sink; then chop the rest of the fruit.

Better Buffalo Wings

GLUTEN-FREE, LOW-CALORIE

PREP TIME:
10 MINUTES

COOK TIME:
4 HOURS ON LOW,
PLUS BROILING TIME

SERVES 8

PER SERVING:
Calories: 294; Fat: 20g;
Saturated Fat: 7g;
Cholesterol: 116mg;
Carbohydrates: 9g;
Fiber: <1g; Protein: 17g;
Sodium: 959mg

These wings are lighter than the traditional deep-fried variety, but they are just as delicious. The wings are broiled after they're cooked, so the skin is crispy and satisfying. There are many varieties of hot sauce on the market; choose your favorite for this recipe.

1 cup hot sauce

2 tablespoons unsalted butter, melted

1 tablespoon honey

1 teaspoon smoked paprika

1 tablespoon minced garlic

½ cup light beer

½ teaspoon sea salt

2 pounds chicken wings, separated into flats and drumettes

1. In a 3-quart slow cooker, whisk together the hot sauce, butter, honey, paprika, and garlic. Whisk in the beer and salt.
2. Add the chicken wings to the slow cooker and stir to coat with the sauce.
3. Cover and cook on low for 4 hours, or until the wings read at least 165°F on a food thermometer.
4. Preheat the broiler.
5. Remove the wings from the sauce and place on a broiler pan in a single layer. Brush them with some of the sauce from the slow cooker.
6. Broil for 3 to 4 minutes, or until crisp; then turn, brush with more sauce, and broil for another 3 to 4 minutes. Serve hot.

GAME PLAN: Serve these wings with a dipping sauce made from ¾ cup low-fat sour cream, ¼ cup low-fat mayonnaise, ¼ cup crumbled blue cheese, 1 teaspoon Worcestershire sauce, and 1 minced garlic clove. Celery sticks are the traditional accompaniment.

Hoisin-Honey Chicken Wings

Wings are a popular entertaining food and are practically expected at tailgating parties or game-day gatherings. With the slow cooker, they're also easy to cook and serve. You'll definitely want to brown the wings after they're finished cooking to add a wonderful crisp crust.

PREP TIME:
15 MINUTES

COOK TIME:
4 HOURS ON LOW,
PLUS BROILING TIME

SERVES 8

PER SERVING:
Calories: 546; Fat: 26g;
Saturated Fat: 8g;
Cholesterol: 163mg;
Carbohydrates: 51g;
Fiber: 1g; Protein: 28g;
Sodium: 1,682mg

3 pounds chicken wings, tips cut off

1 teaspoon paprika

½ teaspoon sea salt

½ teaspoon freshly ground black pepper

1 cup honey

½ cup soy sauce

½ cup hoisin sauce

¼ cup rice wine

2 garlic cloves, minced

1 teaspoon minced fresh ginger

1. Sprinkle the wings with the paprika, salt, and pepper and place them in a 4-quart slow cooker.
2. In a medium bowl, whisk together the honey, soy sauce, hoisin sauce, rice wine, garlic, and ginger.
3. Pour the honey mixture over the wings in the slow cooker and toss to coat.
4. Cover and cook on low for 4 hours, or until the wings register 165°F on a food thermometer.
5. Preheat the broiler.
6. Remove the wings from the sauce and place on a broiler pan in a single layer. Brush them with some of the sauce from the slow cooker.
7. Broil for 3 to 4 minutes, or until crisp; then turn, brush with more sauce, and broil for another 3 to 4 minutes. Serve hot.

INGREDIENT TIP: Most chicken wings have three parts: the drumette (which looks like a mini drumstick), the flat part, and the tip. Cut off and discard the tips before cooking, or save them for making stock. You can sometimes find chicken drumettes in the grocery store. Use these if you can find them because they are very meaty.

Cheese Fondue

LOW-CALORIE, VEGETARIAN

PREP TIME:
15 MINUTES

COOK TIME:
2 HOURS ON LOW

SERVES 8

PER SERVING:
Calories: 237; Fat: 17g;
Saturated Fat: 11g;
Cholesterol: 50mg;
Carbohydrates: 4g;
Fiber: <1g; Protein: 13g;
Sodium: 241mg

Fondue is a classic recipe traditionally served on Christmas Eve. It is decadent and rich and a very celebratory, communal dish. It can be tricky to make on the stovetop, but the cheese melts beautifully in the slow cooker. Offer a variety of dippers to your guests, such as baby carrots, broccoli and cauliflower florets, and French bread cubes.

2 cups shredded Swiss cheese

2 cups shredded sharp Cheddar cheese

1 garlic clove, minced

½ teaspoon dry mustard

¼ teaspoon freshly grated nutmeg

2 tablespoons all-purpose flour

1 cup light beer

1. Place the Swiss cheese, Cheddar cheese, garlic, dry mustard, nutmeg, and flour in a 3-quart slow cooker. Stir to combine. Pour in the beer and stir well.
2. Cover and cook on low for 2 hours, or until the cheese is melted. If you can, stir the mixture occasionally as the cheese melts.
3. Uncover and stir well. Serve the fondue right from the slow cooker, keeping the heat on low or "keep warm" if your slow cooker has that setting.

GAME PLAN: Have all of the dippers prepared ahead of time so when you're ready to eat, you can just put them into bowls and set them on the table.

Caponata

GLUTEN-FREE, LOW-CALORIE, VEGAN

Caponata's original home is Sicily, where the dish is made from eggplant and other vegetables. It can be served as a side dish, a vegetarian entrée, or an appetizer dip or spread. However you enjoy it, sip some wine, close your eyes, and imagine you're enjoying the warm Sicilian breeze.

1 large eggplant, peeled and cubed

2 (14-ounce) cans diced tomatoes, drained

2 yellow onions, chopped

4 celery stalks, sliced

2 red bell peppers, seeded and chopped

6 garlic cloves, sliced

½ cup golden raisins

¼ cup tomato paste

2 tablespoons freshly squeezed lemon juice

1 teaspoon dried Italian seasoning

1 teaspoon sea salt

⅛ teaspoon freshly ground black pepper

PREP TIME:
25 MINUTES

COOK TIME:
8 HOURS ON LOW

SERVES 8

PER SERVING:
Calories: 89; Fat: <1g;
Saturated Fat: <1g;
Cholesterol: 0mg;
Carbohydrates: 21g;
Fiber: 4g; Protein: 3g;
Sodium: 475mg

1. Place all of the ingredients in a 4- to 5-quart slow cooker. Stir well to combine.
2. Cover and cook on low for 8 hours, or until the vegetables are tender and a sauce has formed.
3. Stir gently and serve.

GAME PLAN: Caponata makes a wonderful sandwich spread or a delicious topping for grilled tofu. Add it to soups, stews, or salad dressings for a nice change of pace. It freezes well, too, for later use.

Spiced Cranberry-Apple Cider

GLUTEN-FREE, LOW-CALORIE, VEGAN

PREP TIME:
5 MINUTES

COOK TIME:
1 HOUR ON HIGH

SERVES 8

PER SERVING:
Calories: 125; Fat: 0g;
Saturated Fat: 0g;
Cholesterol: 0mg;
Carbohydrates: 32g;
Fiber: 0g; Protein: 0g;
Sodium: 48mg

This nonalcoholic cider is rich in antioxidants from the cranberry juice. It's a festive winter drink and a warm, welcome treat after caroling, cutting down a Christmas tree, or playing out in the snow. And it makes your home smell wonderful as it cooks.

4 cups apple cider

4 cups cranberry juice

4 cinnamon sticks

2 orange wedges

1 teaspoon whole cloves

1. Place the apple cider, cranberry juice, and cinnamon sticks in a 3-quart slow cooker.
2. Pierce the orange wedges with the cloves and add the studded orange wedges to the slow cooker.
3. Cover and cook on high for 1 hour, or until the mixture is hot and steaming.
4. Uncover the slow cooker, reduce the heat to low, and ladle the warm cider into mugs. Discard the orange wedges before serving.

Spiked Apple Cider

GLUTEN-FREE, LOW-CALORIE, VEGETARIAN

Adults (only!) will enjoy this hot apple cider flavored with butter, nutmeg, and dark rum. It's the perfect addition to keep the mood festive at fall parties and cold winter gatherings. Your driveway needs to be shoveled? Get this drink in the slow cooker before you head out, and it will be ready to enjoy after your hard work.

2 tablespoons unsalted butter

½ cup packed brown sugar

¼ teaspoon freshly grated nutmeg

6 cups unfiltered apple cider

2 cinnamon sticks

1 cup dark rum

PREP TIME:
5 MINUTES

COOK TIME:
1 HOUR ON HIGH

SERVES 6

PER SERVING:
Calories: 309; Fat: 4g;
Saturated Fat: 3g;
Cholesterol: 10mg;
Carbohydrates: 55g;
Fiber: 0g; Protein: 0g;
Sodium: 95mg

1. Place the butter in a small, microwave-safe bowl or cup and microwave on high for 20 to 30 seconds, until melted. Add the brown sugar and nutmeg and stir until combined. Transfer the butter mixture to a 3-quart slow cooker and add the apple cider and cinnamon sticks.
2. Cover and cook on high for 1 hour, or until the mixture is hot and steaming.
3. Uncover the slow cooker, reduce the heat to low, and stir in the rum. Discard the cinnamon sticks. Serve the cider warm, ladled into mugs.

INGREDIENT TIP: There are many different types of rum: dark rum, light rum, gold rum, and spiced rum. Dark rum is aged for longer periods, giving it a complex flavor. Light rum is aged very briefly and is clear. Gold rum is aged in oak barrels and has a more complicated flavor than light rum, and spiced rum has spices added to it. Any type can be used in this recipe.

Mulled Wine

GLUTEN-FREE, LOW-CALORIE, VEGAN

PREP TIME:
5 MINUTES

COOK TIME:
2 HOURS ON LOW

SERVES 6

PER SERVING:
Calories: 271; Fat: 0g;
Saturated Fat: 0g;
Cholesterol: 0mg;
Carbohydrates: 23g;
Fiber: 0g; Protein: 0g;
Sodium: 0g

In Germany, Christmas markets open in every city in December. Vendors offer steaming cups of mulled wine called *glühwein*, which is spicy and warming. This drink is perfect for Christmas or New Year's Eve parties.

2 (750-ml) bottles full-bodied red wine, such as pinot noir

½ cup granulated sugar

2 cinnamon sticks

2 orange slices

1 whole star anise (optional)

1. Place the wine, sugar, cinnamon sticks, orange slices, and star anise (if using) in a 3-quart slow cooker.
2. Cover and cook on low for 2 hours, or until the beverage is hot but not simmering.
3. Remove the cinnamon sticks, orange slices, and star anise (if used) before serving.

INGREDIENT TIP: When you buy the red wine for this recipe, ask for German red wines. The country is famous for white wine but also makes great reds. Some brands include Franz Keller, Meyer-Näkel, and Bernhard Huber. They all make delicious pinot noirs.

Chai Tea

GLUTEN-FREE, LOW-CALORIE, VEGETARIAN

In India, chai is served in tiny disposable clay cups that can be thrown on the ground and broken up into the dirt after use. This recipe is a far richer beverage than what is typically considered chai in the United States. It's delicious served for breakfast or any time of the day.

4 cups hot water

2 whole star anise

2 cinnamon sticks

1 teaspoon ground cardamom

6 black tea bags

¼ cup packed brown sugar

2 cups half-and-half

1. Pour the hot water into a 3-quart slow cooker; then add the star anise, cinnamon sticks, cardamom, and black tea bags.
2. Cover and cook on high for 30 minutes.
3. Using a slotted spoon, remove and discard the tea bags. Stir in the brown sugar and half-and-half.
4. Cover and cook for 15 minutes more, or until the chai is hot. Remove the cinnamon sticks and star anise before serving.

PREP TIME:
5 MINUTES

COOK TIME:
45 MINUTES
ON HIGH

SERVES 4

PER SERVING:
Calories: 211; Fat: 14g;
Saturated Fat: 9g;
Cholesterol: 48mg;
Carbohydrates: 24g;
Fiber: <1g; Protein: 3g;
Sodium: 54mg

Hot Chocolate

GLUTEN-FREE, LOW-CALORIE, VEGETARIAN

PREP TIME:
5 MINUTES

COOK TIME:
1 HOUR ON HIGH

SERVES 4

PER SERVING:
Calories: 328; Fat: 16g;
Saturated Fat:10g;
Cholesterol: 33mg;
Carbohydrates: 41g;
Fiber: 3g; Protein: 9g;
Sodium: 130mg

After a day of sledding or chopping firewood out in the cold, a mug of hot chocolate hits the spot. Simply put the ingredients in the slow cooker before you head outdoors and savor this sweet beverage when you return.

¼ cup granulated sugar

2 tablespoons unsweetened cocoa powder

4 cups whole milk, divided

1 vanilla bean, split, seeds scraped and reserved, or 1 tablespoon pure vanilla extract

3½ ounces dark chocolate, roughly chopped

1. In a small measuring cup, combine the sugar and cocoa powder. Whisk in about ¼ cup of milk until no lumps remain.

2. Pour the cocoa mixture into a 2-quart slow cooker. Add the remaining 3¾ cups of milk, the vanilla bean pod and seeds, and the dark chocolate. Stir gently to combine.

3. Cover and cook on low for 1 hour; then stir with a wire whisk. The mixture should be hot and the chocolate melted. Continue cooking for another 15 to 20 minutes if the chocolate has not melted. Remove the vanilla bean pod before serving.

GAME PLAN: If you plan to make a lot of beverages in your slow cooker, it's worthwhile to invest in a 2-quart-size appliance. Remember that slow cookers should be filled half to two-thirds full for the best results.

**Honey-Dijon
Brussels Sprouts,**
page 62

CHAPTER 4

VEGETABLES AND SIDES

Sweet and Spicy Kale

GLUTEN-FREE, LOW-CALORIE, VEGAN, WEEKNIGHT HERO

PREP TIME:
10 MINUTES

COOK TIME:
8 HOURS ON LOW

SERVES 4

PER SERVING:
Calories: 124; Fat: 1g;
Saturated Fat: <1g;
Cholesterol: 0mg;
Carbohydrates: 29g;
Fiber: 5g; Protein: 5g;
Sodium: 636mg

Adding a little sweetness and a little spice to kale balances out some of the bitterness of this dark, leafy green, making it a really delicious side dish. When preparing the kale, trim away the large center stems, which tend to be on the tough side, leaving only the leaves for the dish.

¼ cup pure maple syrup

1 teaspoon garlic powder

Grated zest and juice
   of 1 orange

1 teaspoon sea salt

¼ to ½ teaspoon red
   pepper flakes

¼ teaspoon freshly
   ground black pepper

2 pounds kale, stems trimmed

1. In a small bowl, whisk together the maple syrup, garlic powder, orange zest and juice, salt, red pepper flakes, and pepper.
2. Place the kale in a 3-quart slow cooker. Add the syrup mixture to the kale, tossing to coat the leaves.
3. Cover and cook on low for 8 hours; then gently stir the kale and serve.

INGREDIENT TIP: Like all dark leafy greens, kale cooks way down. The slow cooker will be full when you start the recipe, but the greens will quickly wilt in the heat and cook until very tender. Six cups of raw kale leaves will cook down to about 2 cooked cups.

Maple-Glazed Carrots

GLUTEN-FREE, LOW-CALORIE, VEGAN, WEEKNIGHT HERO

Using packaged baby carrots makes this recipe a snap. Choose pure maple syrup, not the maple-flavored pancake syrup you find in the pancake aisle. While pure maple syrup is more expensive than the sugar-based, artificially flavored syrups, it makes up for the higher price with its flavor.

¼ **cup pure maple syrup**

½ **teaspoon ground ginger**

¼ **teaspoon ground nutmeg**

½ **teaspoon sea salt**

Juice of 1 orange

1½ **pounds baby carrots**

1. In a small bowl, whisk together the maple syrup, ginger, nutmeg, salt, and orange juice.
2. Place the carrots in a 3-quart slow cooker. Add the syrup mixture to the carrots, tossing to coat.
3. Cover and cook on low for 8 hours, until the carrots are very tender.

PREP TIME:
10 MINUTES

COOK TIME:
8 HOURS ON LOW

SERVES 6

PER SERVING:
Calories: 86; Fat: 0g;
Saturated Fat: 0g;
Cholesterol: 0mg;
Carbohydrates: 21g;
Fiber: 3g; Protein: 1g;
Sodium: 282mg

Garlic-Parmesan Green Beans

GLUTEN-FREE, LOW-CALORIE, VEGETARIAN

When you cook the green beans, broth, butter, garlic, and cheese for this recipe, your kitchen will be filled with incredible aromas. The slow cooker will look pretty full when this starts cooking, but the ingredients will cook down a bit as the hours go by. This is a great recipe to serve alongside grilled chicken or steak.

3 pounds green beans, trimmed

⅓ cup Vegetable Broth (page 264 or store-bought)

4 garlic cloves, minced

⅔ cup shaved Parmesan cheese

½ teaspoon sea salt

¼ teaspoon freshly ground black pepper

1 tablespoon unsalted butter, cut into small pieces

1. Place the green beans in a 4-quart slow cooker.
2. Pour the broth over the top. Sprinkle the garlic, Parmesan cheese, salt, and pepper over the green beans. Top with the pieces of butter.
3. Cover and cook on low for 4 to 6 hours or on high for 2 to 3 hours, or until the beans are tender.

EXTRA EASY: Some grocery stores offer green beans that have already been trimmed and even cut into smaller pieces. Pick up a couple of containers to cut your prep time in half.

PREP TIME:
10 MINUTES

COOK TIME:
4 TO 6 HOURS
ON LOW OR
2 TO 3 HOURS
ON HIGH

SERVES 6

PER SERVING:
Calories: 139; Fat: 6g;
Saturated Fat: 3g;
Cholesterol: 16mg;
Carbohydrates: 17g;
Fiber: 8g; Protein: 10g;
Sodium: 392mg

Sweet and Sour Cabbage and Apples

GLUTEN-FREE, LOW-CALORIE, VEGETARIAN

PREP TIME:
20 MINUTES

COOK TIME:
8 HOURS ON LOW

SERVES 6

PER SERVING:
Calories: 167; Fat: 1g;
Saturated Fat: <1g;
Cholesterol: 0mg;
Carbohydrates: 40g;
Fiber: 9g; Protein: 5g;
Sodium: 309mg

Cabbage and apples make a flavorful combination, and when you add the sweetness of honey and orange, the sourness of vinegar, and a bit of heat from chili garlic sauce, you've got a dish that hits all the high notes. This is a delicious and satisfying side that has an addictive flavor.

¼ cup honey

¼ cup apple cider vinegar

2 tablespoons chili garlic sauce

1 teaspoon grated orange zest

½ teaspoon sea salt

3 sweet-tart apples (such as Braeburn), peeled, cored, and sliced

2 heads green cabbage, cored and shredded

1 red onion, thinly sliced

1. In a small bowl, whisk together the honey, vinegar, chili garlic sauce, orange zest, and salt.
2. Place the apples, cabbage, and onion in a 4-quart slow cooker. Add the honey mixture and stir to coat.
3. Cover and cook on low for 8 hours, or until the cabbage and apples are tender. Serve.

INGREDIENT TIP: Chili garlic sauce is an Asian condiment that you can find in large grocery stores. If you can't find it, substitute chili sauce and add 2 minced garlic cloves.

Cilantro and Lime Rice

GLUTEN-FREE, LOW-CALORIE, VEGETARIAN

This rice cooks in the slow cooker until it is moist and fluffy; then lime zest, lime juice, and a generous amount of cilantro are stirred in. You'll have to stir the rice after the first hour of cooking, so this is a recipe to make when you're at home for the day.

3 cups water

2 tablespoons unsalted butter

1 teaspoon sea salt

1½ cups uncooked long-grain white rice

2 teaspoons grated lime zest

1 tablespoon freshly squeezed lime juice

½ cup chopped fresh cilantro, divided

1. Place the water, butter, salt, and rice in a 2-quart slow cooker. Gently stir to combine.
2. Cover and cook on low for 2½ hours, stirring the rice once after the first 30 minutes, until it's tender.
3. Stir in the lime zest and juice and ¼ cup of cilantro.
4. Top with the remaining ¼ cup of cilantro and serve.

GAME PLAN: You can make a big batch of this recipe and freeze it to use in other recipes. Place 4 cups of long-grain rice in a 4-quart slow cooker and add 8½ cups of water along with 2 teaspoons of sea salt and 3 tablespoons of butter. Cover and cook on low for 3 hours, stirring after the first hour. Add 4 teaspoons of grated lime zest, 2 tablespoons of lime juice, and ½ cup of chopped fresh cilantro. Fluff the rice and divide it into 2-cup portions in freezer bags. Freeze for up to 3 months. To use, let thaw in the refrigerator overnight. Do not thaw on the counter.

PREP TIME:
5 MINUTES

COOK TIME:
2½ HOURS ON LOW

SERVES 6

PER SERVING:
Calories: 206; Fat: 4g;
Saturated Fat: 3g;
Cholesterol: 10mg;
Carbohydrates: 38g;
Fiber: 1g; Protein: 4g;
Sodium: 393mg

Coconutty Brown Rice

GLUTEN-FREE, VEGAN

PREP TIME:
15 MINUTES

COOK TIME:
3 HOURS ON HIGH

SERVES 4 TO 6

PER SERVING:
Calories: 480; Fat: 19g;
Saturated Fat: 14g;
Cholesterol: 0mg;
Carbohydrates: 72g;
Fiber: 4g; Protein: 9g;
Sodium: 314mg

Coconut rice is a restaurant favorite that's easy to make at home. Because brown rice still has its hull, it takes more time and more liquid to cook than white rice, which makes it the perfect choice for the slow cooker. This recipe makes an ideal base for rice bowls, stir-fries, and curries.

2 cups brown rice

3 cups water

1½ cups full-fat coconut milk

½ teaspoon sea salt

½ teaspoon ground ginger

⅛ teaspoon freshly
  ground black pepper

1. Place the rice, water, coconut milk, salt, ginger, and pepper in a 2-quart slow cooker. Stir to combine.
2. Cover and cook on high for 3 hours, until the rice is tender. Fluff with a fork and serve.

GAME PLAN: If you use a lot of rice, cook it according to this recipe and freeze it for later use. Put 2 cups of cooked rice into a freezer bag and gently flatten the rice in a 1-inch layer. Freeze flat, so the rice doesn't clump, for up to six months. To use, let thaw in the refrigerator overnight or add it straight to stir-fries and soups.

Spanish Rice

GLUTEN-FREE, LOW-CALORIE, VEGAN

This classic and delicious dish can be served as a side dish to accompany chicken or fish or as a main dish for vegetarians. The tomatoes and chiles add wonderful flavor and color, and all the spices perk up the plain white rice. You can use any type of green chiles you'd like in this recipe; try minced jalapeños or poblano peppers.

2 cups long-grain white rice

3 cups Vegetable Broth (page 264 or store-bought)

2 tablespoons extra-virgin olive oil

1 (14.5-ounce) can crushed tomatoes

1 (4-ounce) can diced Hatch green chiles

1 medium yellow onion, diced

½ teaspoon sea salt

½ teaspoon ground cumin

½ teaspoon garlic powder

½ teaspoon chili powder

½ teaspoon dried oregano

Freshly ground black pepper

PREP TIME:
15 MINUTES

COOK TIME:
5 TO 6 HOURS
ON LOW

SERVES 6

PER SERVING:
Calories: 300; Fat: 5g;
Saturated Fat: 1g;
Cholesterol: 0mg;
Carbohydrates: 56g;
Fiber: 3g; Protein: 5g;
Sodium: 669mg

1. Place all the ingredients in a 3-quart slow cooker. Stir to combine.
2. Cover and cook on low for 5 to 6 hours, until the rice is tender and has absorbed the liquid. Fluff with a fork and serve.

Mediterranean Quinoa with Pepperoncini

GLUTEN-FREE, LOW-CALORIE, VEGAN, WEEKNIGHT HERO

PREP TIME:
15 MINUTES

COOK TIME:
6 TO 8 HOURS
ON LOW

SERVES 6

PER SERVING:
Calories: 251; Fat: 10g;
Saturated Fat: 1g;
Cholesterol: 0mg;
Carbohydrates: 35g;
Fiber: 4g; Protein: 7g;
Sodium: 529mg

This colorful and tasty side dish can also be served as a main dish for vegetarians since quinoa is a whole and complete protein source. The arugula adds a peppery bite, and the pepperoncini is mildly spicy.

1½ cups quinoa, rinsed and drained

3 cups Vegetable Broth (page 264 or store-bought)

½ teaspoon sea salt

½ teaspoon garlic powder

¼ teaspoon dried oregano

¼ teaspoon dried basil

⅛ teaspoon freshly ground black pepper

3 cups arugula

½ cup diced tomatoes

⅓ cup sliced pepperoncini

¼ cup freshly squeezed lemon juice

3 tablespoons extra-virgin olive oil

1. Place the quinoa, broth, salt, garlic powder, oregano, basil, and black pepper in a 3-quart slow cooker. Stir to combine.
2. Cover and cook on low for 6 to 8 hours, or until the quinoa is tender and has absorbed the liquid.
3. In a large bowl, toss together the arugula, tomatoes, pepperoncini, lemon juice, and olive oil.
4. When the quinoa is done, add it to the arugula salad, mix well, and serve.

INGREDIENT TIP: The arugula will wilt in the heat from the cooked quinoa and become more tender. You can substitute other greens for the arugula if you'd like; try spinach or kale that has been torn into pieces.

Classic Refried Beans

GLUTEN-FREE, LOW-CALORIE, VEGAN, WEEKNIGHT HERO

PREP TIME:
10 MINUTES

COOK TIME:
8 HOURS ON LOW

SERVES 6

PER SERVING:
Calories: 145; Fat: 1g;
Saturated Fat: 0g;
Cholesterol: 0mg;
Carbohydrates: 27g;
Fiber: 11g; Protein: 9g;
Sodium: 389mg

Refried beans are a staple side dish and an accompaniment of many main dishes in Mexican cuisine. They aren't hard to make at all, plus they freeze well for up to three months, so you can make a big batch and freeze it in recipe-size portions for use later on. Always add salt at the very end when cooking beans because salt keeps them from getting tender while they cook. Use these refried beans as a side dish or in burritos, nachos, or enchiladas.

1¼ cups dried pinto beans, rinsed

1 medium yellow onion, chopped

1 jalapeño, seeded and chopped

2 garlic cloves, minced

4 cups water or Vegetable Broth (page 264 or store-bought)

1 teaspoon sea salt

1 teaspoon freshly ground black pepper

½ teaspoon ancho chili powder

¼ teaspoon ground cumin

1. Place the beans, onion, jalapeño, garlic, and water in a 3-quart slow cooker. Stir to combine.
2. Cover and cook on low for 8 hours, or until the beans are tender.
3. Drain and reserve the liquid.
4. Add the salt, black pepper, chili powder, and cumin to the beans, and stir well to combine.
5. Mash the beans with a potato masher, adding the bean liquid as needed to get the correct consistency. Serve warm.

GAME PLAN: To freeze the beans, let them cool for 30 minutes at room temperature. Then separate them into 1-cup portions in freezer containers and freeze them for up to 4 months. Thaw overnight in the refrigerator.

Creamy Mushroom Hash Browns

GLUTEN-FREE, LOW-CALORIE, VEGETARIAN, WEEKNIGHT HERO

You can make your own hash browns by grating the potatoes either in a food processor or on a box grater, but the frozen varieties are of very high quality and much easier—not to mention faster—to use.

1 (30-ounce) package frozen hash brown potatoes

2 yellow onions, chopped

2 cups sliced cremini or shiitake mushrooms

4 garlic cloves, minced

1 cup Vegetable Broth (page 264 or store-bought)

3 tablespoons extra-virgin olive oil

1 teaspoon dried tarragon leaves

1 teaspoon salt

⅛ teaspoon freshly ground black pepper

1 (8-ounce) package cream cheese, cut into cubes

1 cup ricotta cheese

1 cup sour cream

PREP TIME:
15 MINUTES

COOK TIME:
8 HOURS ON LOW,
PLUS 30 MINUTES
ON HIGH

SERVES 8

PER SERVING:
Calories: 373; Fat: 26g;
Saturated Fat: 14g;
Cholesterol: 59mg;
Carbohydrates: 27g;
Fiber: 2g; Protein: 10g;
Sodium: 508mg

1. Place the frozen hash browns, onions, mushrooms, and garlic in a 4- to 5-quart slow cooker. Stir well to combine.
2. Pour the broth and olive oil over the vegetables and sprinkle with the tarragon, salt, and pepper.
3. Cover and cook on low for 8 hours, or until the vegetables are tender.
4. Stir in the cream cheese, ricotta, and sour cream. Cover and cook on high for 20 to 30 minutes, or until the mixture is thickened and bubbly.
5. Stir gently and serve.

IF YOU HAVE A MINUTE: If you are at home during the day, stir this recipe a few times while it's cooking. That way, the brown bits on the sides of the slow cooker will mix into the center and add that much more flavor. But if you can't stir it during cooking, that's okay. Give it a good stir to mix the crusty brown bits on the side into the center of the potatoes before serving.

Honey-Dijon Brussels Sprouts

GLUTEN-FREE, LOW-CALORIE, VEGETARIAN

PREP TIME:
15 MINUTES

COOK TIME:
4 HOURS ON LOW

SERVES 4 TO 6

PER SERVING:
Calories: 85; Fat: <1g;
Saturated Fat: <1g;
Cholesterol: 0mg;
Carbohydrates: 19g;
Fiber: 4g; Protein: 4g;
Sodium: 410mg

Brussels sprouts are delicious, tender, and sweet when prepared properly. The slow cooker is a great way to cook these little cabbages. When they are flavored with honey and Dijon mustard, they will tempt the pickiest eater.

1 pound Brussels sprouts,
  ends trimmed

2 tablespoons honey

1 tablespoon Dijon mustard

½ teaspoon garlic powder

½ teaspoon sea salt

¼ cup water

Grated Pecorino cheese
  (optional), for serving

1. Place all of the ingredients except the Pecorino cheese in a 3-quart slow cooker. Toss together to distribute evenly.

2. Cover and cook on low for 3 to 4 hours, or until the Brussels sprouts are tender and glazed. If desired, grate some Pecorino cheese on top. Serve.

INGREDIENT TIP: To prepare Brussels sprouts, sort through them and remove any with soft or dark spots. Using a sharp knife, trim the very end of the sprout, which is usually dark brown. Then just wash and toss into the slow cooker.

Classic Baked Beans

GLUTEN-FREE, LOW-CALORIE, VEGAN

This is the perfect recipe to bring to a backyard potluck or to serve at your own barbecue party. These sweet and savory baked beans are packed with flavor. Your vegetarian and vegan friends will thank you for a dish free of animal products. But if you can't imagine baked beans without bacon, feel free to fry up a few slices and toss them in before the beans cook.

4 (15-ounce) cans pinto beans, drained and rinsed

1 cup ketchup

¼ cup packed brown sugar

1 tablespoon Dijon mustard

¼ cup apple cider vinegar

¼ teaspoon sea salt

⅛ teaspoon freshly ground black pepper

1. Place the beans, ketchup, brown sugar, mustard, and vinegar in a 3-quart slow cooker. Season with the salt and pepper. Stir to combine.
2. Cover and cook on low for 3 hours, or until the bean mixture is bubbling.

PREP TIME:
5 MINUTES

COOK TIME:
3 HOURS ON LOW

SERVES 8

PER SERVING:
Calories: 260; Fat: 0g;
Saturated Fat: 0g;
Cholesterol: 0mg;
Carbohydrates: 54g;
Fiber: 9g; Protein: 12g;
Sodium: 440mg

Slow Cooker Mashed Potatoes

GLUTEN-FREE, LOW-CALORIE, VEGETARIAN

PREP TIME:
15 MINUTES

COOK TIME:
4 HOURS ON HIGH

SERVES 8

PER SERVING:
Calories: 220; Fat: 9g;
Saturated Fat: 7g;
Cholesterol: 21mg;
Carbohydrates: 34g;
Fiber: 4g; Protein: 6g;
Sodium: 227mg

You don't have to peel the potatoes before you add them to the slow cooker, but peeled potatoes will have a smoother texture after they're mashed. You can add more vegetables to this simple recipe; try some garlic cloves or a chopped onion.

2 tablespoons unsalted butter, at room temperature, divided

3 pounds Yukon gold potatoes, peeled and diced

1 cup Vegetable Broth (page 264 or store-bought)

1 cup sour cream

¼ cup roughly chopped fresh chives

½ teaspoon sea salt

Freshly ground black pepper

1. Grease a 3- to 4-quart slow cooker with about 1 teaspoon of butter. Add the potatoes and broth.
2. Cover and cook on high for 4 hours. Test for doneness by prodding several potatoes with a fork. They should be tender and break apart easily when done.
3. Use a potato masher, immersion blender, or wooden spoon to mash the potatoes until mostly smooth.
4. Beat in the sour cream, chives, and remaining butter and continue beating until the potatoes reach your desired consistency. Season with salt and pepper and serve.

GAME PLAN: You can keep these potatoes warm in the slow cooker until it's time to eat. Just smooth the top of the potatoes while they are in the slow cooker and top with about 3 tablespoons of broth. Cover and turn the slow cooker to "keep warm" for up to 2 hours.

Mashed Sweet Potatoes

GLUTEN-FREE, LOW-CALORIE, VEGETARIAN

Compared with white potatoes, sweet potatoes have a lower glycemic index, more fiber, and fewer calories. They're also rich in vitamin A. So, when you're in the mood for mashed potatoes, give these richly hued spuds a try instead. For variety, season with minced rosemary, butter, and toasted pecans.

3 tablespoons unsalted butter, at room temperature, divided

4 large sweet potatoes, peeled and cubed

½ cup water

½ teaspoon sea salt

⅛ teaspoon freshly ground black pepper

½ cup sour cream

1. Coat the interior of a 3-quart slow cooker with 1 tablespoon of butter. Place the sweet potatoes and water in the slow cooker and season with the salt and pepper.
2. Cover and cook on low for 4 hours.
3. Add the remaining 2 tablespoons of butter and the sour cream to the slow cooker and mash with a wooden spoon or a potato masher until smooth.

PREP TIME:
10 MINUTES

COOK TIME:
4 HOURS ON LOW

SERVES 6

PER SERVING: Calories: 207; Fat: 10g; Saturated Fat: 7g; Cholesterol: 24mg; Carbohydrates: 26g; Fiber: 4g; Protein: 4g; Sodium: 232mg

Herbed Mashed Cauliflower

GLUTEN-FREE, LOW-CALORIE, VEGETARIAN, WEEKNIGHT HERO

PREP TIME:
15 MINUTES

COOK TIME:
8 HOURS ON LOW

SERVES 6 TO 8

PER SERVING:
Calories: 291; Fat: 23g;
Saturated Fat: 14g;
Cholesterol: 72mg;
Carbohydrates: 19g;
Fiber: 8g; Protein: 7g;
Sodium: 579mg

Cauliflower has replaced potatoes in this classic mashed dish, beloved as the ultimate comfort food. Not only does this recipe taste very much like mashed potatoes, it's also high in antioxidants and fiber. Bring on the mashed goodness!

2 large heads cauliflower

1 leek, white and light green part only, chopped

3 garlic cloves, minced

1 cup Vegetable Broth (page 264 or store-bought)

2 thyme sprigs

1 teaspoon sea salt

⅛ teaspoon freshly ground black pepper

⅓ cup unsalted butter or extra-virgin olive oil

1 cup light cream or almond milk

2 tablespoons minced fresh chives

3 tablespoons minced fresh parsley

1. Remove and discard the leaves from the cauliflower. Cut the florets off the cauliflower. Cut the stems into 1-inch pieces.
2. Place the cauliflower, leek, garlic, broth, thyme, salt, and pepper in a 4- to 5-quart slow cooker. Stir well to combine.
3. Cover and cook on low for 8 hours, or until the cauliflower is very tender.
4. Remove and discard the thyme stems. Stir the butter, cream, chives, and parsley into the cauliflower.
5. Purée the cauliflower right in the slow cooker using an immersion blender or potato masher, or purée in 2 or 3 batches in a food processor or blender. Serve.

EXTRA EASY: Like many vegetables, you can find prepared cauliflower florets in the produce aisle of the supermarket. Make sure you look for florets that don't have any brown spots and check the expiration dates.

Vegetarian Stuffing

VEGETARIAN

Making bread stuffing in a slow cooker is a good option because the appliance mimics the moist heat inside a traditional Thanksgiving turkey without the risk of foodborne illness. And vegetarians can enjoy the dish, too. The combination of herbs in this recipe is so delicious that even meat-eaters won't miss the meat!

PREP TIME:
10 MINUTES

COOK TIME:
4 HOURS ON LOW

SERVES 4 TO 6

PER SERVING:
Calories: 412; Fat: 10g;
Saturated Fat: 4g;
Cholesterol: 16mg;
Carbohydrates: 73g;
Fiber: 2g; Protein: 12g;
Sodium: 1,032mg

1 (12- to 18-ounce) loaf white or wheat bread, cubed

2 tablespoons unsalted butter or extra-virgin olive oil

4 celery stalks, diced

1 yellow onion, diced

2 garlic cloves, minced

¼ cup minced fresh sage

1 tablespoon minced fresh thyme

1 tablespoon minced fresh rosemary

¼ cup minced fresh parsley

2 cups Vegetable Broth (page 264 or store-bought)

1. Preheat the oven to 350°F. Spread the bread cubes in a single layer on a rimmed baking sheet. Toast the cubes in the oven for 5 minutes; then flip them and toast for 5 minutes more.

2. Meanwhile, in a large skillet over medium heat, melt the butter. Add the celery and onion and cook for 5 minutes. Add the garlic and cook for 1 minute more.

3. Transfer the onion and celery mixture to a 4-quart slow cooker and add the toasted bread cubes. Add the sage, thyme, rosemary, and parsley and toss gently to combine. Drizzle the vegetable broth evenly over the mixture and toss again.

4. Cover and cook on low for 4 hours, or until the stuffing is hot and the vegetables are tender.

INGREDIENT TIP: Instead of purchasing three separate packages of herbs, consider buying a "poultry blend," which usually contains sage, thyme, and rosemary.

Cornbread Stuffing with Ham and Dried Fruit

WEEKNIGHT HERO

PREP TIME:
15 MINUTES

COOK TIME:
6 TO 8 HOURS
ON LOW

SERVES 6

PER SERVING:
Calories: 479; Fat: 22g;
Saturated Fat: 11g;
Cholesterol: 87mg;
Carbohydrates: 59g;
Fiber: 2g; Protein: 15g;
Sodium: 1,281mg

This cornbread dressing is a tradition for many families around the holidays—and for good reason. It's filled with salty and smoky ham, flavored with fresh herbs, and studded with bits of vegetables and fruit.

4 cups crumbled stale cornbread

1 medium yellow onion, chopped

2 celery stalks, chopped

1 cup diced smoked ham

½ teaspoon sea salt

⅛ teaspoon freshly ground black pepper

¼ cup chopped fresh herbs, such as thyme and rosemary

½ cup chopped dried apricots

½ cup (1 stick) unsalted butter, melted

2 cups Chicken Stock (page 263 or store-bought) or Vegetable Broth (page 264 or store-bought)

½ cup 2% milk

1 large egg, beaten

4 drops hot sauce

1. Place the cornbread, onion, celery, ham, salt, pepper, herbs, and apricots in a 3-quart slow cooker. Stir to combine.
2. Drizzle with the butter and stir again.
3. In a medium bowl, whisk together the stock or broth, milk, egg, and hot sauce. Pour this mixture into the slow cooker and stir gently.
4. Cover and cook on low for 6 to 8 hours, or until the mixture registers at least 160°F on a food thermometer. Serve hot.

INGREDIENT TIP: To stale cornbread, cut it into slices or cubes and let it stand overnight, uncovered, at room temperature. Then crumble it and proceed with the recipe.

Cheesy Spaghetti Squash Casserole

GLUTEN-FREE, LOW-CALORIE, VEGETARIAN

A simple herb blend from your pantry and two kinds of cheese spice up this easy casserole. This is a nice dish to bring to a potluck because people who are following a gluten-free diet can eat it.

1 (2-pound) spaghetti squash

Nonstick cooking spray

1 cup low-sodium or no-salt-added canned diced tomatoes, drained

1¼ teaspoons dried Italian seasoning

½ teaspoon sea salt

¼ teaspoon freshly ground black pepper

4 ounces mozzarella cheese, shredded

⅓ cup grated Parmesan cheese

¼ cup water

PREP TIME:
15 MINUTES

COOK TIME:
4 TO 6 HOURS
ON LOW OR
2 TO 3 HOURS
ON HIGH

SERVES 6

PER SERVING:
Calories: 129; Fat: 6g;
Saturated Fat: 4g;
Cholesterol: 14mg;
Carbohydrates: 13g;
Fiber: 3g; Protein: 8g;
Sodium: 449mg

1. Pierce the spaghetti squash all over with a knife. Place it in a microwave-safe dish and microwave for 7 to 10 minutes, or until soft. Be careful removing it from the microwave; it will be very hot.

2. Cut the squash in half lengthwise. Scoop out and discard the seeds. Use a fork to scrape out the spaghetti-like strands into a large bowl.

3. Coat a 3- to 4-quart slow cooker generously with nonstick cooking spray.

4. Place the spaghetti squash strands, tomatoes, Italian seasoning, salt, pepper, both cheeses, and water in the slow cooker. Stir gently to combine.

5. Cover and cook on low for 4 to 6 hours or on high for 2 to 3 hours, until the casserole is bubbling.

INGREDIENT TIP: Spaghetti squash will release water when it's cooked. To reduce that amount of liquid, place the spaghetti squash strands on a couple of paper towels, sprinkle them with a bit of salt, and let them sit for about 5 minutes. Gently wring the excess water out before adding them to the slow cooker.

Southern-Style Collard Greens

GLUTEN-FREE, LOW-CALORIE, WEEKNIGHT HERO

PREP TIME:
15 MINUTES

COOK TIME:
8 HOURS ON LOW

SERVES 6

PER SERVING:
Calories: 34; Fat: 1g;
Saturated Fat: <1g;
Cholesterol: 3mg;
Carbohydrates: 2g;
Fiber: 1g; Protein: 4g;
Sodium: 451mg

Few vegetables are as ubiquitous in Southern cooking as the humble collard green—and for good reason. Collard greens are packed with nutrients and may even help lower cholesterol and reduce the risk of cancer. Enjoy this dish with Barbecue Pork Ribs (page 194) and a cool glass of sweet tea.

2 slices bacon

1 large bunch collard greens

2 garlic cloves, minced

4 cups Chicken Stock (page 263 or store-bought)

¼ teaspoon sea salt

⅛ teaspoon freshly ground black pepper

1. In a medium skillet over medium-low heat, cook the bacon for about 10 minutes, until it is crispy, turning frequently. Crumble the bacon and set it aside.
2. Rinse the collard greens thoroughly. Cut out and discard the tough ribs of the collard greens. Roughly chop the greens and place them in a 3-quart slow cooker along with the garlic, stock, and bacon. Season with the salt and pepper. Stir to combine.
3. Cover and cook on low for 8 hours, or until the greens are very tender and deep green.
4. Use tongs to transfer the cooked collard greens to a serving platter. Serve.

GAME PLAN: Don't toss that bacon grease! Store it in a covered container in the refrigerator and use it for cooking eggs or searing meat. It adds a delicious flavor to other foods.

Ground Beef Chili,
page 99

CHAPTER 5

SOUPS, STEWS, AND CHILIS

Garlicky Chicken and Kale Soup

GLUTEN-FREE, LOW-CALORIE

PREP TIME:
15 MINUTES

COOK TIME:
6 HOURS ON LOW

SERVES 4

PER SERVING:
Calories: 290; Fat: 12g;
Saturated Fat: 3g;
Cholesterol: 135mg;
Carbohydrates: 19g;
Fiber: 5g; Protein: 28g;
Sodium: 599mg

The garlic and red pepper flakes liven up the kale and tender meat in this flavorful soup. Season to taste—you may want more or less garlic and red pepper flakes. You may be accustomed to cooking with the leaner white meat of the chicken, but the thighs add a negligible amount of fat and calories to the dish and a lot more flavor.

6 boneless, skinless chicken thighs

2 small yellow onions, halved lengthwise and sliced thin

4 carrots, diced

6 garlic cloves, roughly chopped

4 cups Chicken Stock (page 263 or store-bought)

¼ teaspoon sea salt

¼ teaspoon red pepper flakes

Grated zest and juice of 1 lemon

4 cups shredded kale

1. Place the chicken, onions, carrots, garlic, stock, salt, red pepper flakes, and lemon zest in a 4-quart slow cooker. Stir to combine.
2. Cover and cook on low for 6 hours, until the chicken is very tender.
3. Using tongs, remove the chicken from the slow cooker and shred it with a fork. Stir the shredded chicken back into the soup.
4. Stir in the lemon juice and kale just before serving.

A LITTLE LIGHTER: You can substitute two bone-in, skinless chicken breasts for the chicken thighs in this recipe. The bones will let you cook the soup for a longer period of time. When the chicken is cooked, remove and discard the bones; then shred the chicken and continue with the recipe.

Chicken Noodle Soup

LOW-CALORIE, WEEKNIGHT HERO

The bones helps keep the chicken moist during the long, slow cooking time and imbue the broth with body and rich flavor. They also let you cook the soup for a longer time period. But if you prefer the convenience, use a large boneless, skinless chicken breast instead. The aroma of this soup is warm and welcoming after a long day of work.

PREP TIME:
15 MINUTES

COOK TIME:
8 HOURS ON LOW

SERVES 4

PER SERVING:
Calories: 334; Fat: 10g;
Saturated Fat: 2g;
Cholesterol: 127mg;
Carbohydrates: 30g;
Fiber: 4g; Protein: 33g;
Sodium: 505mg

2 (8- to 12-ounce)
  bone-in, skinless
  chicken breasts
2 cups sliced carrots
2 cups sliced celery
4 garlic cloves, minced
2 thyme sprigs

4 cups Chicken Stock
  (page 263 or store-bought)
¼ teaspoon sea salt
4 ounces (1 cup) egg noodles
2 teaspoons red wine vinegar
Freshly ground black pepper

1. Place the chicken, carrots, celery, garlic, thyme, stock, and salt in a 4-quart slow cooker. Stir to combine.
2. Cover and cook on low for 8 hours, or until the chicken is cooked and the vegetables are tender.
3. Using tongs, remove the chicken from the slow cooker. Discard the bones and shred the meat with a fork.
4. Add the egg noodles to the slow cooker, cover, and cook for 10 to 15 minutes, until the noodles are tender. Return the shredded chicken to the slow cooker and stir in the vinegar. Season with black pepper and serve.

Chicken and Tortilla Soup

GLUTEN-FREE, WEEKNIGHT HERO

This hearty dish is made with shredded chicken, black beans, and corn, flavored with plenty of garlic and cilantro. You can adjust the spicy heat of this dish by adding or reducing the amount of ancho chili powder or jalapeños to taste. The tortilla chips not only add crunch, but they also thicken the soup and add flavor.

PREP TIME:
15 MINUTES

COOK TIME:
8 HOURS ON LOW
OR
4 HOURS ON HIGH

SERVES 6

PER SERVING:
Calories: 587; Fat: 23g;
Saturated Fat: 11g;
Cholesterol: 114mg;
Carbohydrates: 54g;
Fiber: 11g; Protein: 46g;
Sodium: 609mg

1½ pounds boneless, skinless chicken breasts or thighs

2 yellow onions, chopped

4 garlic cloves, minced

1 medium bell pepper (any color), seeded and chopped

2 teaspoons chili powder

1 teaspoon dried oregano

1 teaspoon ancho chili powder

4 large tomatoes, diced

3 medium jalapeños, seeded and chopped

4 cups Chicken Stock (page 263 or store-bought)

2 cups fresh or frozen corn (optional)

2 (15-ounce) cans black beans, drained and rinsed

½ cup chopped fresh cilantro

1 cup coarsely broken tortilla chips, for serving

2 cups grated Cheddar cheese, for serving

½ cup sour cream, for serving

Avocado, sliced (optional)

Cilantro sprigs, for garnish (optional)

1. Place the chicken, onions, garlic, bell pepper, chili powder, oregano, ancho chili powder, tomatoes, jalapeños, stock, corn, black beans, and cilantro in a 4- to 5-quart slow cooker. Stir well to combine.

2. Cover and cook on low for 8 hours or on high for 4 hours, until the vegetables and chicken are tender.

3. Using tongs, remove the chicken from the slow cooker and shred it with a fork. Stir the shredded chicken back into the soup.

4. Ladle the soup into bowls and top with the chips, cheese, and sour cream. You may also top with avocado slices and garnish with cilantro sprigs.

EXTRA EASY: You can replace the fresh tomatoes and jalapeños with 3 (14.5-ounce) cans of diced tomatoes with chiles to save you about 6 minutes of preparation time. Don't drain the tomatoes before you add them to the soup.

Red Curry Butternut Squash Soup

GLUTEN-FREE, LOW-CALORIE, WEEKNIGHT HERO

PREP TIME:
15 MINUTES

COOK TIME:
8 HOURS ON LOW
OR
4 HOURS ON HIGH

SERVES 4

PER SERVING:
Calories: 224; Fat: 12g;
Saturated Fat: 9g;
Cholesterol: 0mg;
Carbohydrates: 28g;
Fiber: 7g; Protein: 4g;
Sodium: 462mg

If you're not familiar with Thai red curry paste, you're in for a treat. It is a time-saving and economical way to imbue your food with traditional Thai flavors—red chile pepper, lemongrass, galangal root, and makrut lime—without having to scour a specialty market. The aromas of this soup are tantalizing.

4 cups cubed butternut squash

1 cup diced yellow onion

2 teaspoons minced garlic

2 teaspoons minced ginger

4 cups Chicken Stock (page 263 or store-bought)

1 to 2 teaspoons Thai red curry paste

2 teaspoons fish sauce

1 cup coconut milk

2 teaspoons freshly squeezed lime juice

½ cup fresh cilantro, for garnish

1. Place the butternut squash, onion, garlic, ginger, stock, curry paste, fish sauce, and coconut milk in a 4-quart slow cooker. Stir gently to combine.

2. Cover and cook on low for 8 hours or on high for 4 hours, until the squash is tender.

3. Just before serving, stir in the lime juice. Garnish each serving with the cilantro.

EXTRA EASY: You can often find prepared butternut squash that has been seeded and chopped in the produce aisle of the grocery store. This should save at least 10 minutes of preparation time.

French Onion Soup

WEEKNIGHT HERO

Is there anything more comforting on a blustery day than a steaming bowl of French onion soup? Yes—not having to slave over a hot stove stirring onions to make it! Serve this soup with toasted bread topped with shredded Gruyère cheese for an authentic French feast.

2 tablespoons unsalted butter, at room temperature, divided

4 yellow onions, thinly sliced

1 tablespoon extra-virgin olive oil

Pinch sugar

½ teaspoon sea salt

½ cup dry red wine

2 thyme sprigs

4 cups beef broth

1⅓ cups shredded Gruyère cheese, for serving

4 slices French bread, toasted, for serving

1. Grease a 3-quart slow cooker with about 1 teaspoon of butter.
2. Place the onions, olive oil, and the remaining butter in the slow cooker and season with the sugar and sea salt.
3. Cover and cook on low for 8 hours, or until the onions are very tender.
4. Add the wine, thyme, and beef broth and stir gently to combine. Cover and cook on high for 30 minutes more.
5. Meanwhile, preheat the broiler. Divide the cheese among the bread slices. Broil the bread for 2 to 4 minutes, watching carefully, until the cheese is melted and starts to turn golden in spots.
6. Divide the soup among 4 large soup bowls and top with the cheesy bread.

PREP TIME:
15 MINUTES

COOK TIME:
8 HOURS ON LOW, PLUS 30 MINUTES ON HIGH, PLUS BROILING TIME

SERVES 4

PER SERVING:
Calories: 425; Fat: 20g; Saturated Fat: 11g; Cholesterol: 49mg; Carbohydrates: 36g; Fiber: 3g; Protein: 20g; Sodium: 959mg

Split Pea Soup

GLUTEN-FREE, WEEKNIGHT HERO

PREP TIME:
10 MINUTES

COOK TIME:
8 HOURS ON LOW

SERVES 4

PER SERVING:
Calories: 487; Fat: 6g;
Saturated Fat: 2g;
Cholesterol: 14mg;
Carbohydrates: 97g;
Fiber: 39g;
Protein: 41g;
Sodium: 1,0153mg

The ham hock or bone adds a wonderful porky flavor to this classic soup. Ask the butcher in your grocery store for a hock or bone; they may have to order it. The split peas soften completely as they cook, thickening the soup and making this a meal that is perfect for a cold winter day.

1 ham hock or ham bone

4 cups dried green split peas, picked over for debris

2 large carrots, sliced

1 yellow onion, diced

3 garlic cloves, minced

1 teaspoon herbes de Provence

6 cups Vegetable Broth (page 264 or store-bought)

¼ teaspoon sea salt

⅛ teaspoon freshly ground black pepper

1. Place the ham, split peas, carrots, onion, garlic, herbes de Provence, and broth in a 4-quart slow cooker.
2. Cover and cook on low for 8 hours, until the split peas and vegetables are tender.
3. Remove the ham and set it aside on a cutting board until cool enough to handle. Remove the meat and finely dice it; discard the bone.
4. Stir the diced ham into the soup and season it with the salt and pepper before serving.

INGREDIENT TIP: Split peas are legumes. They're peas that are grown specifically for drying. They split naturally in the middle, which means the peas can absorb liquid and almost dissolve into the soup.

Cream of Mushroom Soup

GLUTEN-FREE, LOW-CALORIE, VEGETARIAN, WEEKNIGHT HERO

You'll never go back to the gloppy canned stuff again after trying this rich, flavorful cream of mushroom soup. Not only does it taste better, but it's also better for you—with far less sodium and saturated fat than the store-bought variety. And it's so simple to make!

2 ounces dried mushrooms

2 cups hot water

2 (8-ounce) packages sliced button or cremini mushrooms

4 cups Vegetable Broth (page 264 or store-bought)

¼ cup dry sherry (optional)

1 tablespoon unsalted butter

1 yellow onion, diced

4 garlic cloves, smashed

4 thyme sprigs

½ teaspoon sea salt

⅛ teaspoon freshly ground black pepper

½ cup heavy (whipping) cream

PREP TIME:
15 MINUTES

COOK TIME:
8 HOURS ON LOW

SERVES 6

PER SERVING:
Calories: 133; Fat: 10g;
Saturated Fat: 6g;
Cholesterol: 32mg;
Carbohydrates: 10g;
Fiber: 2g; Protein: 3g;
Sodium: 573mg

1. Place the dried mushrooms in a small bowl and add the hot water. Let them soak for 10 minutes while you prepare the remaining ingredients.
2. Drain the dried mushrooms, reserving the soaking liquid. Strain the soaking liquid through cheesecloth to remove any grit. Remove and discard the stems from the mushrooms and coarsely chop the caps.
3. Place the chopped rehydrated mushrooms, strained soaking liquid, sliced mushrooms, broth, sherry (if using), butter, onion, garlic, thyme, salt, and pepper in a 4-quart slow cooker. Stir to mix well.
4. Cover and cook on low for 8 hours. Discard the thyme sprigs.
5. Transfer 2 cups of the mixture to a blender or food processor and purée until smooth. Pour back into the slow cooker and stir to combine. Stir in the cream and serve warm.

INGREDIENT TIP: Some types of dried mushrooms you might find at the store include shiitakes, chanterelles, porcini, and morels. They will all add deep and rich flavor to this soup.

Lentil Soup with Sausage

GLUTEN-FREE, WEEKNIGHT HERO

PREP TIME:
15 MINUTES

COOK TIME:
8 HOURS ON LOW

SERVES 4

PER SERVING:
Calories: 446; Fat: 16g;
Saturated Fat: 5g;
Cholesterol: 30mg;
Carbohydrates: 46g;
Fiber: 21g;
Protein: 28g;
Sodium: 1,074mg

A little sausage goes a long way in this flavorful, fiber-rich soup. The heat of the sausage adds zip to the soup, while the lentils add texture and nutrition. It's wonderful to come home to the scent of this soup cooking on a cold winter day.

1 tablespoon extra-virgin olive oil

2 hot Italian sausage links, casings removed

1 cup sliced carrots

1 cup sliced celery

1 yellow onion, diced

2 garlic cloves, minced

4 cups Chicken Stock (page 263 or store-bought)

½ cup dry white wine

1½ cups green lentils

½ teaspoon sea salt

⅛ teaspoon freshly ground black pepper

1. Place a large skillet over medium heat and add the olive oil. Once hot, crumble the sausage into the skillet and cook for 5 to 7 minutes, using a wooden spoon to break up the meat, until browned and cooked through. Drain if necessary.

2. Place the sausage in a 4-quart slow cooker. Add the carrots, celery, onion, garlic, stock, wine, lentils, salt, and pepper. Stir well to combine.

3. Cover and cook on low for 8 hours, or until the lentils and vegetables are tender.

GAME PLAN: You can brown the sausage and prepare the vegetables the night before; store them in covered containers in the refrigerator. Measure out the lentils, too. Then, in the morning, just combine all of the ingredients in the slow cooker, turn it on, and go about your day.

Turkey and Wild Rice Soup

GLUTEN-FREE

This soup is a simple and delicious way to use up leftover holiday turkey. You can also make it from a rotisserie chicken since each chicken has about 4 cups of meat.

5 cups Chicken Stock (page 263 or store-bought)

4 cups cooked turkey, cut into bite-size pieces

1 cup wild rice

1 yellow onion, diced

2 garlic cloves, minced

2 carrots, diced

2 celery stalks, sliced

1 teaspoon dried Italian seasoning

½ teaspoon sea salt

⅛ teaspoon freshly ground black pepper

PREP TIME:
15 MINUTES

COOK TIME:
6 HOURS ON LOW

SERVES 4

PER SERVING:
Calories: 407; Fat: 2g; Saturated Fat: 1g; Cholesterol: 108mg; Carbohydrates: 42g; Fiber: 5g; Protein: 53g; Sodium: 880mg

1. Place the stock, turkey, wild rice, onion, garlic, carrots, celery, Italian seasoning, salt, and pepper in a 4-quart slow cooker. Stir to mix well.

2. Cover and cook on low for 6 hours, or until the wild rice is tender.

INGREDIENT TIP: Wild rice is actually a grass seed, not a grain. It grows wild in Minnesota, and the best kind is harvested by Native Americans, who have licenses to harvest it while gliding through the lakes in canoes. It adds a wonderful nutty flavor and texture to this soup.

Chickpea and Spinach Soup

GLUTEN-FREE, LOW-CALORIE, VEGETARIAN

PREP TIME:
25 MINUTES

COOK TIME:
8 TO 10 HOURS
ON LOW

SERVES 8

PER SERVING:
Calories: 201; Fat: 1g;
Saturated Fat: 0g;
Cholesterol: 0mg;
Carbohydrates: 41g;
Fiber: 10g;
Protein: 9g;
Sodium: 684mg

Chickpeas and spinach are a great combination for a hearty soup. The potatoes, carrots, fennel, and tomatoes—and spinach, of course—add delightful pops of color to the recipe. You'll love it even more knowing that it has lots of vitamins A and C.

2 (15-ounce) cans chickpeas, drained and rinsed

2 yellow onions, chopped

1 fennel bulb, peeled and chopped

3 carrots, sliced

3 Yukon Gold potatoes, cubed

4 garlic cloves, minced

5 cups Vegetable Broth (page 264 or store-bought)

2 large tomatoes, seeded and chopped

1 bay leaf

1 teaspoon dried marjoram

1 teaspoon sea salt

⅛ teaspoon freshly ground black pepper

6 cups baby spinach leaves

1. Place the chickpeas, onions, fennel, carrots, potatoes, garlic, broth, tomatoes, bay leaf, marjoram, salt, and pepper in a 4- to 5-quart slow cooker. Stir well to combine.
2. Cover and cook on low for 8 to 10 hours, or until the flavors have blended.
3. Remove and discard the bay leaf. Transfer 1 cup of the soup to a blender or food processor and purée. Stir the purée back into the soup.
4. Tear the spinach into 2-inch pieces. Add the spinach to the slow cooker and stir.
5. Cover and cook on low for another 10 to 15 minutes, or until the spinach is wilted.
6. Stir gently and serve.

GAME PLAN: You can prepare the fennel, carrots, garlic, and tomatoes ahead of time and store them in the refrigerator. Don't peel and cube the potatoes ahead of time, however, or they will turn brown.

Creamy Tomato Bisque

GLUTEN-FREE, LOW-CALORIE, VEGETARIAN, WEEKNIGHT HERO

"Bisque" is simply a smooth soup that has some cream added for richness. It is traditionally made from shell-fish, but the term can refer to any creamy puréed soup. This bisque is delicious, whether you make it from canned tomatoes or tomatoes fresh from your garden.

1 (28-ounce) can crushed tomatoes in purée

1 (8-ounce) can tomato sauce

3 tablespoons tomato paste

2 shallots, minced

1 garlic clove, minced

3 cups Vegetable Broth (page 264 or store-bought)

2 tablespoons unsalted butter

1 teaspoon sea salt

⅛ teaspoon freshly ground black pepper

1 bay leaf

1 teaspoon dried thyme

1 teaspoon dried marjoram

1 cup heavy (whipping) cream

1 cup grated Parmesan cheese

PREP TIME:
15 MINUTES

COOK TIME:
7 TO 8 HOURS
ON LOW

SERVES 6 TO 8

PER SERVING:
Calories: 304; Fat: 24g;
Saturated Fat: 15g;
Cholesterol: 78mg;
Carbohydrates: 14g;
Fiber: 3g; Protein: 14g;
Sodium: 1,460mg

INGREDIENT TIP:
When fresh, ripe, red tomatoes are in season, use them instead of the canned crushed tomatoes in this recipe. Use about 2½ pounds of tomatoes, seeded and roughly chopped.

1. Place the crushed tomatoes, tomato sauce, tomato paste, shallots, garlic, broth, butter, salt, pepper, bay leaf, thyme, and marjoram in a 4-quart slow cooker. Stir well to combine.
2. Cover and cook on low for 7 to 8 hours, or until the soup is blended and bubbling. Remove and discard the bay leaf.
3. Using an immersion blender, purée the soup right in the slow cooker. You can also transfer the soup, in 2 or 3 batches, to a food processor or blender and blend it until smooth. Return the blended soup to the slow cooker.
4. Stir in the cream and Parmesan cheese.
5. Cover and cook on low for another 20 to 25 minutes, or until the soup is hot.
6. Stir gently and serve.

Beer-Cheese Soup

VEGETARIAN

PREP TIME:
20 MINUTES

COOK TIME:
8¼ HOURS
ON LOW

SERVES 6 TO 8

PER SERVING:
Calories: 410; Fat: 27g;
Saturated Fat: 18g;
Cholesterol: 79mg;
Carbohydrates: 19g;
Fiber: 3g; Protein: 16g;
Sodium: 1,109mg

Beer-cheese soup is a classic. The mellow, slightly nutty flavor of beer pairs so well with melted cheese. This is really a meal, so don't serve it as part of a larger menu; you'll just end up with leftovers of everything else after this soup fills you up!

3 tablespoons unsalted butter

2 yellow onions, chopped

5 garlic cloves, minced

3 carrots, sliced

2 celery stalks, sliced

4 cups Vegetable Broth (page 264 or store-bought)

1 (12-ounce) bottle mild beer, such as a lager

½ teaspoon sea salt

⅛ teaspoon freshly ground black pepper

2 cups shredded Cheddar cheese

1 cup shredded Havarti cheese

3 tablespoons cornstarch

1 tablespoon vegetarian Worcestershire sauce

1 tablespoon Dijon mustard

1 cup light cream

1. Place the butter, onion, garlic, carrots, celery, broth, beer, salt, and pepper in a 4- to 5-quart slow cooker. Stir well to combine.

2. Cover and cook on low for 8 hours, or until the vegetables are very tender.

3. In a large bowl, toss the Cheddar and Havarti cheeses with the cornstarch. Add the cheese mixture to the slow cooker and stir well.

4. In a small bowl, whisk together the Worcestershire sauce, mustard, and cream. Add it to the slow cooker and stir well.

5. Cover and cook on low for another 10 to 15 minutes, or until the cheese is melted and the soup is slightly thickened.

6. Stir gently and serve.

INGREDIENT TIP: The mildest beer varieties include lagers, pale ales, and pilsners. A strong-tasting beer, such as a stout, would overwhelm the other flavors here. If you don't like beer, you can use broth instead and add a tablespoon of lemon juice.

Black Bean Soup with Chipotle

GLUTEN-FREE, LOW-CALORIE, VEGAN, WEEKNIGHT HERO

PREP TIME:
10 MINUTES

COOK TIME:
10 HOURS ON LOW

SERVES 8

PER SERVING:
Calories: 98; Fat: 1g;
Saturated Fat: 0g;
Cholesterol: 0mg;
Carbohydrates: 18g;
Fiber: 5g; Protein: 4g;
Sodium: 254mg

These black beans are cooked with tomatoes, garlic, spices, and a generous amount of smoky chipotle for a simple and hearty soup everyone will love. You'll need an immersion or traditional blender to make the soup smooth before serving, or you can use a potato masher. You can also just serve the soup as is.

1 (15-ounce) can black beans, drained and rinsed

6 Roma tomatoes, diced

2 garlic cloves, chopped

3 tablespoons chopped chipotle chiles in adobo sauce

1 teaspoon ground cinnamon

1 tablespoon ground cumin

Juice of 1 orange

3 limes, 1 juiced and 2 cut into wedges, for serving

5 cups Vegetable Broth (page 264 or store-bought)

½ cup chopped fresh cilantro

1. Place the beans, tomatoes, garlic, chipotle chiles in adobo sauce, cinnamon, cumin, orange juice, lime juice, and broth in a 4-quart slow cooker. Stir to combine well.

2. Cover and cook on low for 10 hours, or until the soup is simmering.

3. Using a handheld immersion blender, blend the soup until smooth. You can also transfer the soup, in 2 or 3 batches, to a food processor or blender and blend until smooth. Return the blended soup to the slow cooker. Or you can just leave the soup unblended.

4. Stir in the chopped cilantro. Ladle the soup into bowls and serve hot with the lime wedges.

GAME PLAN: You can use dried beans in this recipe. First, sort and pick over the dried black beans and rinse them. Cover with water (right in the slow cooker insert if you want) and let them soak overnight. Drain and rinse the beans in the morning; then continue with the recipe.

Vegetarian Borscht

GLUTEN-FREE, LOW-CALORIE, VEGAN

Borscht is an Eastern European soup made from beets. Beets are naturally sweet, which makes this soup slightly sweet with a beautiful deep pink color. You can serve this soup hot or cold. Add a delicious tart contrast with a dollop of sour cream or crème fraîche. This soup is as wonderful on a warm summer evening as it is on the coldest of winter days.

PREP TIME:
25 MINUTES

COOK TIME:
9 HOURS ON LOW

SERVES 6

PER SERVING:
Calories: 129; Fat: <1g;
Saturated Fat: <1g;
Cholesterol: 0mg;
Carbohydrates: 28g;
Fiber: 7g; Protein: 4g;
Sodium: 1,118mg

6 large red beets, peeled and chopped

2 yellow onions, chopped

5 garlic cloves, minced

1 large sweet potato, peeled and chopped

5 cups Vegetable Broth (page 264 or store-bought)

1 (14-ounce) can diced tomatoes, undrained

3 tablespoons tomato paste

1 teaspoon dried dill seed

1 teaspoon dried dill weed

1 teaspoon sea salt

⅛ teaspoon freshly ground black pepper

1 teaspoon grated lemon zest

2 tablespoons freshly squeezed lemon juice

2 tablespoons chopped fresh dill weed

1. Place the beets, onions, garlic, sweet potato, broth, diced tomatoes with their juices, tomato paste, dill seed, dried dill weed, salt, and pepper in a 5-quart slow cooker. Stir well to combine.

2. Cover and cook on low for 9 hours, or until the vegetables are very tender.

3. Stir in the lemon zest, lemon juice, and fresh dill weed, and serve.

IF YOU HAVE A MINUTE: You can serve this soup as is, or you can purée it for a wonderful variation. Use an immersion blender right in the slow cooker or transfer the soup, in 2 or 3 batches, to a food processor or blender and blend until smooth. Return it to the slow cooker, stir, and serve.

Ginger-Carrot Bisque

GLUTEN-FREE, LOW-CALORIE, WEEKNIGHT HERO

The ginger and tangy lime juice give this creamy soup a surprising zing. The carrots and potatoes get really soft after this long cooking time, so they purée into a velvety soup. This is comfort in a bowl and is a wonderful soup to serve to guests.

1 cup diced yellow onion

½ cup diced celery

2 tablespoons minced
   fresh ginger

4 cups Chicken Stock
   (page 263 or store-bought)

4 cups diced carrots

2 russet potatoes,
   peeled and sliced

2 teaspoons curry powder

¼ teaspoon sea salt

2 tablespoons freshly
   squeezed lime juice

¼ cup heavy (whipping) cream

½ cup roughly chopped
   fresh cilantro

PREP TIME:
15 MINUTES

COOK TIME:
8 HOURS ON LOW

SERVES 4

PER SERVING:
Calories: 203; Fat: 7g;
Saturated Fat: 4g;
Cholesterol: 20mg;
Carbohydrates: 32g;
Fiber: 6g; Protein: 5g;
Sodium: 619mg

1. Place the onion, celery, ginger, stock, carrots, potatoes, curry powder, and salt in a 4-quart slow cooker. Stir to combine.

2. Cover and cook on low for 8 hours.

3. Add the lime juice to the slow cooker and purée the bisque with an immersion blender. You can also purée the soup, in batches if needed, in a blender or food processor. Return the blended soup to the slow cooker. Be careful, since the hot soup will expand while it's being blended.

4. Swirl in the heavy cream just before serving. Garnish each bowl with the cilantro.

GAME PLAN: This soup is delicious hot or cold. You can save the leftovers in the refrigerator to eat the next day for lunch. Try it cold, thinned with a little more chicken stock if you'd like, or reheat until it's steaming hot and top it with the cream and cilantro.

Corn Chowder

GLUTEN-FREE, LOW-CALORIE, VEGETARIAN

PREP TIME:
10 MINUTES

COOK TIME:
4 HOURS ON LOW
OR 1 TO 2 HOURS
ON HIGH, PLUS
30 MINUTES
ON LOW

SERVES 4

PER SERVING:
Calories: 277; Fat: 15g;
Saturated Fat: 9g;
Cholesterol: 48mg;
Carbohydrates: 31g;
Fiber: 5g; Protein: 7g;
Sodium: 1,180mg

Enjoy this creamy and flavorful soup in the summer when fresh corn on the cob is plentiful at the farmers' markets. Serve it with a crisp green salad for a flavorful vegetarian meal. But when it's not summer, you can still make this recipe using four cups of frozen sweet corn. It's warm and hearty on a crisp fall day.

1 leek

4 ears sweet corn, husks and silks removed

1 yellow onion, diced

1 teaspoon sea salt

4 thyme sprigs

4 cups Vegetable Broth (page 264 or store-bought)

1 tablespoon white wine vinegar

2 cups half-and-half

2 scallions, green parts only, thinly sliced, for garnish

INGREDIENT TIP:
When buying sweet corn, look for ears that are plump and firm with moist-looking husks. Older husks with dried leaves and slightly shriveled kernels are still edible, but they won't be as sweet since the sugar in the kernels starts to turn to starch as soon as the corn is harvested.

1. Trim and discard the dark green portion and roots of the leek. Halve the trimmed leek lengthwise and rinse it under cool running water until it is completely free from dirt and grit. Slice it crosswise into half-moons and place them in a 4-quart slow cooker.
2. Cut the kernels from the corncobs and place both the kernels and the scraped cobs in the slow cooker. Add the onion, salt, thyme, and broth.
3. Cover and cook on low for 4 hours or on high for 1 to 2 hours.
4. Discard the corncobs and thyme sprigs. Using an immersion blender, purée the soup. Or transfer the soup, in 2 or 3 batches, to a food processor or and blend until smooth. Return the blended soup to the slow cooker. Stir in the vinegar and half-and-half.
5. Cover and cook on low for another 30 minutes, or until the soup is steaming.
6. Ladle into soup bowls and garnish with the scallion greens.

Spicy Coconut and Shrimp Chowder

GLUTEN-FREE, LOW-CALORIE

This spicy chowder is a treat with sweet and briny shrimp, creamy coconut milk, and hot chile peppers. It's a hearty soup that freezes well and makes an excellent meal on the go. You can play with the amount and type of chile peppers in this recipe, depending on whether your family likes things spicier or milder.

PREP TIME:
20 MINUTES

COOK TIME:
8½ HOURS
ON LOW

SERVES 6

PER SERVING:
Calories: 263; Fat: 13g;
Saturated Fat: 10g;
Cholesterol: 97mg;
Carbohydrates: 21g;
Fiber: 3g; Protein: 16g;
Sodium: 676mg

5 cups Chicken Stock
   (page 263 or store-
   bought) or fish stock
½ cup chopped chile
   peppers of your choice
   (jalapeños, Anaheim, etc.)
2 sweet potatoes,
   peeled and cubed
1 yellow onion, chopped
2 carrots, sliced
1 teaspoon garlic powder
½ teaspoon sea salt

1 teaspoon ground ginger
Grated zest of 1 lime,
   plus 2 tablespoons lime
   juice, for garnish
1 (13-ounce) can unsweetened
   coconut milk
3 tablespoons cornstarch
1 pound small shrimp
   (51- to 60-count per pound),
   peeled and deveined
¼ cup chopped fresh cilantro

1. Place the stock, chiles, sweet potatoes, onion, carrots, garlic powder, salt, ginger, and lime zest in a 3- to 4-quart slow cooker. Stir to combine.
2. Cover and cook on low for 8 hours, or until the vegetables are tender.
3. In a small bowl, whisk the coconut milk and cornstarch until smooth. Stir this into the slow cooker along with the shrimp.
4. Cover and cook on low for 30 minutes longer, until the shrimp curl and turn pink and the soup thickens slightly. Serve the soup topped with the cilantro and lime juice.

INGREDIENT TIP: Coconut milk separates into a thick top layer and runny bottom layer in the can. Pour it all out into a bowl, whisk to combine, and then proceed with the recipe.

Classic Beef Stew

GLUTEN-FREE, LOW-CALORIE, WEEKNIGHT HERO

PREP TIME:
15 MINUTES

COOK TIME:
8 HOURS ON LOW

SERVES 4

PER SERVING:
Calories: 370; Fat: 10g;
Saturated Fat: 5g;
Cholesterol: 82mg;
Carbohydrates: 32g;
Fiber: 6g; Protein: 28g;
Sodium: 760mg

For those mornings when you only have a few minutes to prepare dinner on your way out the door, this beef stew comes to the rescue. Simply throw all the ingredients in the slow cooker, cover, and let it simmer all day long. The wonderful aroma will welcome you home. All you'll need to add are some toasted rolls and a green salad.

1 cup sliced carrots

1 cup diced yellow onions

1 cup sliced celery

1 pound beef chuck, cut
  into 1-inch pieces

4 cups fingerling potatoes

1 cup dry white wine

2 cups beef broth or water

1 bay leaf

½ teaspoon sea salt

⅛ teaspoon freshly
  ground black pepper

1 to 2 tablespoons
  unsalted butter

1. In a 4-quart slow cooker, layer the ingredients in the following order: carrots, onions, celery, beef, and potatoes. Pour the wine and broth over them. Add the bay leaf, salt, and pepper.
2. Cover and cook on low for 8 hours, or until the potatoes and beef are tender.
3. To serve, transfer the beef and potatoes to a serving platter. Discard the bay leaf.
4. Using a stand or immersion blender, purée the remaining vegetables and cooking liquid with the butter until smooth. Return the beef and potatoes to the slow cooker and stir to combine. Serve.

EXTRA EASY: If you purchase sliced carrots and celery and diced onions from the grocery store, you can cut the prep time for this recipe by at least 5 minutes.

Chili Verde

GLUTEN-FREE, WEEKNIGHT HERO

This green chili is spicy with chiles and has tangy tomatillos to add a bit of acidity. You can find tomatillos in the produce section; they look like small green tomatoes with a papery skin. The skin should not be dried and shriveled. Just pull it off with your hands before rinsing and chopping the tomatillos. While the recipe calls for pork shoulder, you can replace it with any fatty meat or poultry of your choice. The cooked chili freezes well.

PREP TIME:
15 MINUTES

COOK TIME:
8 HOURS ON LOW

SERVES 6

PER SERVING:
Calories: 425; Fat: 31g; Saturated Fat: 11g; Cholesterol: 107mg; Carbohydrates: 6g; Fiber: 1g; Protein: 30g; Sodium: 650mg

2 pounds pork shoulder, cut into 1-inch cubes

3 cups Bone Broth (page 262 or store-bought)

1 yellow onion, chopped

½ cup chopped green chiles of your choice (jalapeños, Anaheim, etc.)

6 tomatillos, papery skin removed, chopped

1 teaspoon garlic powder

1 teaspoon ground cumin

1 teaspoon ground coriander

½ teaspoon sea salt

Juice of 1 lime

¼ cup chopped fresh cilantro

1. Place the pork, broth, onion, chiles, tomatillos, garlic powder, cumin, coriander, and salt in a 4-quart slow cooker. Stir to combine.
2. Cover and cook on low for 8 hours, or until the pork is very tender.
3. Stir in the lime juice and cilantro and serve.

INGREDIENT TIP: If you don't have Bone Broth, you can substitute an equal amount of Chicken Stock (page 263) or beef broth.

Moroccan Lamb Stew

GLUTEN-FREE, LOW-CALORIE

PREP TIME:
20 MINUTES

COOK TIME:
8 HOURS ON LOW

SERVES 8

PER SERVING:
Calories: 320; Fat: 9g;
Saturated Fat: 3g;
Cholesterol: 101mg;
Carbohydrates: 26g;
Fiber: 3g; Protein: 35g;
Sodium: 447mg

This stew has exotic flavors that blend together to make a fragrant, tasty dish. The lamb is juicy and tender, and the scents of the spices and citrus will fill your home. Like all good stews, this one gets even better on the second or third day, after the flavors have had time to meld together.

Grated zest and juice
  of 1 orange
2 tablespoons cornstarch
2 pounds boneless leg of
  lamb, cut into 1-inch pieces
2 yellow onions, chopped
2 carrots, chopped
1 (14-ounce) can
  crushed tomatoes

1 cup chopped pitted dates
1 teaspoon garlic powder
1 teaspoon ground ginger
1 teaspoon ground cumin
1 teaspoon sea salt
¼ teaspoon freshly ground
  black pepper
¼ cup chopped fresh parsley

1. In a small bowl, whisk together the orange zest, orange juice, and cornstarch.
2. Pour the juice mixture in a 4-quart slow cooker. Place the lamb, onions, carrots, crushed tomatoes, dates, garlic powder, ginger, cumin, salt, and pepper in the slow cooker. Stir to combine.
3. Cover and cook on low for 8 hours, or until the lamb is very tender.
4. Stir in the parsley just before serving.

IF YOU HAVE A MINUTE: Add deeper flavor by browning the lamb cubes before adding them to the slow cooker. Heat 2 tablespoons of fat or oil in a skillet over medium-high heat. Working in batches, brown the lamb for about 3 minutes per side; then add it to the slow cooker and continue with the recipe.

Chicken Taco Chili

GLUTEN-FREE, LOW-CALORIE, WEEKNIGHT HERO

This chili blends two favorites into one soul-warming dish, making it perfect for blustery winter days. The chipotles in adobo make this chili spicy; if you'd prefer it milder, cut back on the chipotles or leave them out altogether. Chicken thighs are less expensive and stand up better to the bold flavors of this dish, but you can certainly use chicken breasts instead if you prefer white meat.

PREP TIME:
15 MINUTES

COOK TIME:
8 HOURS ON LOW
OR
4 HOURS ON HIGH

SERVES 6

PER SERVING:
Calories: 341; Fat: 16g;
Saturated Fat: 6g;
Cholesterol: 140mg;
Carbohydrates: 18g;
Fiber: 4g; Protein: 32g;
Sodium: 542mg

2 pounds boneless, skinless chicken thighs

1 tablespoon chili powder

2 teaspoons low-sodium taco seasoning mix

2 garlic cloves, minced

1 teaspoon ground cumin

2 large tomatoes, diced

1 large poblano chile, seeded and diced

1 tablespoon chopped chipotle chiles in adobo sauce

1 (15-ounce) can red kidney beans, drained and rinsed

1½ cups Chicken Stock (page 263 or store-bought)

1 cup grated Cheddar cheese

1. Place the chicken, chili powder, taco seasoning mix, garlic, cumin, tomatoes, poblano chile, chipotle chiles in adobe sauce, kidney beans, and stock in a 4-quart slow cooker. Stir to combine.
2. Cover and cook on low for 8 hours or on high for 4 hours, until the chicken is very tender.
3. Using tongs, remove the chicken and shred it with a fork. Stir the shredded chicken back into the soup.
4. Ladle the soup into bowls; then top each serving with the cheese.

INGREDIENT TIP: Chipotle chiles in adobo sauce are fired-roasted jalapeño peppers that are packed in a spicy red sauce. You can use the chiles and the sauce separately or together. They add a nice spicy punch and subtle smoky flavor to any Tex-Mex recipe.

Turkey and Sweet Potato Chili

GLUTEN-FREE, LOW-CALORIE, WEEKNIGHT HERO

PREP TIME:
15 MINUTES

COOK TIME:
6 TO 8 HOURS
ON LOW

SERVES 4

PER SERVING:
Calories: 383; Fat: 13g;
Saturated Fat: 3g;
Cholesterol: 90mg;
Carbohydrates: 39g;
Fiber: 8g; Protein: 26g;
Sodium: 1,245mg

Chili is not always made with beans. This hearty version is delicious with tender ground turkey and velvety sweet potatoes. What makes it a "chili" is the green chiles and chili powder. Adjust the seasoning to suit your family's tastes.

1 tablespoon extra-virgin olive oil

1 pound ground turkey

3 cups sweet potato cubes

1 (28-ounce) can diced tomatoes, undrained

1 red bell pepper, seeded and chopped

1 (4-ounce) can diced green chiles, drained

1 medium red onion, diced

3 cups Chicken Stock (page 263 or store-bought)

1 tablespoon freshly squeezed lime juice

1 tablespoon chili powder

1 teaspoon garlic powder

1 teaspoon unsweetened cocoa powder

1 teaspoon ground cumin

½ teaspoon sea salt

½ teaspoon ground cinnamon

Pinch cayenne pepper

1. Place a large skillet over medium-high heat and add the olive oil. Once hot, add the ground turkey and cook, using a wooden spoon to break up the meat, until cooked through. Drain if necessary.

2. Place the cooked ground turkey, sweet potato cubes, tomatoes with their juices, bell pepper, green chiles, onion, stock, lime juice, chili powder, garlic powder, cocoa powder, cumin, salt, cinnamon, and cayenne pepper in a 4-quart slow cooker. Stir to combine.

3. Cover and cook on low for 6 to 8 hours, or until the vegetables are tender.

4. Stir the chili well and serve.

EXTRA EASY: You can find sweet potatoes that have been peeled and cut into chunks in most grocery stores. Using this shortcut will save about 5 minutes of preparation time.

Ground Beef Chili

GLUTEN-FREE, LOW-CALORIE, WEEKNIGHT HERO

Chili is a classic slow cooker recipe; it's hard to imagine making this flavorful dish any other way. The cocoa powder adds depth of flavor. Serve topped with sour cream, pickled onions, and cilantro for a lovely mix of flavors and textures.

1½ pounds lean ground beef

1 large yellow onion, chopped

5 garlic cloves, minced

2 jalapeño peppers, seeded and minced

1 teaspoon sea salt

¼ teaspoon cayenne pepper

1 tablespoon chili powder

2 (15-ounce) cans kidney beans, drained and rinsed

1 (28-ounce) can crushed tomatoes

4 cups beef broth

3 tablespoons tomato paste

2 tablespoons unsweetened cocoa powder

PREP TIME:
15 MINUTES

COOK TIME:
8 HOURS ON LOW

SERVES 6

PER SERVING:
Calories: 384; Fat: 11g;
Saturated Fat: 4g;
Cholesterol: 70mg;
Carbohydrates: 35g;
Fiber: 9g; Protein: 40g;
Sodium: 1,091mg

1. In a large skillet over medium heat, brown the ground beef with the onion, using a wooden spoon to break up the meat, until the beef is cooked through. Drain if necessary.
2. Place the cooked ground beef and onion in a 4-quart slow cooker. Add the garlic, jalapeños, salt, cayenne pepper, chili powder, beans, crushed tomatoes, broth, tomato paste, and cocoa powder. Stir to combine.
3. Cover and cook on low for 8 hours, or until the chili is simmering. Serve.

INGREDIENT TIP: Chile peppers are rated on what is called the Scoville scale, which tells you how hot they are—the higher the number, the more heat. Poblano peppers score 1,250 Scoville Heat Units (SHU), while jalapeños are 5,000 SHU. Cayenne pepper is 50,000 SHU, habanero peppers score 150,000 SHU, and Scotch bonnets are 400,000 SHU. Choose the pepper you want to use based on how spicy you like it.

Spicy Red Vegetarian Chili

GLUTEN-FREE, LOW-CALORIE, VEGAN, WEEKNIGHT HERO

PREP TIME:
15 MINUTES

COOK TIME:
8 HOURS ON LOW

SERVES 8

PER SERVING:
Calories: 160; Fat: 1g;
Saturated Fat: <1g;
Cholesterol: 0mg;
Carbohydrates: 31g;
Fiber: 8g; Protein: 8g;
Sodium: 773mg

The more beans, the better! This chili is rich and filled with lots of vegetables and seasonings. Adjust the spice level in this recipe to suit your taste. This version has a kick already, but you can certainly add more chiles, red pepper flakes, or hot sauce to spice it up even more.

1 (15-ounce) can kidney beans, drained and rinsed

1 (15-ounce) pinto beans, drained and rinsed

2 yellow onions, chopped

4 garlic cloves, minced

2 red bell peppers, seeded and chopped

4 large tomatoes, seeded and chopped

¼ cup tomato paste

2 jalapeño peppers, seeded and minced

6 cups Vegetable Broth (page 264 or store-bought)

1 tablespoon chili powder

1 teaspoon ground cumin

1 teaspoon dried oregano

1 teaspoon sea salt

⅛ teaspoon freshly ground black pepper

⅛ teaspoon red pepper flakes

1. Place all of the ingredients in a 5-quart slow cooker. Stir well to combine.
2. Cover and cook on low for 8 hours, or until the chili is simmering.
3. Stir gently and serve.

EXTRA EASY: In place of the chopped fresh tomatoes and jalapeño peppers, use two cans of chopped tomatoes with chiles (with their juices). Rotel is a good brand. That will save you about 5 minutes of preparation time.

Green Chile and Pork Pozole

GLUTEN-FREE, LOW-CALORIE, WEEKNIGHT HERO

Pozole is Mexican comfort food soup made with pork, hominy, and dried chiles. This version is quite spicy. The broth is flavorful with a lot of heat and a fresh flavor that comes from the limes and cilantro. Leftovers freeze well in airtight containers for up to 6 months.

2½ pounds lean, boneless pork, cut into 1-inch pieces

2 teaspoons ground cumin

3 cups Chicken Stock (page 263 or store-bought)

3 medium yellow onions, chopped

3 jalapeños peppers, seeded and chopped

1 (28-ounce) can white hominy, drained

2 (28-ounce) cans tomatillos, drained

1 bunch fresh cilantro, chopped, plus more for garnish

1 teaspoon sugar (optional)

2 limes, cut into wedges

PREP TIME:
15 MINUTES

COOK TIME:
10 HOURS ON LOW
OR
5 HOURS ON HIGH

SERVES 8

PER SERVING:
Calories: 333; Fat: 12g;
Saturated Fat: 4g;
Cholesterol: 69mg;
Carbohydrates: 27g;
Fiber: 5g; Protein: 31g;
Sodium: 761mg

1. Place the pork, cumin, stock, onions, jalapeños, hominy, tomatillos, and 1 bunch of chopped cilantro in a 4- to 5-quart slow cooker. Stir well to combine.
2. Cover and cook on low for 10 hours or on high for 5 hours, until the pork is tender.
3. Taste the broth and add sugar if needed to balance the acidity of the tomatillos.
4. Serve in bowls, garnished with more cilantro and limes wedges for squeezing into the soup.

INGREDIENT TIP: Tomatillos are small, round fruits that resemble green tomatoes wrapped in papery husks. They have a tart, tangy flavor and are used for green salsa. Many large grocery stores carry them fresh or canned, but if you can't find them, commercially prepared green salsa is a good substitute. And hominy is corn that has been soaked in a lime solution to remove the outer shell. It's puffy and white and tender—delicious in this soup.

Kale and White Bean Chili

GLUTEN-FREE, LOW-CALORIE, VEGAN, WEEKNIGHT HERO

PREP TIME:
15 MINUTES

COOK TIME:
6 TO 8 HOURS
ON LOW

SERVES 4 TO 6

PER SERVING:
Calories: 391; Fat: 14g;
Saturated Fat: 2g;
Cholesterol: 0mg;
Carbohydrates: 52g;
Fiber: 17g; Protein: 16g;
Sodium: 674mg

Cannellini beans are white and have a smooth and velvety texture. They are delicious combined with vegetables and hearty kale in this unique chili. You can add more veggies to this recipe if you'd like, like chopped bell peppers, sliced zucchini, summer squash, or corn.

2 (15-ounce) cans cannellini beans, drained and rinsed

1 small bunch kale, ribs removed, chopped

1 medium yellow onion, diced

½ green bell pepper, seeded and chopped

1 (4-ounce) can diced green chiles, drained

4 cups Vegetable Broth (page 264 or store-bought)

½ teaspoon garlic powder

1 teaspoon chili powder

½ teaspoon ground cumin

2 tablespoons extra-virgin olive oil

1 avocado, peeled, pitted, and chopped

1. Place the beans, kale, onion, bell pepper, chiles, broth, garlic powder, chili powder, and cumin in a 3- to 4-quart slow cooker. Stir well to combine.
2. Cover and cook on low for 6 to 8 hours, or until the vegetables are tender.
3. Ladle the chili into bowls. Drizzle each serving with the olive oil and top with avocado. Serve.

EXTRA EASY: You can often find prepared kale in the produce aisle of the supermarket. This will save about 5 minutes of preparation time.

Beef Bourguignon

LOW-CALORIE, WEEKNIGHT HERO

This rich and hearty French stew flavors beef chuck with red wine and herbs for a gourmet meal that is sure to become your favorite winter supper.

2 to 3 tablespoons bacon fat or unsalted butter

2 pounds beef chuck, cut into 2-inch cubes

3 tablespoons all-purpose flour

1 teaspoon sea salt

¼ teaspoon freshly ground black pepper

1 (8-ounce) package button or cremini mushrooms, halved

2 cups dry red wine, divided

2 large carrots, sliced

1 (16-ounce) bag frozen pearl onions

2 thyme sprigs

1 rosemary sprig

3 cups beef broth

2 tablespoons tomato paste

1 garlic clove, minced

PREP TIME:
15 MINUTES

COOK TIME:
8 TO 10 HOURS
ON LOW

SERVES 6

PER SERVING:
Calories: 373; Fat: 14g;
Saturated Fat: 6g;
Cholesterol: 109mg;
Carbohydrates: 14g;
Fiber: 2g; Protein: 33g;
Sodium: 886mg

1. In a large skillet over medium-high heat, melt 2 tablespoons of bacon fat.
2. Pat the beef cubes dry; sprinkle them all over with the flour, salt, and pepper. Working in batches, brown the beef on all sides for about 4 minutes. Do not overcrowd the pan. Transfer the browned beef to a 4- to 5-quart slow cooker.
3. In the same skillet, brown the mushrooms; do not overcrowd the pan. If needed, add more bacon fat or butter. Transfer the mushrooms to the slow cooker.
4. Add about ½ cup of red wine to the pan, scraping up the browned bits from the bottom. Pour this into the slow cooker, along with the remaining 1½ cups of wine and all the remaining ingredients. Stir gently to combine.

CONTINUED

5. Cover and cook on low for 8 to 10 hours, or until the beef is very tender. Remove the herb sprigs; discard. Serve.

IF YOU HAVE A MINUTE: To make the sauce even more delicious, after the recipe is done, reduce the cooking liquid in a medium pan over medium-low heat by about half. Then add 4 tablespoons of unsalted butter, 1 tablespoon at a time, whisking continuously. Pour the sauce back into the slow cooker and stir to combine.

Ribollita

LOW-CALORIE, VEGETARIAN, WEEKNIGHT HERO

Ribollita is an Italian soup recipe that is thickened with bread. Kale, chard, and cannellini beans merge beautifully in this hearty stew. Serve it with a dollop of mascarpone cheese and a green salad for a satisfying meal.

PREP TIME:
15 MINUTES

COOK TIME:
8 HOURS ON LOW

SERVES 6

PER SERVING:
Calories: 372; Fat: 1g;
Saturated Fat: 0g;
Cholesterol: 0mg;
Carbohydrates: 72g;
Fiber: 14g; Protein: 17g;
Sodium: 958mg

3 carrots, sliced

1 yellow onion, diced

Pinch red pepper flakes

4 garlic cloves, smashed

4 thyme sprigs

1 bunch kale, stems removed, leaves roughly chopped

½ bunch Swiss chard, roughly chopped

1 (28-ounce) can plum tomatoes, undrained

4 cups Vegetable Broth (page 264 or store-bought)

2 (15-ounce) cans cannellini beans, drained and rinsed

3 cups torn ciabatta bread

1. Place the carrots, onion, red pepper flakes, garlic, thyme, kale, chard, tomatoes, broth, and beans in a 4-quart slow cooker. Stir gently to combine.
2. Cover and cook on low for 8 hours, or until the vegetables are tender.
3. Stir the torn bread into the soup, cover, and let stand for 10 to 15 minutes, or until the bread is softened. Stir and serve.

INGREDIENT TIP: Ciabatta bread is a white Italian bread that has a crisp and firm crust and tender interior with lots of holes. The name *ciabatta* means "slipper," and the bread does look like a slipper. If you can't find it, any firm bread will do.

Beef Pho

GLUTEN-FREE, LOW-CALORIE, WEEKNIGHT HERO

PREP TIME:
15 MINUTES

COOK TIME:
6 TO 8 HOURS
ON LOW

SERVES 4

PER SERVING:
Calories: 353; Fat: 8g;
Saturated Fat: 3g;
Cholesterol: 65mg;
Carbohydrates: 31g;
Fiber: 2g; Protein: 38g;
Sodium: 1,310mg

Once you try it, this Vietnamese soup will become your new favorite with its rich flavors and many spices. It's traditionally made by spooning beef stock over steak and rice noodles. This simpler method still provides authentic flavor in an all-day cooking method.

- 1 large yellow onion, thinly sliced
- 2 teaspoons minced fresh ginger
- 1 teaspoon ground coriander
- 1 teaspoon ground cloves
- ¼ teaspoon ground cinnamon
- 1 tablespoon fennel seeds or 2 star anise pods
- 1 pound beef sirloin steak
- 4 cups Vegetable Broth (page 264 or store-bought) or beef broth
- 2 tablespoons fish sauce
- 4 ounces Vietnamese rice noodles
- Chopped fresh cilantro, for serving

1. Place the onion, ginger, coriander, cloves, cinnamon, and fennel seeds in a 3-quart slow cooker. Stir to combine. Top with the steak and pour the broth over.
2. Cover and cook on low for 6 to 8 hours.
3. About 10 minutes before serving, take the steak out and slice it thinly or shred it. Return it to the slow cooker and stir in the fish sauce.
4. Add the rice noodles, stir, and cover the slow cooker. Set it aside, covered, for 2 to 3 minutes, or until the noodles have softened.
5. Serve with fresh cilantro.

INGREDIENT TIP: Fish sauce, also called *nuoc mam*, is made of anchovies that have fermented in salt. The fish break down and produce a liquid that is intensely salty and savory. It can be found in most large grocery stores in the international or Asian foods aisle.

Mushroom-Barley Stew

GLUTEN-FREE, LOW-CALORIE, VEGAN

Barley is the perfect grain for soup. It adds wonderful texture and is loaded with fiber and minerals such as manganese, selenium, and magnesium. Mushrooms and barley go hand in hand. This hearty soup features three kinds of mushrooms for rich, satisfying, and complex flavors.

1 ounce dried shiitake
  mushrooms

1 cup hot water

2 cups sliced button
  mushrooms

2 cups sliced cremini
  mushrooms

3 carrots, sliced

1 cup hulled barley

1 yellow onion, chopped

4 garlic cloves, minced

5 cups Vegetable Broth
  (page 264 or store-bought)

1 teaspoon dried marjoram

1 teaspoon sea salt

⅛ teaspoon freshly
  ground black pepper

3 cups baby spinach leaves

PREP TIME:
20 MINUTES

COOK TIME:
8¼ HOURS ON LOW

SERVES 6

PER SERVING:
Calories: 169; Fat: 1g;
Saturated Fat: 0g;
Cholesterol: 0mg;
Carbohydrates: 36g;
Fiber: 7g; Protein: 6g;
Sodium: 871mg

EXTRA EASY:
Many grocery stores carry all kinds of washed and sliced mushrooms, which will save about 5 minutes of preparation time. One 8-ounce package is equal to 2 cups sliced mushrooms.

1. In a small bowl, cover the dried shiitake mushrooms with the hot water and let them soak for 30 minutes. Strain the mushrooms, reserving the soaking liquid. Strain the liquid through cheesecloth to remove any grit. Remove and discard the tough mushroom stems. Meanwhile, prepare the remaining ingredients.
2. Place the rehydrated shiitakes, the soaking liquid, the button and cremini mushrooms, carrots, barley, onion, garlic, broth, marjoram, salt, and pepper in a 4- to 5-quart slow cooker. Stir well to combine.
3. Cover and cook on low for 8 hours, or until the barley is tender.
4. Stir in the spinach, cover, and cook on low for another 10 to 15 minutes, or until the spinach is wilted.
5. Stir gently and serve.

Vegetarian Minestrone

LOW-CALORIE, VEGETARIAN

PREP TIME:
25 MINUTES

COOK TIME:
8 TO 10 HOURS
ON LOW

SERVES 8

PER SERVING:
Calories: 192; Fat: 2g;
Saturated Fat: 1g;
Cholesterol: 5mg;
Carbohydrates: 32g;
Fiber: 6g; Protein: 13g;
Sodium: 982mg

Minestrone is a classic Italian vegetable soup. It's rich, flavorful, and healthy and should be in everyone's repertoire; it's definitely one of my go-to soups. You can use just about any vegetable you can think of in minestrone. As with all slow cooker soups that call for pasta, it should be added at the end of the cooking time so it doesn't overcook.

1 yellow onion, chopped

5 garlic cloves, minced

3 celery stalks, sliced

2 carrots, sliced

1 cup sliced cremini mushrooms

1 (14-ounce) can cannellini beans, drained and rinsed

1 (28-ounce) can crushed tomatoes in purée

1 (14-ounce) can diced tomatoes, undrained

3 tablespoons tomato paste

4 cups Vegetable Broth (page 264 or store-bought)

2 teaspoons dried Italian seasoning

1 teaspoon sea salt

⅛ teaspoon freshly ground black pepper

1 cup small shell pasta

2 cups baby spinach leaves

½ cup grated Parmesan cheese

1. Place the onion, garlic, celery, carrots, mushrooms, beans, crushed tomatoes, diced tomatoes with their juices, tomato paste, broth, Italian seasoning, salt, and pepper in a 5-quart slow cooker. Stir well to combine.
2. Cover and cook on low for 8 to 10 hours, or until the vegetables are tender.
3. Stir in the pasta and spinach leaves.
4. Cover and cook on low for another 15 to 20 minutes, or until the pasta is tender.
5. Stir in the Parmesan cheese and serve.

Greek Lentil and Vegetable Stew

GLUTEN-FREE, LOW-CALORIE, VEGETARIAN

The alluring flavors of Greek cuisine include lemon, feta cheese, oregano, garlic, and olive oil. Here, these wonderful ingredients combine in your slow cooker for a fragrant lentil stew that is simple to make and delicious to eat.

1½ cups French lentils

1 yellow onion, chopped

1 fennel bulb, peeled and chopped

4 beefsteak tomatoes, seeded and chopped

5 garlic cloves, sliced

5 cups Vegetable Broth (page 264 or store-bought)

2 cups water

¼ cup freshly squeezed lemon juice

1 teaspoon dried oregano

1 teaspoon sea salt

⅛ teaspoon freshly ground black pepper

2 cups fresh green beans, roughly chopped

½ cup crumbled feta cheese

6 tablespoons extra-virgin olive oil

PREP TIME:
25 MINUTES

COOK TIME:
8 TO 9 HOURS
ON LOW, PLUS
30 MINUTES
ON HIGH

SERVES 8

PER SERVING:
Calories: 278; Fat: 13g;
Saturated Fat: 3g;
Cholesterol: 8mg;
Carbohydrates: 30g;
Fiber: 13g; Protein: 12g;
Sodium: 758mg

1. Sort the lentils, removing any grit. Rinse well and drain. Place them in a 4- to 5-quart slow cooker.
2. Add the onion, fennel, tomatoes, garlic, broth, water, lemon juice, oregano, salt, and pepper. Stir well to combine.
3. Cover and cook on low for 8 to 9 hours, until the lentils are very soft and the vegetables are tender.
4. Stir in the green beans, cover, and cook on high for another 20 to 30 minutes.
5. Stir the stew and ladle it into bowls. Garnish each with feta cheese and a drizzle of olive oil and serve.

INGREDIENT TIP: French lentils, or Puy lentils, are grown in a specific region of France. The flavor of these lentils is more peppery than green or brown lentils. They stand up well to long cooking times, too. If you can't find them, substitute brown lentils.

Indian Chickpeas with Yogurt and Cardamom, page 136

CHAPTER 6

SEAFOOD AND VEGETARIAN MEALS

Salmon with Lime Butter

GLUTEN-FREE, LOW-CALORIE

PREP TIME:
5 MINUTES

COOK TIME:
4 HOURS ON LOW
OR
2 HOURS ON HIGH

SERVES 4

PER SERVING:
Calories: 200; Fat: 7g;
Saturated Fat: 1g;
Cholesterol: 83mg;
Carbohydrates: 1g;
Fiber: <1g;
Protein: 35g;
Sodium: 349mg

This recipe allows you to use the slow cooker to its greatest advantage, slowly infusing the salmon with citrus flavor, resulting in a fresh, delicious, and light fish dish. Served with Slow Cooker Rice (page 258), Basic Quinoa (page 257), or any other whole grain, this dish is a simple winner.

4 (6- to 8-ounce) salmon fillets

1 tablespoon extra-virgin olive oil

1 tablespoon freshly squeezed lime juice

3 garlic cloves, minced

1 tablespoon finely chopped fresh parsley

¼ teaspoon sea salt

¼ teaspoon freshly ground black pepper

1. Spread a length of aluminum foil onto the counter-top and put the salmon fillets directly in the middle.
2. In a small bowl, whisk together the olive oil, lime juice, garlic, parsley, salt, and pepper. Brush the mixture over the fillets. Fold the foil over and crimp the sides to make a packet.
3. Place the packet in a 3½-quart slow cooker. Cover and cook on low for 4 hours or on high for 2 hours, until the salmon flakes easily when tested with a fork.

INGREDIENT TIP: You can cook other dense fillets of fish this way. Try using cod, halibut, or haddock. Just cook the fish until it flakes when tested with a fork.

Clams in White Wine Butter Sauce

GLUTEN-FREE, LOW-CALORIE

Clams in wine and butter sauce is a popular choice on appetizer menus around the world. Unfortunately, it's typically loaded with added fat and salt. This recipe uses a fraction of the butter typically used in restaurants and instead relies on quality seafood and fresh herbs for its fantastic flavor.

4 tablespoons cold unsalted butter, divided

1 cup Chicken Stock (page 263 or store-bought) or Vegetable Broth (page 264 or store-bought)

1 cup dry white wine

¼ cup minced shallots

1 teaspoon fresh thyme

2 garlic cloves, minced

Juice of 1 lemon

½ teaspoon sea salt

⅛ teaspoon freshly ground black pepper

2 pounds fresh clams, scrubbed

Chopped fresh parsley, for garnish

1. Grease a 4-quart slow cooker with 1 tablespoon of butter.
2. Place the stock, wine, shallots, thyme, garlic, lemon juice, salt, and pepper in the slow cooker. Stir to combine. Gently add the clams.
3. Cover and cook on high for 30 minutes, or until all the clams have opened. Discard any that do not open.
4. Using a slotted spoon, transfer the clams to a serving platter. Continue to cook the sauce, uncovered, for another 10 minutes on high to reduce a bit.
5. Whisk the remaining 3 tablespoons of butter, 1 tablespoon at a time, into the liquid to thicken the sauce. Carefully pour the sauce over the clams and garnish with parsley.

PREP TIME:
10 MINUTES

COOK TIME:
40 MINUTES
ON HIGH

SERVES 4

PER SERVING:
Calories: 195; Fat: 12g;
Saturated Fat: 7g;
Cholesterol: 48mg;
Carbohydrates: 5g;
Fiber: <1g; Protein: 8g;
Sodium: 407mg

INGREDIENT TIP:
To prepare fresh clams, soak them in cold water for about 30 minutes before cooking. Then scrub the shells with a brush under cool running water. Examine the clams; all should be tightly closed. If any are not, tap on their shells. If the clams still won't close, discard them.

Mussels in Saffron Curry Sauce

GLUTEN-FREE

PREP TIME:
10 MINUTES

COOK TIME:
30 MINUTES ON LOW

SERVES 4

PER SERVING:
Calories: 504; Fat: 13g;
Saturated Fat: 4g;
Cholesterol: 135mg;
Carbohydrates: 21g;
Fiber: 1g; Protein: 56g;
Sodium: 1,358mg

Mussels are blue-black bivalves with a sweet taste. The combination of saffron and curry gives these mussels a delicious and savory flavor. Serve them with Slow Cooker Rice (page 258) as a main course or as an appetizer with toasted whole-grain bread.

1 tablespoon unsalted butter, at room temperature

2 cups Chicken Stock (page 263 or store-bought)

1 cup dry vermouth

½ cup diced yellow onion

2 plum tomatoes, diced

2 garlic cloves, minced

1 bay leaf

1 teaspoon curry powder

Pinch saffron threads

1 lemon, halved

½ teaspoon sea salt

⅛ teaspoon freshly ground black pepper

2 pounds fresh mussels, scrubbed and debearded

¼ cup roughly chopped fresh parsley, for serving

1. Grease a 4-quart slow cooker with the butter.
2. Place the stock, vermouth, onion, tomatoes, garlic, and bay leaf in the slow cooker. Stir to combine. Stir in the curry powder, saffron, lemon halves, salt, and pepper.
3. Gently add the mussels to the broth mixture.
4. Cover and cook on low for 30 minutes, or until the mussels open. Discard the bay leaf and any mussels that remain closed. Serve sprinkled with the parsley.

INGREDIENT TIP: Saffron is the most expensive spice in the world, but it adds fabulous color and flavor to food. It is the red pistils of the saffron crocus. There are only three pistils per flour, so 190 flowers must be plucked to obtain a single gram of saffron. Saffron powder is less expensive, so you can use that if you don't want to splurge on the threads.

Shrimp Scampi with Orzo

LOW-CALORIE

This one-dish meal is easy to prepare in the slow cooker, leaving you free to do other things while it cooks. Whole-wheat orzo is used because it has a longer cooking time and will cook to al dente perfection.

1 pound large shrimp, peeled and deveined

1 cup whole-wheat orzo pasta

¼ cup minced fresh parsley

4 garlic cloves, minced

3 cups Chicken Stock (page 263 or store-bought)

½ cup dry white wine

¼ teaspoon sea salt

⅛ teaspoon freshly ground black pepper

PREP TIME:
10 MINUTES

COOK TIME:
2 HOURS ON LOW

SERVES 4

PER SERVING:
Calories: 260; Fat: 2g; Saturated Fat: 0g; Cholesterol: 145mg; Carbohydrates: 32g; Fiber: 7g; Protein: 25g; Sodium: 594mg

1. Place the shrimp, pasta, parsley, and garlic in a 3-quart slow cooker and stir to combine. Pour in the stock and wine. Season with the salt and pepper. Stir gently.
2. Cover and cook on low for 2 hours, or until the pasta is tender and the shrimp are cooked through.

Low Country Seafood Boil

GLUTEN-FREE, LOW-CALORIE

A traditional low country boil includes sausage, seafood, corn, and potatoes combined in a delicious one-pot meal that is full of flavor. Old Bay seasoning gives this dish the aromas and flavors of the South. Serve it with lots of crusty bread to soak up the wonderful sauce. Omit the potatoes and corn if you're following a low-carb diet.

1½ pounds Yukon Gold potatoes, cut into 1-inch cubes (optional)

1 pound kielbasa sausage, cut into 1-inch pieces

5 cups water

1½ cups Vegetable Broth (page 264 or store-bought)

2 tablespoons Old Bay Seasoning

2 lemons, sliced

2 celery stalks, chopped

1 yellow onion, chopped

3 garlic cloves, minced

2 pounds large shrimp in shells

2 cups frozen corn (optional)

1. Place the potatoes (if using), sausage, water, broth, seasoning, lemons, celery, onion, and garlic in a 4- to 5-quart slow cooker.
2. Cover and cook on low for 4 to 5 hours or on high for 2 to 2½ hours, until the potatoes are tender when pierced with a fork.
3. Add the shrimp and corn (if using) and cook for an additional 15 to 20 minutes on high, until the shrimp are cooked through and the sausage registers 165°F with a food thermometer.

IF YOU HAVE A MINUTE: You don't have to do this because kielbasa is sold fully cooked, but browning the sausages in a skillet before you cut them into pieces adds more flavor, and the sausage looks nicer, too. Add some of the water to the skillet after you remove the sausages and bring it to a boil, scraping the bottom of the pan to get all the delicious drippings. Add the drippings to the slow cooker.

PREP TIME:
20 MINUTES

COOK TIME:
4 TO 5 HOURS ON LOW OR 2 TO 2½ HOURS ON HIGH, PLUS 20 MINUTES ON HIGH

SERVES 8

PER SERVING:
Calories: 356; Fat: 17g; Saturated Fat: 6g; Cholesterol: 218mg; Carbohydrates: 22g; Fiber: 4g; Protein: 29g; Sodium: 1,943mg

INGREDIENT TIP:
Large shrimp usually have 21 to 30 in a pound. Extra-large shrimp have 16 to 20 in a pound. Either large or extra-large shrimp will work in this recipe.

Shrimp Fajitas

GLUTEN-FREE, LOW-CALORIE

PREP TIME:
15 MINUTES

COOK TIME:
2 HOURS, PLUS
15 MINUTES
ON HIGH

SERVES 6

PER SERVING:
Calories: 194; Fat: 6g;
Saturated Fat: 1g;
Cholesterol: 193mg;
Carbohydrates: 9g;
Fiber: 2g; Protein: 25g;
Sodium: 352mg

Shrimp fajitas are a classic Tex-Mex dish. Enjoy this spicy and flavorful fajita filling with warmed whole-wheat tortillas or over hot cooked rice.

1 green bell pepper, sliced

2 yellow, red, or orange bell peppers, sliced

2 yellow onions, halved and thinly sliced

2 tablespoons extra-virgin olive oil

1 tablespoon ground cumin

¼ teaspoon cayenne pepper

½ teaspoon sea salt

⅛ teaspoon freshly ground black pepper

½ cup dry white wine

2 pounds large shrimp, peeled and deveined

Corn tortillas, warmed, for serving

1. Place the bell peppers, onions, and oil in a 3½-quart slow cooker. Stir to coat the vegetables in the oil. Add the cumin, cayenne pepper, salt, and black pepper and stir to combine.
2. Cover and cook on high for 2 hours.
3. Add the white wine and shrimp and stir to combine. Cover and cook on high for another 15 minutes, or until the shrimp curl and turn pink. Use tongs to put the mixture into the warmed tortillas.

INGREDIENT TIP: To warm the tortillas, stack 5 or fewer on paper towels and microwave them in 30-second intervals until they are soft and warm. You can also warm them in the oven: Wrap 5 or fewer in aluminum foil and place them in a preheated 350°F oven for 5 to 10 minutes until warm.

Cioppino

GLUTEN-FREE, LOW-CALORIE

This seafood dish is loaded with flavor and fragrant with Italian herbs and sweet tomato broth. Serve this dish over pasta or with lots of crusty bread.

1 (15-ounce) can
  tomato sauce

7 cups fish stock or
  Chicken Stock (page
  263 or store-bought)

1 yellow onion, chopped

1 tablespoon Italian seasoning

1 teaspoon garlic powder

½ teaspoon sea salt

¼ teaspoon freshly
  ground black pepper

Pinch red pepper flakes

8 ounces skinless cod or
  halibut fillets, cut
  into 1-inch pieces

1 pound medium (41- to
  50-count) shrimp,
  peeled and deveined

1 pound mussels, cleaned
  and debearded

¼ cup chopped fresh parsley

Grated zest of 1 lemon

PREP TIME:
20 MINUTES

COOK TIME:
8 HOURS ON LOW,
PLUS 30 MINUTES
ON HIGH

SERVES 6

PER SERVING:
Calories: 275; Fat: 5g;
Saturated Fat: 1g;
Cholesterol: 160mg;
Carbohydrates: 16g;
Fiber: 2g; Protein: 42g;
Sodium: 1,813mg

1. Place the tomato sauce, stock, onion, Italian seasoning, garlic powder, salt, black pepper, and red pepper flakes in a 4- to 5-quart slow cooker. Stir to combine.

2. Cover and cook on low for 8 hours. Stir in the fish, shrimp, mussels, parsley, and lemon zest.

3. Cover and cook on high for an additional 25 to 30 minutes, or until the fish is cooked through, and serve.

INGREDIENT TIP: Mussels are delicious, inexpensive, and sustainable, but there are a few tricks to prepping them. To clean and debeard mussels, scrub the shells under cool running water. Examine each one to make sure it is not broken and that each closes when tapped with your fingers. If there are black strings poking out of the mussel (the beard), pull them off with your fingers and a paring knife and discard them. Never use a mussel that is open before cooking because it's dead.

Lemon-Dijon Salmon with Dill Barley

GLUTEN-FREE, LOW-CALORIE

PREP TIME:
15 MINUTES

COOK TIME:
2 HOURS ON LOW

SERVES 6

PER SERVING:
Calories: 359; Fat: 12g;
Saturated Fat: 2g;
Cholesterol: 85mg;
Carbohydrates: 23g;
Fiber: 3g; Protein: 39g;
Sodium: 706mg

The lemon-Dijon flavor combination is a classic for fish. It originates in the Mediterranean cuisine of southern France. Fresh dill livens up the healthy barley, and you end up with a hearty yet light-tasting meal that's special enough to serve to company.

FOR THE FISH

1 medium yellow onion, diced

2 teaspoons minced garlic

2 teaspoons extra-virgin olive oil

2 cups Vegetable Broth (page 264 or store-bought)

1 cup quick-cooking barley

1 tablespoon minced fresh dill

6 (6- to 8-ounce) salmon fillets

Sea salt

Freshly ground black pepper

FOR THE LEMON-DIJON SAUCE

⅓ cup Dijon mustard

3 tablespoons extra-virgin olive oil

3 tablespoons freshly squeezed lemon juice

⅓ cup plain Greek yogurt

1 garlic clove, minced

TO MAKE THE FISH

1. Combine the onion, garlic, and oil in a small microwave-safe bowl. Heat in the microwave on 70 percent power for 4 to 5 minutes, stirring occasionally, until the vegetables are softened. Place this mixture in a 3½-quart slow cooker.

2. Add the broth, barley, and dill to the slow cooker and stir to combine. Season the salmon fillets with salt and pepper and place them on top of the barley mixture.

3. Cover and cook on low for about 2 hours, until the salmon flakes when tested with a fork and the barley is tender.

4. In a small bowl, whisk together the Dijon mustard, olive oil, lemon juice, Greek yogurt, and garlic. Set aside and allow the flavors to blend.

5. To serve, place some barley on a plate and top it with a salmon fillet. Spoon the lemon-Dijon sauce over the top of the salmon.

INGREDIENT TIP: Barley is available in several different varieties. Each takes a different time to cook. Pearl barley has the outer husk and bran layer removed. It takes about 45 minutes to cook on the stovetop and 4 to 6 hours in the slow cooker. Quick-cooking barley has been pre-steamed, so it cooks in just 10 minutes or 2 hours in the slow cooker. Hulled barley has only the outer inedible husk removed, and it takes a long time to cook. Choose pearl or hulled barley for longer-cooking slow cooker recipes.

Halibut in Mango-Pineapple Chutney

GLUTEN-FREE, LOW-CALORIE

PREP TIME:
15 MINUTES

COOK TIME:
4 TO 6 HOURS
ON LOW

SERVES 4

PER SERVING:
Calories: 351; Fat: 6g;
Saturated Fat: 1g;
Cholesterol: 70mg;
Carbohydrates: 28g;
Fiber: 4g; Protein: 47g;
Sodium: 418mg

Enjoy the flavors of India with tender fish cooked in this spicy curried chutney. This recipe makes fresh chutney, which cooks to perfection in the slow cooker. You can substitute 2½ cups of prepared chutney for the fruits and spices in this recipe.

1 cup diced fresh pineapple

2 large mangos, peeled, pitted, and diced

2 tomatoes, seeded and diced

1 red onion, diced

1 teaspoon curry powder

1 teaspoon ground ginger

1 teaspoon ground coriander

½ teaspoon sea salt

⅛ teaspoon freshly ground black pepper

½ cup red wine vinegar

4 (6-ounce) halibut fillets

1. Place the pineapple, mangos, tomatoes, onion, curry powder, ginger, coriander, salt, and pepper in a 3-quart slow cooker. Stir to combine. Pour in the vinegar and stir to combine.
2. Cover and cook on low for 4 to 6 hours.
3. In the last 30 minutes of cooking, add the halibut fillets. Cover and cook until the fish flakes easily with a fork.

INGREDIENT TIP: Mangos are a bit tricky to prepare because they have a large oval stone in the center. The easiest way is to cut the mango in half lengthwise, avoiding the stone. Cut a lattice pattern into the fruit's flesh, but don't cut through the skin. Push the mango half inside out and cut off the cubes. Cut the remaining flesh from around the stone and continue with the recipe.

Citrus Swordfish

GLUTEN-FREE, LOW-CALORIE

It may seem strange to cook swordfish fillets in the slow cooker, but the low and moist heat results in fish that is tender and velvety. While it cooks, you can relax with a glass of wine. The orange and lemon add a tart flavor, and the onion adds a sharp note to this delicious recipe.

Nonstick cooking spray

4 (8-ounce) swordfish fillets

Sea salt

Freshly ground black pepper

1 yellow onion, chopped

5 tablespoons chopped fresh parsley, plus parsley sprigs, for garnish

1 tablespoon extra-virgin olive oil

2 teaspoons grated lemon zest

2 teaspoons grated orange zest

Orange and lemon slices, for garnish

PREP TIME:
10 MINUTES

COOK TIME:
1½ TO 2 HOURS ON LOW

SERVES 4

PER SERVING:
Calories: 394; Fat: 15g; Saturated Fat: 4g; Cholesterol: 113mg; Carbohydrates: 3g; Fiber: 1g; Protein: 58g; Sodium: 264mg

1. Coat a 3-quart slow cooker with nonstick cooking spray.
2. Season the fish fillets with salt and pepper.
3. Distribute the onion, 5 tablespoons of chopped parsley, olive oil, lemon zest, and orange zest in the bottom of the slow cooker. Place the fish fillets on top.
4. Cover and cook on low for 1½ to 2 hours, or until the fish flakes when tested with a fork.
5. Serve hot, garnished with orange and lemon slices and sprigs of fresh parsley.

Lemon-Poached Cod with Chimichurri

GLUTEN-FREE

Garlicky chimichurri sauce is a staple in Argentina and is typically served with steak. But the flavors are a bright, flavorful complement to fish. You can use any sturdy white fish fillet in this recipe, including halibut, cod, and haddock.

½ cup Chicken Stock (page 263 or store-bought)

½ cup dry white wine

Grated zest and juice of 1 lemon

1½ pounds cod

½ teaspoon sea salt, plus additional for the chimichurri

⅛ teaspoon freshly ground black pepper, plus additional for the chimichurri

1 cup chopped fresh parsley

¼ cup chopped fresh cilantro

½ cup extra-virgin olive oil

¼ cup white wine vinegar

2 garlic cloves, peeled

¼ teaspoon red pepper flakes

PREP TIME:
10 MINUTES

COOK TIME:
30 MINUTES TO
HOUR ON HIGH

SERVES 4

PER SERVING:
Calories: 451; Fat: 29g;
Saturated Fat: 4g;
Cholesterol: 94mg;
Carbohydrates: 3g;
Fiber: 1g; Protein: 39g;
Sodium: 491mg

1. Place the stock, wine, and lemon zest and juice in a 3-quart slow cooker. Stir to combine. Sprinkle the cod with the salt and pepper and add it to the slow cooker.
2. Cover and cook on high for 30 minutes to 1 hour (depending on the thickness of the fillets), or until the fish flakes easily with a fork.
3. To make the chimichurri sauce, place the parsley, cilantro, oil, vinegar, garlic, and red pepper flakes in a blender and pulse until smooth. Season with salt and pepper.
4. Serve the poached cod with a spoonful of chimichurri sauce.

GAME PLAN: You can make the chimichurri sauce the day ahead and refrigerate it in an airtight container. Bring it to room temperature before serving it with the fish.

Carbonara Risotto

GLUTEN-FREE, VEGETARIAN

PREP TIME:
15 MINUTES

COOK TIME:
5 TO 6 HOURS ON
LOW, PLUS 15 MIN-
UTES ON LOW

SERVES 6 TO 8

PER SERVING:
Calories: 502; Fat: 11g;
Saturated Fat: 5g;
Cholesterol: 83mg;
Carbohydrates: 92g;
Fiber: 10g; Protein: 15g;
Sodium: 1,015mg

Carbonara is one of my favorite dishes. The combination of egg, cream, and cheese adds richness to plain old pasta. Risotto gets the same treatment in this easy recipe using short-grain brown rice, transforming it into a lush and delicious dish.

3 cups short-grain brown rice

2 cups sliced cremini mushrooms

1 yellow onion, chopped

2 garlic cloves, minced

5 cups Vegetable Broth (page 264 or store-bought)

1 teaspoon dried thyme

1 teaspoon sea salt

⅛ teaspoon freshly ground black pepper

2 cups frozen baby peas

2 large eggs, beaten

⅓ cup light cream

½ cup grated Parmesan cheese

1. Place the rice, mushrooms, onion, garlic, broth, thyme, salt, and pepper in a 4-quart slow cooker. Stir well to combine.
2. Cover and cook on low for 5 to 6 hours, or until the rice is tender.
3. Stir in the peas.
4. In a small bowl, beat the eggs and cream together. Stir the mixture into the slow cooker, and then stir in the Parmesan cheese.
5. Cover and cook on low for another 10 to 15 minutes, or until hot.
6. Stir gently and serve.

GAME PLAN: Leftover risotto makes wonderful little risotto cakes. Just form the cold mixture into patties, dip them in a beaten egg, and roll them in dried bread crumbs. Melt a little butter in a frying pan over medium-high heat, add the risotto patties, and fry them until golden brown on both sides.

Barley-Vegetable Risotto

VEGETARIAN, WEEKNIGHT HERO

Barley risotto is delicious, although it doesn't achieve the creaminess of a true rice-based risotto. That's okay—I added some light cream to give the sauce a velvety texture. This recipe is the perfect dinner served with a green salad studded with grape tomatoes.

1 tablespoon extra-
  virgin olive oil

1 yellow onion, finely chopped

2 cups hulled barley

5 cups Vegetable Broth
  (page 264 or store-
  bought), divided

2 cups sliced button mushrooms

3 garlic cloves, minced

1 teaspoon sea salt

⅛ teaspoon freshly
  ground black pepper

1 cup grated Parmesan cheese

2 tablespoons unsalted butter

⅓ cup light cream

PREP TIME:
15 MINUTES

COOK TIME:
6 TO 8 HOURS
ON LOW

SERVES 6 TO 8

PER SERVING:
Calories: 422; Fat: 16g;
Saturated Fat: 9g;
Cholesterol: 38mg;
Carbohydrates: 56g;
Fiber: 10g; Protein: 15g;
Sodium: 1,146mg

1. In a large skillet over medium heat, add the olive oil. Once hot, add the onion and sauté for 10 to 15 minutes, until it starts to brown.
2. Add the barley and cook, stirring frequently, for 2 to 4 minutes, until it is toasted.
3. Add 1 cup of broth and bring it to a simmer. Turn off the heat.
4. Transfer the mixture to a 4- to 5-quart slow cooker. Add the mushrooms, garlic, salt, pepper, and the remaining 4 cups of broth. Stir well to combine.
5. Cover and cook on low for 6 to 8 hours, or until the barley is tender.
6. Stir in the Parmesan cheese, butter, and cream. Cover, turn off the slow cooker, and let the risotto stand for 10 minutes.
7. Stir gently and serve.

INGREDIENT TIP: Hulled barley is a bit more nutritious than pearl barley because less of the bran has been removed. It does take longer to cook, which makes it perfect for the slow cooker.

Ratatouille

GLUTEN-FREE, LOW-CALORIE, VEGETARIAN

PREP TIME:
20 MINUTES

COOK TIME:
8 HOURS ON LOW

SERVES 6 TO 8

PER SERVING:
Calories: 138; Fat: 1g;
Saturated Fat: <1g;
Cholesterol: 0mg;
Carbohydrates: 31g;
Fiber: 8g; Protein: 6g;
Sodium: 868mg

GAME PLAN:
Leftover ratatouille
makes a great
pizza topping.
Spread the mixture
on a prepared
pizza crust, top
with cheese, and
bake at 400°F for
15 to 20 minutes,
or until hot.

Ratatouille is a classic French stew that is rich with vegetables. It makes an excellent side dish, or it can be a vegetarian main dish when served with some toasted bread and a green salad. Whichever way you serve it, it's vegetable heaven.

1 large eggplant, peeled and cut into 1-inch cubes

1½ teaspoons sea salt, divided

2 yellow onions, chopped

5 garlic cloves, minced

2 cups sliced cremini mushrooms

2 red bell peppers, seeded and chopped

2 yellow summer squash, chopped

5 large tomatoes, seeded and chopped

1 (6-ounce) can tomato paste

1 tablespoon honey

1 tablespoon freshly squeezed lemon juice

1 bay leaf

2 thyme sprigs

1 teaspoon dried marjoram

⅛ teaspoon freshly ground black pepper

1. Put the eggplant cubes in a large colander or strainer in the sink. Sprinkle 1 teaspoon of salt over the eggplant. Let stand for 15 minutes while you prepare the remaining ingredients.
2. Rinse the eggplant and drain well; pat dry with paper towels.
3. Place the eggplant, onions, garlic, mushrooms, bell peppers, summer squash, tomatoes, tomato paste, honey, lemon juice, bay leaf, thyme, marjoram, black pepper, and the remaining ½ teaspoon of salt in a 5-quart slow cooker. Stir well to combine.
4. Cover and cook on low for 8 hours, or until the vegetables are tender.
5. Remove and discard the thyme stems and bay leaf. Stir gently and serve.

Vegetarian Lasagna

VEGETARIAN

This may be the best lasagna recipe you ever try, and it doesn't have a bit of meat in it.

8 cups Basic Marinara Sauce (page 261 or store-bought)

2 yellow onions, finely chopped

5 garlic cloves, minced

1 tablespoon coarsely ground fennel seed

Pinch red pepper flakes

1 tablespoon extra-virgin olive oil

16 ounces no-boil lasagna noodles

16 ounces cottage cheese

4 cups shredded mozzarella cheese, divided

1 cup grated Parmesan cheese

2 large eggs

2 cups roughly chopped fresh basil, divided

PREP TIME:
20 MINUTES

COOK TIME:
4 HOURS ON LOW

SERVES 8

PER SERVING:
Calories: 595; Fat: 22g;
Saturated Fat: 12g;
Cholesterol: 94mg;
Carbohydrates: 60g;
Fiber: 7g; Protein: 37g;
Sodium: 1,425mg

1. In a bowl, mix together the marinara sauce, onions, garlic, fennel seed, red pepper flakes, and oil. Ladle about ½ cup of the mixture into a 5-quart slow cooker (enough to thoroughly coat the bottom of the insert).

2. Arrange a layer of lasagna noodles in the slow cooker. Ladle additional sauce over the noodles.

3. In a large bowl, mix the cottage cheese, 3½ cups of mozzarella cheese, the Parmesan cheese, and the eggs. Layer about half of the cheese mixture on top of the noodles. Top with 1 cup of basil.

4. Repeat with a layer of noodles, marinara sauce, the remainder of the cheese mixture, and the remaining 1 cup of basil.

5. Finish with the remaining pasta, marinara sauce, and the remaining ½ cup of mozzarella cheese.

CONTINUED

6. Cover and cook on low for 4 hours, or until the noodles are tender and the lasagna is bubbling around the edges. Uncover and let rest for at least 15 minutes before serving.

INGREDIENT TIP: In place of the cooked lasagna noodles, substitute no-boil noodles. These are available at most grocery stores. That will save you about 10 minutes of preparation time. The slow cooker cooking time is the same as with cooked regular noodles. Just test the noodles with a fork before you serve the lasagna to make sure they are tender.

Quinoa-Stuffed Tomatoes

GLUTEN-FREE, LOW-CALORIE, VEGETARIAN

Sometimes, you just want to round up the leftover veggies in your refrigerator and use them up all at once. This is the perfect dish for the job, but it doesn't taste like leftovers. The seasonings and quinoa combine with the veggies to make an ideal filling for tender and meaty tomatoes.

4 large tomatoes (preferably beefsteak), top ½ inch sliced off, seeded, and cored

½ teaspoon sea salt

1 cup cooked quinoa (see following Ingredient Tip)

1 cup diced vegetables, such as carrots, zucchini, or spinach

1 garlic clove, minced

1 teaspoon dried Italian seasoning

Freshly ground black pepper

1 teaspoon extra-virgin olive oil

¼ cup grated Parmesan cheese

⅓ cup water

PREP TIME:
15 MINUTES

COOK TIME:
4 HOURS ON LOW

SERVES 4

PER SERVING:
Calories: 145; Fat: 5g;
Saturated Fat: 1g;
Cholesterol: 5mg;
Carbohydrates: 21g;
Fiber: 4g; Protein: 7g;
Sodium: 439mg

1. Sprinkle the inside of each tomato with the salt; then place them upside down in a colander to drain for 10 minutes.
2. Meanwhile, in a medium mixing bowl, mix together the quinoa, vegetables, garlic, Italian seasoning, and pepper. Spoon the mixture evenly into the tomatoes.
3. Lightly grease a 3-quart slow cooker with the olive oil. Place the tomatoes in the slow cooker in a single layer and sprinkle each with the Parmesan cheese. Pour the water around the tomatoes.
4. Cover and cook on low for 4 hours, until the filling is hot and the tomatoes are tender.

INGREDIENT TIP: To get 1 cup of cooked quinoa, rinse ⅓ cup of dried quinoa. Combine the quinoa with ⅔ cup of water in a medium saucepan. Simmer over low heat for 25 to 30 minutes or until the quinoa is tender. Drain if necessary and continue with the recipe. You can cook the quinoa the day before you want to make this recipe; just cover and refrigerate. Fluff it with a fork before using.

Spicy Peanut Rice Bake

GLUTEN-FREE, VEGAN

PREP TIME:
20 MINUTES

COOK TIME:
6 TO 8 HOURS
ON LOW

SERVES 4

PER SERVING:
Calories: 686; Fat: 26g;
Saturated Fat: 4g;
Cholesterol: 0mg;
Carbohydrates: 96g;
Fiber: 13g; Protein: 21g;
Sodium: 705mg

Ginger, tomato paste, peanut butter, and hot sauce are classic flavors of North and West Africa. If you've never had this type of dish before, you're in for a treat. This recipe is a meal in one, or you can serve it as a side dish.

1 tablespoon extra-virgin olive oil

2 cups long-grain brown rice

5 cups Vegetable Broth (page 264 or store-bought), divided

8 collard green leaves, ribs removed, sliced into thin ribbons

1 cup minced red onion

½ cup unsalted creamy peanut butter

¼ cup tomato paste

2 tablespoons minced fresh ginger

1 to 2 teaspoons Sriracha

¼ teaspoon sea salt

½ cup chopped fresh cilantro, for garnish

Lime wedges, for garnish

¼ cup chopped roasted peanuts, for garnish

1. Grease a 4-quart slow cooker with the olive oil.
2. Place the rice, 4 cups of broth, the collard greens, and the onion in the slow cooker. Stir to combine.
3. In a medium bowl, whisk together the remaining 1 cup of broth, peanut butter, tomato paste, ginger, Sriracha, and salt. Stir this mixture into the slow cooker.
4. Cover and cook on low for 6 to 8 hours, or until the rice and vegetables are tender. Garnish each serving with fresh cilantro, a lime wedge, and the chopped peanuts.

INGREDIENT TIP: Sriracha is a very hot sauce made with chile peppers, vinegar, garlic, sugar, and salt. If you aren't a fan of spicy food, you could omit it or use a couple of dashes of Tabasco sauce or some red pepper flakes instead.

Artichoke and Swiss Chard Ragout

GLUTEN-FREE, LOW-CALORIE, VEGAN, WEEKNIGHT HERO

A ragout is a seasoned stew made with meat and vegetables, but you can make it with a lot of hearty vegetables instead. This recipe works well as a main dish or as a side dish for your meal. It also freezes and reheats well for meals on the go. If you can't find Swiss chard, try substituting kale or spinach.

PREP TIME:
15 MINUTES

COOK TIME:
8 HOURS ON LOW

SERVES 6

PER SERVING:
Calories: 117; Fat: <1g;
Saturated Fat: 0g;
Cholesterol: 0mg;
Carbohydrates: 25g;
Fiber: 8g; Protein: 6g;
Sodium: 871mg

2 (14-ounce) cans artichoke hearts, drained and quartered

1 red onion, chopped

1½ pounds Swiss chard, thick stems removed

1½ teaspoons garlic powder

2 large carrots, chopped

2 (8-ounce) jars roasted red peppers, drained and chopped

3 cups Vegetable Broth (page 264 or store-bought)

2 tablespoons cornstarch

1 teaspoon dried thyme

½ teaspoon sea salt

¼ teaspoon freshly ground black pepper

¼ cup chopped fresh parsley

1. Place the artichoke hearts, onion, chard, garlic powder, carrots, and roasted peppers in a 4-quart slow cooker. Stir to combine.
2. In a small bowl, whisk together the broth, cornstarch, thyme, salt, and pepper. Pour the broth mixture over the vegetables in the slow cooker.
3. Cover and cook on low for 8 hours, or until the vegetables are tender.
4. Stir in the parsley just before serving.

INGREDIENT TIP: Hearty leafy greens include Swiss chard, mustard greens, collard greens, kale, and spinach. They're all full of vitamins, fiber, and minerals, and they cook beautifully in the slow cooker.

Vegan Mushroom Bolognese

GLUTEN-FREE, LOW-CALORIE, VEGAN, WEEKNIGHT HERO

PREP TIME:
15 MINUTES

COOK TIME:
8 TO 9 HOURS
ON LOW

MAKES 10 CUPS

PER ½-CUP SERVING:
Calories: 40; Fat: <1g;
Saturated Fat: 0g;
Cholesterol: 0mg;
Carbohydrates: 8g;
Fiber: 2g; Protein: 4g;
Sodium: 346mg

INGREDIENT TIP:
Tamari is used here as a gluten-free alternative to soy sauce. Though many brands of tamari are completely gluten-free, it's important for those with celiac disease or gluten allergies to check the label before using it.

Traditional Bolognese sauce is made with beef and pork, but this vegetarian version is equally hearty with a rich, deep flavor. Lots of mushrooms add meaty flavor and texture, while dried herbs perk up the sauce. Serve it over pasta for a wonderful, comforting meal.

2 ounces dried porcini mushrooms

1 cup hot water

2 cups chopped cremini mushrooms

1 cup chopped shiitake mushrooms

2 yellow onions, finely chopped

2 carrots, chopped

2 (28-ounce) cans crushed tomatoes

3 tablespoons tomato paste

2 tablespoons tamari

1 teaspoon sea salt

1 teaspoon dried oregano

1 teaspoon dried basil

1. In a small bowl, cover the porcini mushrooms with the hot water. Let them soak for 15 minutes. Meanwhile, prepare the remaining ingredients.
2. Drain the mushrooms, reserving the soaking liquid. Strain the mushroom liquid through cheesecloth to remove any grit. Remove and discard the mushroom stems and chop the tops.
3. Place the porcini mushrooms, mushroom soaking liquid, cremini and shiitake mushrooms, onions, carrots, crushed tomatoes, tomato paste, tamari, salt, oregano, and basil in a 4- to 5-quart slow cooker. Stir well to combine.
4. Cover and cook on low for 8 to 9 hours, or until the sauce is thickened.
5. Serve immediately, or cool at room temperature for 30 minutes and then refrigerate it in an airtight container for up to 1 week. Freeze for longer storage. To reheat, place in a saucepan over medium-low heat and cook until hot and steaming.

Spinach and Black Bean Enchilada Pie

GLUTEN-FREE, VEGETARIAN, WEEKNIGHT HERO

This savory vegetarian dish is a favorite. The combination of green spinach with black beans and yellow corn tortillas is colorful and delicious. You can use full-fat versions of the cheeses in this recipe if you'd like.

4 ounces low-fat cream cheese

½ cup shredded low-fat Cheddar cheese

2 (15-ounce) cans black beans, drained and rinsed

1 cup minced yellow onion

2 teaspoons minced garlic

1 teaspoon ground cumin

2 teaspoons smoked paprika

4 cups shredded fresh spinach

2 teaspoons extra-virgin olive oil

2 cups enchilada sauce, divided

8 corn tortillas, divided

½ cup chopped fresh cilantro, for garnish

1. In a large bowl, beat the cream cheese with the Cheddar cheese until combined. Stir in the black beans, onion, garlic, cumin, and paprika. Stir in the spinach.
2. Grease a 4-quart slow cooker with the olive oil.
3. Spread ⅔ cup of the enchilada sauce across the bottom of the slow cooker. Place 2 corn tortillas on top of the sauce in a single layer. Top the tortillas with a third of the black bean and spinach mixture. Top this with 2 more corn tortillas and then slather them with ⅔ cup of enchilada sauce. Then layer two more tortillas and another third of the bean mixture. Place two tortillas on top of that, and then top with the remaining bean mixture and ⅔ cup of enchilada sauce.
4. Cover and cook on low for 6 to 8 hours, or until the mixture is bubbling around the edges. Garnish with the cilantro just before serving.

PREP TIME:
15 MINUTES

COOK TIME:
6 TO 8 HOURS ON LOW

SERVES 4

PER SERVING:
Calories: 503; Fat: 14g; Saturated Fat: 5g; Cholesterol: 23mg; Carbohydrates: 72g; Fiber: 15g; Protein: 24g; Sodium: 1,051mg

IF YOU HAVE A MINUTE: For added flavor, use whole cumin seeds in place of the ground cumin. Toast 1½ teaspoons of cumin seeds in a dry skillet for a couple of minutes, and then grind them a spice grinder or with a mortar and pestle just before adding to the slow cooker.

Indian Chickpeas with Yogurt and Cardamom

GLUTEN-FREE, LOW-CALORIE, VEGETARIAN, WEEKNIGHT HERO

PREP TIME:
15 MINUTES

COOK TIME:
8 HOURS ON LOW

SERVES 4

PER SERVING:
Calories: 318; Fat: 5g;
Saturated Fat: 2g;
Cholesterol: 8mg;
Carbohydrates: 55g;
Fiber: 13g; Protein: 16g;
Sodium: 476mg

GAME PLAN: If you
want to make
this recipe often,
measure out four
or five times the
amount of spices
and store them
in a small plastic
bag or airtight
container in a cool
and dry place.
Then, when you
want to make this
dish, just measure
out 2 tablespoons
of the mixture
and continue
with the recipe.

Indian cooking uses lots of yogurt. This ingredient tenderizes proteins and adds great flavor and texture. And the spices in this recipe provide a wonderful flavor and aroma. This protein- and fiber-rich entrée is delicious served over Slow Cooker Rice (page 258) or Basic Quinoa (page 257) or with naan.

2 teaspoons garam masala

1 teaspoon ground turmeric

1 teaspoon ground cumin

1 teaspoon ground coriander

1 teaspoon ground ginger

¼ teaspoon ground cardamom

½ teaspoon ground cinnamon

2 (15-ounce) cans chickpeas, drained and rinsed

2 cups Vegetable Broth (page 264 or store-bought)

1 yellow onion, diced

2 garlic cloves, minced

½ teaspoon sea salt

⅛ teaspoon freshly ground black pepper

1 large tomato, seeded and diced

4 cups fresh spinach, cut into thin ribbons

1 cup plain full-fat yogurt

Chopped fresh cilantro, for garnish

1. In a small bowl, whisk together the garam masala, turmeric, cumin, coriander, ginger, cardamom, and cinnamon.
2. Place the prepared spice blend, chickpeas, broth, onion, garlic, salt, and pepper in a 3-quart slow cooker. Stir to mix well.
3. Cover and cook on low for 8 hours.
4. Uncover and let rest for about 10 minutes before serving.
5. Stir in the tomato, spinach, and yogurt. Garnish with fresh cilantro and serve.

Mushroom Cassoulet

GLUTEN-FREE, LOW-CALORIE, VEGAN, WEEKNIGHT HERO

Traditionally, cassoulet is made with pork and duck, but mushrooms make an admirable substitute. Mushrooms have a compound that activates the umami taste buds on your tongue, providing an intense meaty flavor.

2 ounces dried wild mushrooms

1½ cups hot water

2 (15-ounce) cans navy beans, drained and rinsed

1 cup Vegetable Broth (page 264 or store-bought)

1 (8-ounce) package sliced cremini or button mushrooms

1 cup sliced carrots

1 cup diced yellow onions

1 cup sliced celery

1 tablespoon herbes de Provence

½ teaspoon sea salt

⅛ teaspoon freshly ground black pepper

PREP TIME:
15 MINUTES

COOK TIME:
8 HOURS ON LOW

SERVES 4

PER SERVING:
Calories: 297; Fat: <1g;
Saturated Fat: <1g;
Cholesterol: 0mg;
Carbohydrates: 53g;
Fiber: 16g; Protein: 19g;
Sodium: 480mg

1. Place the dried mushrooms in a medium bowl and add the hot water. Let them soak for 15 minutes while you prepare the remaining ingredients.
2. Drain the mushrooms, reserving the soaking liquid. Strain the liquid through cheesecloth to remove any grit. Remove the mushroom stems and discard.
3. Place the beans, broth, wild and cremini mushrooms, strained soaking liquid, carrots, onions, celery, herbes de Provence, salt, and pepper in a 4-quart slow cooker. Stir well to mix.
4. Cover and cook on low for 8 hours, until the vegetables are tender.

Eggplant Parmesan Casserole

LOW-CALORIE, VEGETARIAN

PREP TIME:
45 MINUTES

COOK TIME:
8 HOURS ON LOW

SERVES 6

PER SERVING:
Calories: 317; Fat: 15g;
Saturated Fat: 5g;
Cholesterol: 20mg;
Carbohydrates: 37g;
Fiber: 6g; Protein: 14g;
Sodium: 798mg

Typical eggplant Parmesan is usually made from slices of eggplant that are coated in egg and bread crumbs and fried. When made in the slow cooker, this recipe is much better for you and just as tasty.

1 large eggplant, peeled and cut into 1-inch cubes

1½ teaspoons sea salt, divided

1 yellow onion, chopped

2 cups sliced shiitake or cremini mushrooms

3 large tomatoes, seeded and chopped

3 garlic cloves, sliced

1 cup Basic Marinara Sauce (page 261 or store-bought)

3 tablespoons tomato paste

2 teaspoons dried Italian seasoning

⅛ teaspoon freshly ground black pepper

1½ cups shredded Parmesan cheese, divided

3 tablespoons extra-virgin olive oil

1½ cups fresh bread crumbs

1. Put the eggplant cubes in a large colander or strainer in the sink. Sprinkle 1 teaspoon of salt over the eggplant. Let stand for 30 minutes.
2. Rinse the eggplant and drain well; pat dry with paper towels.
3. Place the eggplant, onion, mushrooms, tomatoes, garlic, marinara sauce, tomato paste, Italian seasoning, pepper, and the remaining ½ teaspoon of salt in a 4-quart slow cooker. Stir well to combine.
4. Cover and cook on low for 8 hours, or until the vegetables are tender. Stir in 1 cup of Parmesan cheese. Sprinkle the top with the remaining ½ cup of cheese.
5. In a small saucepan over medium-high heat, add the olive oil. Once hot, add the bread crumbs and toast them, stirring frequently, for about 5 minutes, until crispy.
6. Sprinkle the bread crumbs over each serving.

Tex-Mex Potato Strata

GLUTEN-FREE, LOW-CALORIE, VEGETARIAN

Potatoes are wonderful in this dish, cooked until tender with lots of spicy flavors and creamy cheese. Serve this with sour cream, some salsa, and chopped avocados. I guarantee you'll do a little salsa dance in your chair while you eat this.

PREP TIME:
25 MINUTES

COOK TIME:
8 HOURS ON LOW

SERVES 8

PER SERVING:
Calories: 345; Fat: 19g;
Saturated Fat: 13g;
Cholesterol: 48mg;
Carbohydrates: 32g;
Fiber: 5g; Protein: 12g;
Sodium: 645mg

2 (20-ounce) bags refrigerated sliced potatoes

1 yellow onion, chopped

3 garlic cloves, minced

2 jalapeño peppers, seeded and minced

2 red bell peppers, seeded and chopped

2 cups shredded pepper Jack cheese

1½ cups sour cream

2 cups Vegetable Broth (page 264 or store-bought)

1 tablespoon chili powder

1 teaspoon sea salt

⅛ teaspoon freshly ground black pepper

⅓ cup grated cotija cheese

1. Layer the potatoes, onion, garlic, jalapeños, red bell peppers, and pepper Jack cheese in a 4- to 5-quart slow cooker.
2. In a large bowl, combine the sour cream, broth, chili powder, salt, and pepper and mix well. Pour the sour cream mixture into the slow cooker. If needed, use a knife to lift and loosen the layers to make sure that the sauce has penetrated through the vegetables.
3. Sprinkle with the cotija cheese.
4. Cover and cook on low for 8 hours, or until the potatoes are tender.
5. Uncover and let stand for 10 minutes.
6. Carefully cut and scoop to serve.

Vegetarian Italian Stuffed Peppers

GLUTEN-FREE, LOW-CALORIE, VEGETARIAN

PREP TIME:
15 MINUTES

COOK TIME:
6 HOURS ON LOW

SERVES 4

PER SERVING:
Calories: 235; Fat: 14g;
Saturated Fat: 7g;
Cholesterol: 81mg;
Carbohydrates: 12g;
Fiber: 2g; Protein: 18g;
Sodium: 542mg

If you're craving lasagna but want a low-carb option, try these stuffed peppers. They have all the flavors of a traditional lasagna but without the noodles, which makes them naturally gluten-free, too. Use a variety of bell pepper colors for visual interest.

1 teaspoon extra-virgin olive oil

4 bell peppers (any color), top ½ inch sliced off, seeded, and cored

1 cup small-curd cottage cheese

1 cup shredded Italian cheese blend

¼ cup minced fresh basil

1 teaspoon dried Italian seasoning

1 large egg, whisked

¼ cup freshly grated Parmesan cheese

1. Lightly grease a 3-quart slow cooker with the oil. Arrange the bell peppers inside (you may need to slice a small portion off the bottom of each pepper to help them stand up, but be careful not to make a hole that would allow the filling to escape).

2. In a small mixing bowl, combine the cottage cheese, Italian cheese blend, basil, Italian seasoning, and egg. Spoon the mixture evenly into the peppers. Sprinkle each pepper with Parmesan cheese.

3. Cover and cook on low for 6 hours, or until the peppers are tender.

Asian Mushroom Lettuce Wraps

GLUTEN-FREE, LOW-CALORIE, VEGETARIAN

Finely chopped mushrooms cooked with Asian flavors make a savory filling for lettuce cups. If you have a food processor, you can save time by pulsing the mushrooms and veggies along with the herbs and spices 10 to 20 times. Otherwise, chop your vegetables finely with a knife. To make this vegetarian, skip the fish sauce and add an extra teaspoon of tamari instead.

PREP TIME:
20 MINUTES

COOK TIME:
8 HOURS ON LOW

SERVES 6

PER SERVING:
Calories: 75; Fat: 1g;
Saturated Fat: <1g;
Cholesterol: 0mg;
Carbohydrates: 15g;
Fiber: 3g; Protein: 4g;
Sodium: 871mg

8 ounces cremini mushrooms, finely chopped

8 ounces shiitake mushrooms, finely chopped

1 yellow onion, finely chopped

6 scallions, sliced on an angle

6 garlic cloves, minced

1 tablespoon grated fresh ginger

2 tablespoons chili garlic sauce, divided

1 teaspoon grated orange zest

4 tablespoons chopped fresh cilantro, divided

1 teaspoon fish sauce (if non-vegetarian)

1 teaspoon extra-virgin olive oil

4 tablespoons tamari, divided (plus an additional 1 teaspoon, if vegetarian)

1 tablespoon honey

6 to 8 large butter lettuce or iceberg lettuce leaves

1. Place the cremini and shiitake mushrooms, onion, scallions, garlic, ginger, 1 tablespoon of chili garlic sauce, orange zest, 2 tablespoons of cilantro, fish sauce, olive oil, and 2 tablespoons of tamari in a 3-quart slow cooker. Stir well to combine.
2. Cover and cook on low for 8 hours.
3. In a small bowl, whisk together the remaining 1 tablespoon of chili garlic sauce, 2 tablespoons of cilantro, 2 tablespoons of tamari, and the honey.
4. To serve, spoon the mushroom mixture into the lettuce leaves using a slotted spoon. Use the honey and chili garlic sauce mixture as a dipping sauce.

Cheesy Brown Rice Casserole

GLUTEN-FREE, VEGETARIAN

PREP TIME:
25 MINUTES

COOK TIME:
6 TO 7 HOURS
ON LOW

SERVES 6

PER SERVING:
Calories: 500; Fat: 10g;
Saturated Fat: 5g;
Cholesterol: 25mg;
Carbohydrates: 80g;
Fiber: 14g; Protein: 23g;
Sodium: 672mg

Brown rice is combined with lentils and lots of aromatic vegetables and herbs in this hearty and satisfying casserole. Cheese adds richness and provides the perfect finishing touch. This is really a one-dish meal, but you can serve a fruit salad with it for a cooling contrast.

1 yellow onion, chopped

1 leek, white and light green parts, chopped

3 garlic cloves, minced

2 cups sliced button or cremini mushrooms

3 carrots, sliced

3 tomatoes, seeded and chopped

2 cups long-grain brown rice

1 cup green lentils

5 cups Vegetable Broth (page 264 or store-bought)

1 bay leaf

1 teaspoon sea salt

1 teaspoon dried thyme

⅛ teaspoon freshly ground black pepper

1½ cups shredded Havarti or Swiss cheese

1. Place the onion, leek, garlic, mushrooms, carrots, tomatoes, rice, lentils, broth, bay leaf, salt, thyme, and pepper in a 4- to 5-quart slow cooker. Stir well to combine.
2. Cover and cook on low for 6 to 7 hours, or until the rice, lentils, and vegetables are tender.
3. Stir in the cheese and let it stand, covered, for 10 minutes.
4. Stir gently and serve.

INGREDIENT TIP: Rice comes in three lengths: short, medium, and long. Short-grain rice is used to make sticky rice for many Asian recipes and for risotto since it releases starch as it cooks. Medium-grain rice is also fairly sticky when cooked and is used in recipes like paella. Long-grain rice is best for the slow cooker. It results in a fluffier finished dish as the grains stay better separated when cooked.

Moroccan Chickpeas with Chard

GLUTEN-FREE, LOW-CALORIE, VEGAN, WEEKNIGHT HERO

The fragrant spices in this healthy vegan dish create a warm, enticing aroma. The Swiss chard cooks way down, so don't worry if it's challenging to fit everything into the slow cooker at first. Look for rainbow chard when you're shopping for this recipe; its multicolored stems offer a great array of nutrients.

1 bunch Swiss chard,
  stems diced and leaves
  roughly chopped

2 (16-ounce) cans chickpeas,
  drained and rinsed

1 cup diced yellow onion

1 cup sliced carrots

½ cup diced dried apricots

¼ cup roughly chopped
  preserved lemons (optional)

2 tablespoons tomato paste

2 teaspoons minced
  fresh ginger

½ teaspoon red pepper flakes

1 teaspoon smoked paprika

1 teaspoon ground cinnamon

½ teaspoon ground cumin

¼ teaspoon sea salt

PREP TIME:
15 MINUTES

COOK TIME:
8 HOURS ON LOW

SERVES 4

PER SERVING:
Calories: 315; Fat: 2g;
Saturated Fat: <1g;
Cholesterol: 0mg;
Carbohydrates: 63g;
Fiber: 17g; Protein: 15g;
Sodium: 470mg

1. Place all of the ingredients in a 4- to 5-quart slow cooker. Stir everything together thoroughly.
2. Cover and cook on low for 8 hours, or until the chard is wilted and the vegetables are tender.

INGREDIENT TIP: Preserved lemons are a specialty product that comes from North Africa. The lemons are diced or quartered and pickled in salt, lemon juice, and water. They add a spicy, salty, and sharp note to any recipe. If you don't want to add them to this recipe, stir in a tablespoon or two of freshly squeezed lemon juice just before serving.

Coq au Vin,
page 177

CHAPTER 7

POULTRY

Chicken with Mushrooms and Shallots

GLUTEN-FREE, LOW-CALORIE, WEEKNIGHT HERO

PREP TIME:
15 MINUTES

COOK TIME:
6 TO 8 HOURS
ON LOW

SERVES 4

PER SERVING:
Calories: 326; Fat: 15g;
Saturated Fat: 6g;
Cholesterol: 188mg;
Carbohydrates: 8g;
Fiber: 1g; Protein: 36g;
Sodium: 250mg

Sherry is a classic cooking ingredient in France and Spain. It adds complexity and flavor to any recipe. Most of the alcohol cooks out, but remember that the slow cooker lid traps volatile ingredients, so some alcohol will remain. If you are serving this to kids, think about substituting chicken stock instead of the wine. Never buy cooking sherry, which is made with a lot of salt.

1 tablespoon unsalted butter, at room temperature, or extra-virgin olive oil

4 cups cremini mushrooms, thinly sliced

2 teaspoons fresh thyme

4 garlic cloves, minced

2 shallots, minced

5 tablespoons dry sherry or Chicken Stock (page 263 or store-bought)

4 (6-ounce) bone-in, skinless chicken thighs

¼ teaspoon sea salt

Freshly ground black pepper

1. Grease a 4-quart slow cooker with the butter.
2. Place the mushrooms, thyme, garlic, and shallots in the slow cooker, tossing them gently to combine. Pour in the sherry.
3. Season the chicken with the salt and pepper and place the thighs on top of the mushroom mixture.
4. Cover and cook on low for 6 to 8 hours, or until the chicken is tender and reads at least 165°F on a food thermometer.

EXTRA EASY: You can often find sliced mushrooms at the grocery store. This could shave up to 10 minutes off your preparation time. You can use a mix of cremini and button mushrooms in this recipe if you'd like.

Cashew Chicken and Snap Peas

GLUTEN-FREE, LOW-CALORIE

It's the sweet, sour, and spicy sauce that will make you want more of this classic Chinese takeout recipe. This dish is nice on its own for a low-carbohydrate meal, or serve it with Slow Cooker Rice (page 258).

4 (8- to 12-ounce) boneless, skinless chicken breasts

3 cups sugar snap peas, strings removed

2 teaspoons grated fresh ginger

2 teaspoons minced garlic

3 tablespoons tamari

2 tablespoons ketchup

2 tablespoons rice vinegar

2 teaspoons honey

Pinch red pepper flakes

½ cup toasted cashews

2 scallions, white and green parts, thinly sliced

PREP TIME:
15 MINUTES

COOK TIME:
6 HOURS ON LOW

SERVES 4

PER SERVING:
Calories: 398; Fat: 13g; Saturated Fat: 3g; Cholesterol: 130mg; Carbohydrates: 21g; Fiber: 3g; Protein: 53g; Sodium: 1,199mg

1. Place the chicken and sugar snap peas in a 4-quart slow cooker.
2. In a measuring cup or small bowl, whisk together the ginger, garlic, tamari, ketchup, vinegar, honey, and red pepper flakes. Pour the mixture over the chicken and snap peas.
3. Cover and cook on low for 6 hours. The snap peas should be tender but not mushy. The chicken should be tender and read at least 165°F on a food thermometer.
4. Just before serving, stir in the cashews and scallions.

INGREDIENT TIP: When you cook whole chicken breasts or thighs, you can cook the dish for a longer period of time. Most often, the chicken will be so tender that it will break up on its own, or you can remove and shred the meat just before serving.

Shredded Buffalo Chicken

GLUTEN-FREE, LOW-CALORIE

This is perhaps one of the easiest slow cooker recipes you'll ever make. It produces tender, shredded, spicy buffalo chicken that you can use on sandwiches, quesadillas, pizzas, and more. Serve it with some creamy blue cheese dressing for an authentic pairing.

Nonstick cooking spray
½ cup (1 stick) unsalted butter, melted

5 large bone-in, skinless chicken breasts
½ cup hot sauce
½ teaspoon sea salt

1. Grease a 3-quart slow cooker with nonstick cooking spray.
2. Add the melted butter to the slow cooker. Add the chicken breasts, layering as you go with the hot sauce and salt.
3. Cover and cook on low for 5 to 6 hours.
4. Using tongs, remove the chicken and shred it with two forks, discarding the bones. Return the chicken to the slow cooker and stir to coat it with the buttery buffalo sauce. Taste and season with additional salt, if needed. Serve warm.

INGREDIENT TIP: You can make this recipe with 12 bone-in, skinless chicken thighs instead of the breasts. The cook time will change to 6 to 7 hours on low.

PREP TIME:
5 MINUTES

COOK TIME:
5 TO 6 HOURS ON LOW

SERVES 6

PER SERVING:
Calories: 331; Fat: 23g;
Saturated Fat: 11g;
Cholesterol: 141mg;
Carbohydrates: 4g;
Fiber: 0g; Protein: 28g;
Sodium: 715mg

Whole Roasted Chicken

GLUTEN-FREE, LOW-CALORIE

PREP TIME:
10 MINUTES

COOK TIME:
4 TO 5 HOURS
ON LOW

SERVES 6

PER SERVING:
Calories: 236; Fat: 17g;
Saturated Fat: 6g;
Cholesterol: 80mg;
Carbohydrates: 2g;
Fiber: 1g; Protein: 19g;
Sodium: 477mg

Purchasing a whole chicken saves money and allows every member of the family to enjoy light or dark meat as they choose. The chicken is cooked with the skin on to keep the meat moist. The skin should be discarded after cooking because it won't be crisp.

1 yellow onion, cut crosswise in rings

1 (3- to 4-pound) whole chicken, giblets and neck removed

1 tablespoon unsalted butter, at room temperature

1 teaspoon sea salt

⅛ teaspoon freshly ground black pepper

1 tablespoon herbes de Provence or other dried herb blend

1. Place the onion rings in the bottom of a 4-quart slow cooker.
2. Coat the outside of the chicken with the butter and season generously with the salt, pepper, and herbes de Provence. Place the chicken on top of the onions.
3. Cover and cook on high for about 4 hours. Test for doneness by inserting a food thermometer into the thickest part of the chicken thigh (be careful not to touch the bone). It should read at least 165°F. If it doesn't, cover and cook for 45 minutes more before testing the temperature again.

IF YOU HAVE A MINUTE: To add more flavor and beautiful browned color to this chicken, coat it with the butter and sprinkle with the salt and pepper. Heat a large skillet over medium heat and brown the chicken on all sides, turning carefully with tongs and a spatula, for 3 to 4 minutes per side. Place the chicken in the slow cooker, sprinkle it with the herbs, and continue with the recipe.

Turkey Breast with Root Vegetables

GLUTEN-FREE, LOW-CALORIE

This turkey breast is simple and delicious. Flavored with fragrant herbs, the turkey juices drip down to the root vegetables, adding wonderful flavor. To store the cooked turkey breast, you can cut it into single-size portions and freeze it in zip-top bags.

2 cups baby carrots

2 fennel bulbs, peeled and sliced

1 yellow onion, chopped

1 (8-ounce) package button mushrooms

1 teaspoon dried thyme

1 teaspoon dried rosemary

1 teaspoon sea salt

¼ teaspoon freshly ground black pepper

Grated zest of 1 lemon

1 (4- to 6-pound) bone-in, skin-on turkey breast

PREP TIME:
25 MINUTES

COOK TIME:
8 HOURS ON LOW

SERVES 8

PER SERVING: Calories: 346; Fat: 2g; Saturated Fat: 1g; Cholesterol: 188mg; Carbohydrates: 9g; Fiber: 3g; Protein: 70g; Sodium: 456mg

1. Arrange the baby carrots, fennel, onion, and mushrooms in the bottom of a 4- to 5-quart slow cooker.
2. In a small bowl, combine the thyme, rosemary, salt, pepper, and lemon zest.
3. Rub the turkey breast with the seasoning mixture.
4. Place the turkey, skin-side up, in the slow cooker on top of the vegetables.
5. Cover and cook on low for 8 hours, or until the turkey registers at least 165°F on a food thermometer. Let the turkey stand, covered, for 10 minutes before slicing. Remove the turkey skin before serving.

IF YOU HAVE A MINUTE: You can brown the turkey skin before you add it to the slow cooker for more flavor and color. Just heat a couple of tablespoons of olive oil in a large skillet over medium heat. Add the turkey, skin-side down, and brown it for 5 to 7 minutes. No need to brown the other side. Add the turkey to the slow cooker and continue with the recipe. Or you can broil the turkey breast after it's finished cooking for 4 to 6 minutes to brown and crisp the skin.

Cranberry Turkey Roast

GLUTEN-FREE, LOW-CALORIE, WEEKNIGHT HERO

If you consider the best parts of Thanksgiving dinner the turkey and cranberry sauce, this recipe is for you. But don't wait until November to enjoy it: Turkey is delicious anytime, and this recipe is easy to make year-round.

1 (3-pound) bone-in, skin-on turkey breast

1 teaspoon sea salt

¼ teaspoon freshly ground black pepper

2 tablespoons extra-virgin olive oil

1 cup apple cider

1 (16-ounce) bag fresh cranberries

Grated zest and juice of 1 orange

1 rosemary sprig

1. Season the turkey breast with the salt and pepper.
2. Heat the olive oil in a large skillet over medium heat. Add the turkey, skin-side down, and cook for 5 to 7 minutes, until the skin is browned. Place the turkey, skin-side up, in a 4-quart slow cooker.
3. Add the apple cider to the skillet and bring it to a boil, scraping the brown bits from the bottom of the pan with a spatula or wooden spoon. Pour this into the slow cooker.
4. Add the cranberries, orange zest and juice, and rosemary to the slow cooker.
5. Cover and cook on low for 8 hours, or until the turkey registers at least 165°F on a food thermometer. Let the turkey stand, covered, for 10 minutes before you carve and serve with the cranberry mixture.

PREP TIME:
15 MINUTES

COOK TIME:
8 HOURS ON LOW

SERVES 8

PER SERVING:
Calories: 340; Fat: 16g; Saturated Fat: 4g; Cholesterol: 110mg; Carbohydrates: 10g; Fiber: 1g; Protein: 36g; Sodium: 1,299mg

GAME PLAN: Even if you have a small family, make this recipe on Thanksgiving. Turkey leftovers are wonderful in sandwiches the next day. If you still have some leftover after 3 days, slice or cube the meat and freeze it for up to 4 months.

Turkey Joes

PREP TIME:
15 MINUTES

COOK TIME:
4 TO 6 HOURS
ON LOW OR
2 TO 3 HOURS
ON HIGH

SERVES 4

PER SERVING:
Calories: 544; Fat: 24g;
Saturated Fat: 10g;
Cholesterol: 145mg;
Carbohydrates: 39g;
Fiber: 6g; Protein: 47g;
Sodium: 1,253mg

This delicious and kid-friendly recipe is a twist on the classic sloppy joe sandwich, which is made with ground beef. It's lightened up with ground turkey and some veggies for more nutrition. Toast the buns before you add the turkey mixture for a bit of crunch.

1½ pounds lean ground turkey

¼ cup tomato paste

6 tablespoons ketchup

2 tablespoons yellow mustard

½ cup water

½ small yellow onion, finely chopped

2 garlic cloves, minced

1 carrot, finely chopped

1 teaspoon paprika

1 teaspoon ground cumin

½ teaspoon sea salt

¼ teaspoon freshly ground black pepper

4 hamburger or onion buns, split and toasted

1 cup shredded Cheddar cheese

1. Place a large skillet over medium heat. Add the ground turkey and cook, breaking up the meat with a wooden spoon, until it is light brown. Drain if necessary.

2. Place the cooked ground turkey, tomato paste, ketchup, mustard, water, onion, garlic, carrot, paprika, cumin, salt, and black pepper in a 3-quart slow cooker. Stir to mix well.

3. Cover and cook on low for 4 to 6 hours or on high for 2 to 3 hours.

4. To serve, spoon about ½ cup of the turkey mixture on the bottom of each bun and top evenly with the cheese. Add the top half of the bun and serve.

INGREDIENT TIP: Use your favorite cheese instead of Cheddar. Try shredded Swiss, Colby, Muenster, provolone, or even pepper Jack for a bit of heat.

Salsa Chicken

GLUTEN-FREE, LOW-CALORIE, WEEKNIGHT HERO

This dish could not be easier: You put uncooked chicken thighs in the bottom of the slow cooker and add salsa. The heat of the salsa will determine the heat of the final dish. The acids in the salsa tenderize and flavor the meat. Let it cook until dinnertime, and you'll have the most tender, flavorful chicken you've ever tasted. You can eat the chicken thighs whole with whatever side dishes you like, or you can shred them and put them in crispy or soft taco shells.

2 pounds boneless, skinless chicken thighs

2 cups Red Salsa (page 268 or store-bought)

1. Place the chicken in a 3-quart slow cooker and pour the salsa over it.
2. Cover and cook on low for 8 hours or on high for 4 hours, until the chicken reads 165°F on a food thermometer.

A LITTLE LIGHTER: You can use boneless, skinless chicken breasts in this recipe for less fat, but the dish should be done in about 4 hours on low. For a longer cooking time, use bone-in chicken breasts and remove the skin. The cooking time will increase to 5 to 6 hours on low.

PREP TIME:
5 MINUTES

COOK TIME:
8 HOURS ON LOW
OR
4 HOURS ON HIGH

SERVES 6

PER SERVING:
Calories: 216; Fat: 10g;
Saturated Fat: 3g;
Cholesterol: 120mg;
Carbohydrates: 9g;
Fiber: 2g; Protein: 23g;
Sodium: 231mg

Chicken Piccata

GLUTEN-FREE, LOW-CALORIE, WEEKNIGHT HERO

PREP TIME:
15 MINUTES

COOK TIME:
6 TO 8 HOURS
ON LOW OR
3 TO 4 HOURS
ON HIGH

SERVES 4

PER SERVING:
Calories: 267; Fat: 14g;
Saturated Fat: 4g;
Cholesterol: 180mg;
Carbohydrates: 2g;
Fiber: <1g;
Protein: 33g;
Sodium: 885mg

Capers and lemon juice provide a classic sauce for this chicken recipe that is light but very flavorful. Use your favorite cut of dark meat, whether it be legs, thighs, bone-in, boneless, skin-on, or skinless. If you choose bone-in, skin-on chicken, it will need to cook longer to reach a safe temperature. Add another hour to the time and check the temperature before serving.

2 pounds boneless, skinless chicken thighs

½ teaspoon sea salt

⅛ teaspoon freshly ground black pepper

¼ cup freshly squeezed lemon juice

3 tablespoons capers, undrained

1 bay leaf

¾ cup Chicken Stock (page 263 or store-bought)

1. Season the chicken with the salt and pepper. Place the chicken, lemon juice, capers, bay leaf, and stock in a 4-quart slow cooker. Stir to mix well.
2. Cover and cook on low for 6 to 8 hours or on high for 3 to 4 hours, until the chicken reads 165°F on a food thermometer.
3. Remove and discard the bay leaf before serving.

GAME PLAN: If you cook extra chicken in this recipe (add up to another pound), you can use the leftovers for a chicken salad or sandwiches the next day.

Chicken Thighs with Grape Tomatoes

GLUTEN-FREE, LOW-CALORIE, WEEKNIGHT HERO

This simple recipe is brimming with Mediterranean flavor. The smaller, sweeter grape tomatoes have more flavor and are more tender, but if you cannot find them, you can use cherry tomatoes. Serve this delicious recipe over Slow Cooker Rice (page 258), Basic Quinoa (page 257), or Slow Cooker Mashed Potatoes (page 64).

PREP TIME:
15 MINUTES

COOK TIME:
8 HOURS ON LOW

SERVES 4

PER SERVING:
Calories: 309; Fat: 16g;
Saturated Fat: 5g;
Cholesterol: 180mg;
Carbohydrates: 9g;
Fiber: 2g; Protein: 35g;
Sodium: 257mg

2 pints grape tomatoes
6 garlic cloves, minced
Grated zest of 1 lemon
1 tablespoon extra-virgin olive oil
4 (6-ounce) bone-in, skinless chicken thighs

2 teaspoons fresh thyme leaves
1 teaspoon fresh rosemary, chopped
¼ teaspoon sea salt
Freshly ground black pepper

1. Place the tomatoes, garlic, lemon zest, and olive oil in a 3½-quart slow cooker. Gently stir to mix.
2. Place the chicken thighs over the tomato mixture and season them with the thyme, rosemary, salt, and a few grinds of black pepper.
3. Cover and cook on low for 8 hours, or until the chicken is tender and reads at least 165°F on a food thermometer. Serve the chicken with the tomatoes and garlic.

INGREDIENT TIP: To remove the skin from chicken thighs or drumsticks, use a paper towel and grasp one end of the skin. Pull it off and discard.

IF YOU HAVE A MINUTE: You can remove the bones from the chicken after it's cooked. Shred the meat and return it to the slow cooker, stirring it into the tomatoes and sauce.

Turkey Sausage with Red Beans and Rice

GLUTEN-FREE

PREP TIME:
20 MINUTES

COOK TIME:
6 TO 8 HOURS
ON LOW

SERVES 6 TO 8

PER SERVING:
Calories: 586; Fat: 9g;
Saturated Fat: 2g;
Cholesterol: 35mg;
Carbohydrates: 92g;
Fiber: 9g; Protein: 33g;
Sodium: 1,178mg

This classic dish of the American South is a little lighter with turkey sausage. The long cooking time means you don't need to soak the beans.

8 cups Chicken Stock (page 263 or store-bought) or fish stock

1 pound dried red beans

1½ cups long-grain brown rice

½ teaspoon extra-virgin olive oil

¾ pound smoked turkey sausage, cut into ½-inch slices

3 celery stalks, chopped

1 green bell pepper, seeded and chopped

1 red bell pepper, seeded and chopped

1 sweet onion, chopped

3 garlic cloves, minced

2 tablespoons Creole seasoning

Finely chopped scallions and/or red onions, for garnish (optional)

1. Place the stock, red beans, and rice in a 5-quart slow cooker.
2. Place a medium skillet over medium-high heat and add the olive oil. Once hot, add the sausage slices and sauté for about 4 minutes, turning once, until browned. Add the sausage to the slow cooker.
3. Add the celery, bell peppers, sweet onion, and garlic to the slow cooker. Stir to combine. Sprinkle in the Creole seasoning and stir.
4. Cover and cook on low for 6 to 8 hours, or until the beans and rice are tender.
5. Stir well. Serve garnished with the scallions and/or red onions, if desired.

Thai Chicken Lettuce Wraps

GLUTEN-FREE

Everyone loves this recipe. The rich flavors of Thailand, which include coconut milk, ginger, lime juice, garlic, and cilantro, add fabulous flavor to this easy and healthy recipe. You can substitute boneless, skinless chicken thighs for the bone-in breasts; add an extra hour of cooking time on low.

2 pounds bone-in, skin-on chicken breasts

1 (15-ounce) can coconut milk

¼ cup chopped fresh cilantro

½ red onion, chopped, divided

3 garlic cloves, minced

1 tablespoon freshly squeezed lime juice

1 teaspoon minced fresh ginger

1 teaspoon ground turmeric

¾ teaspoon sea salt

½ teaspoon freshly ground black pepper

8 ounces butter lettuce leaves

Julienned carrots, for garnish

1 serrano chile, sliced (optional)

1. Place the chicken, coconut milk, cilantro, half of the onion, garlic, lime juice, ginger, turmeric, salt, and black pepper in a 3-quart slow cooker. Stir to mix well.

2. Cover and cook on low for 4 to 6 hours or on high for 2 to 3 hours, until the chicken registers at least 165°F on a food thermometer.

3. Using tongs, remove the chicken from the slow cooker. Remove and discard the skin and bones. Shred the meat using two forks. Place the shredded chicken back in the slow cooker and mix well.

4. Spoon the chicken mixture onto the lettuce leaves using a slotted spoon, and garnish with the carrots, chile (if using), and the remaining red onion. Wrap and serve.

PREP TIME:
15 MINUTES

COOK TIME:
4 TO 6 HOURS ON LOW OR 2 TO 3 HOURS ON HIGH

6 SERVINGS

PER SERVING:
Calories: 425; Fat: 28g; Saturated Fat: 15g; Cholesterol: 143mg; Carbohydrates: 4g; Fiber: 1g; Protein: 40g; Sodium: 391mg

INGREDIENT TIP:
Serve these wraps topped with extra chopped cilantro and avocado slices. Serrano chiles are quite hot, so if you don't like your food very spicy, leave it out or use a milder pepper, like a jalapeño or a poblano. Remove the seeds from the pepper for a milder flavor.

Jerk Chicken with Sweet Potatoes

GLUTEN-FREE, WEEKNIGHT HERO

PREP TIME:
15 MINUTES

COOK TIME:
8 HOURS ON LOW

SERVES 4

PER SERVING:
Calories: 798; Fat: 56g;
Saturated Fat: 15g;
Cholesterol: 225mg;
Carbohydrates: 18g;
Fiber: 2g; Protein: 58g;
Sodium: 816mg

INGREDIENT TIP:
You can remove the skin before cooking and simply season the meat with the spice rub. In that case, don't brown the chicken before cooking it in the slow cooker. Or broil the skin-on chicken after it's done cooking for a crisp finish.

Jerk cooking comes from Jamaica, and it refers to a certain way of cooking and seasoning meat. The meat is marinated in a spicy mixture made with Scotch bonnet peppers, which are extremely hot, and then slow smoked. This recipe substitutes a dry rub for the marinade and slow cooking for smoking, but the flavors are similar.

**2 sweet potatoes,
 peeled and cubed**

1 teaspoon garlic powder

1 teaspoon onion powder

1 teaspoon brown sugar

1 teaspoon sea salt

½ teaspoon smoked paprika

½ teaspoon ground allspice

¼ teaspoon cayenne pepper

**¼ teaspoon freshly
 ground black pepper**

¼ teaspoon ground nutmeg

Pinch ground cinnamon

3 pounds chicken parts

**3 tablespoons extra-
 virgin olive oil**

1. Arrange the sweet potatoes in the bottom of a 4-quart slow cooker.
2. In a small bowl, combine the garlic powder, onion powder, brown sugar, salt, paprika, allspice, cayenne pepper, black pepper, nutmeg, and cinnamon.
3. Rub the spice mixture onto the chicken pieces.
4. Place a large skillet over medium heat and add the olive oil. Once hot, add the chicken pieces, skin-side down, and cook for 4 to 6 minutes, or until the skin is browned.
5. Arrange the chicken in the slow cooker, skin-side up, on top of the sweet potatoes.
6. Cover the slow cooker and cook on low for 8 hours, or until the chicken reads 165°F on a food thermometer and the potatoes are tender.

Bacon-Wrapped Drumsticks

GLUTEN-FREE, LOW-CALORIE, WEEKNIGHT HERO

Nothing makes chicken taste better than smoky bacon. This recipe is super easy, and it's always popular at potlucks. Serve it with steamed veggies, Herbed Mashed Cauliflower (page 66), or a leafy salad for a healthy, complete meal. This also makes an excellent meal on the go as it reheats quickly.

12 chicken drumsticks, skin removed   **12 slices thin-cut bacon**

1. Place a large skillet over medium heat and add the bacon slices. Partially cook them for 2 to 4 minutes, until some of the fat renders out. Make sure the bacon is still flexible.
2. Wrap each drumstick in a bacon slice and place them in a 4- to 5-quart slow cooker.
3. Cover and cook on low for 8 hours, until the chicken reads at least 165°F on a food thermometer.

PREP TIME:
15 MINUTES

COOK TIME:
8 HOURS ON LOW

SERVES 6

PER SERVING:
Calories: 323; Fat: 19g;
Saturated Fat: 6g;
Cholesterol: 138mg;
Carbohydrates: <1g;
Fiber: 0g; Protein: 35g;
Sodium: 447mg

Barbecue Chicken Drumsticks

GLUTEN-FREE, LOW-CALORIE, WEEKNIGHT HERO

PREP TIME:
15 MINUTES

COOK TIME:
8 HOURS ON LOW

SERVES 6

PER SERVING:
Calories: 259; Fat: 8g;
Saturated Fat: 4g;
Cholesterol: 190mg;
Carbohydrates: 16g;
Fiber: 2g; Protein: 38g;
Sodium: 812mg

A simple, sticky barbecue sauce adds a smoky, sweet flavor to chicken drumsticks (or any other chicken parts you choose). Serve these with some crisp coleslaw for a tasty picnic-style dinner. This recipe is mild enough that even children will like it, and you can add or subtract seasonings as you see fit.

1 (6-ounce) can tomato paste

¼ cup pure maple syrup

¼ cup apple cider vinegar

1 teaspoon smoked paprika

1 teaspoon garlic powder

1 teaspoon chili powder

1 teaspoon onion powder

1 teaspoon sea salt

½ teaspoon liquid smoke (optional)

½ teaspoon ground cumin

12 chicken drumsticks, skin removed

1. In a small bowl, whisk together the tomato paste, maple syrup, vinegar, paprika, garlic powder, chili powder, onion powder, salt, liquid smoke (if using), and cumin.
2. Arrange the drumsticks in a 4-quart slow cooker and pour the sauce over the top.
3. Cover and cook on low for 8 hours, until the chicken reads 165°F on a food thermometer. Serve with any sauce remaining in the slow cooker.

Chicken Drumsticks with Fennel and Sausage

GLUTEN-FREE

With just a few ingredients, this hearty and delicious recipe is easy to prepare. But it's so much more than the sum of its parts. The synergy between the sweet roasted fennel, spicy sausage, and savory chicken makes this dish sing. Who knew simplicity could taste so good?

1 fennel bulb, peeled and sliced

1 yellow onion, chopped

4 hot Italian sausages, cut into 2-inch pieces

4 chicken drumsticks, skin removed

2 tablespoons extra-virgin olive oil

½ teaspoon sea salt

⅛ teaspoon freshly ground black pepper

PREP TIME:
15 MINUTES

COOK TIME:
6 HOURS ON LOW

SERVES 4

PER SERVING:
Calories: 445; Fat: 32g;
Saturated Fat: 11g;
Cholesterol: 155mg;
Carbohydrates: 10g;
Fiber: 2g; Protein: 33g;
Sodium: 972mg

1. Place the fennel, onion, sausages, and chicken in a 4-quart slow cooker. Drizzle the olive oil over the top and toss until everything is fully coated. Season with the salt and pepper.

2. Cover and cook on low for 6 hours, or until the chicken is tender and reads 165°F on a food thermometer.

INGREDIENT TIP: Fennel is a large root vegetable with a flat root and leafy fronds that has a slight licorice taste. To prepare it, cut the fronds off (reserve the fronds if you like and use them as a garnish), and then remove the outer layer. Rinse it well; then slice it and proceed with the recipe.

Pesto Chicken with Summer Vegetables

GLUTEN-FREE

PREP TIME:
20 MINUTES

COOK TIME:
6 TO 8 HOURS
ON LOW

SERVES 4

PER SERVING:
Calories: 563; Fat: 34g;
Saturated Fat: 8g;
Cholesterol: 248mg;
Carbohydrates: 18g;
Fiber: 6g; Protein: 50g;
Sodium: 609mg

This recipe is a great way to serve all of the wonderful vegetables that are in their prime in summer. You can use any fresh thin-skinned vegetable you'd like in this recipe, like yellow summer squash, other colors of bell peppers, or even green beans. This recipe isn't an exact formula—it's about using whatever is fresh and seasonal.

2 zucchini, cut into 1-inch pieces

2 cups grape tomatoes

2 red bell peppers, seeded and thinly sliced

1 red onion, halved and thinly sliced

2 tablespoons chopped mixed fresh herbs

2 teaspoons extra-virgin olive oil

¼ teaspoon sea salt

Freshly ground black pepper

4 (8-ounce) bone-in, skinless chicken thighs

½ cup basil pesto

1. Place the zucchini, grape tomatoes, bell peppers, onion, and herbs in a 4-quart slow cooker. Gently stir together. Drizzle the vegetables with the olive oil and season with the salt and a few grinds of black pepper.

2. In a medium bowl, coat the chicken on all sides with the pesto and then place it on top of the vegetables.

3. Cover and cook on low for 6 to 8 hours, until the vegetables are tender and the chicken reads 165°F on a food thermometer. Serve the chicken as is, or you can remove it from the slow cooker, take the meat from the bone, shred it, and return the chicken to the slow cooker for a one-dish meal.

Maple-Glazed Chicken Thighs

LOW-CALORIE, WEEKNIGHT HERO

Quick prep and a slow cook truly make this dish a weeknight hero. The maple glaze is sweet and a little spicy, which perfectly complements the rich flavor of the chicken thighs. When served with a veggie side, it makes a tasty meal.

12 bone-in, skinless chicken thighs

¼ cup pure maple syrup

¼ cup low-sodium soy sauce

2 tablespoons tomato paste

1 teaspoon garlic powder

½ teaspoon sea salt

⅛ teaspoon freshly ground black pepper

Pinch cayenne pepper

1. Arrange the chicken thighs in the bottom of a 3-quart slow cooker.
2. In a small bowl, whisk together the maple syrup, soy sauce, tomato paste, garlic powder, salt, black pepper, and cayenne pepper. Pour the mixture over the thighs.
3. Cover and cook on low for 8 hours, until the chicken is tender and a food thermometer reads 165°F.

A LITTLE LIGHTER: You could substitute 6 bone-in, skinless chicken breasts for the thighs in this recipe. The cook time will reduce to 5 to 6 hours on low.

PREP TIME:
10 MINUTES

COOK TIME:
8 HOURS ON LOW

SERVES 6

PER SERVING:
Calories: 367; Fat: 16g;
Saturated Fat: 6g;
Cholesterol: 240mg;
Carbohydrates: 11g;
Fiber: <1g;
Protein: 45g;
Sodium: 752mg

Cheater's Chicken Pot Pie

WEEKNIGHT HERO

PREP TIME:
15 MINUTES

COOK TIME:
8 HOURS ON LOW

SERVES 4

PER SERVING:
Calories: 482; Fat: 15g;
Saturated Fat: 4g;
Cholesterol: 90mg;
Carbohydrates: 61g;
Fiber: 8g; Protein: 28g;
Sodium: 1,224mg

This classic and comforting chicken pot pie is perfect for a cold winter night. The cheater name comes from serving the dish with biscuits that are store-bought or baked from a tube. So much easier! The traditional peas, onions, and carrots are used in this recipe, but you could substitute other ingredients such as frozen corn.

4 boneless, skinless chicken thighs

2 cups diced, peeled Yukon Gold potatoes

2 cups frozen peas

2 cups diced yellow onions

2 cups sliced carrots

2 teaspoons fresh thyme

¼ teaspoon sea salt

Freshly ground black pepper

2 tablespoons all-purpose flour

2 cups Chicken Stock (page 263 or store-bought)

4 biscuits, warmed and split

1. Place the chicken, potatoes, peas, onions, carrots, and thyme in a 4-quart slow cooker. Season with the salt and a few grinds of black pepper.
2. In a medium bowl, whisk together the flour and stock. Pour this into the slow cooker and stir.
3. Cover and cook on low for 8 hours, or until the vegetables are tender. Using tongs, remove the chicken from the slow cooker and shred it with two forks. Return the shredded chicken to the slow cooker, stir, and serve spooned over the biscuits.

Chicken and Dumplings

Chicken and dumplings is the original comfort food. There's nothing better than tender chicken and veggies enveloped in a creamy sauce, topped with fluffy dumplings. There are two tricks to making good dumplings: Don't overwork the dough, and drop the dough onto simmering liquid so it starts cooking immediately.

PREP TIME:
25 MINUTES

COOK TIME:
8 HOURS ON LOW

SERVES 6

PER SERVING:
Calories: 456; Fat: 20g;
Saturated Fat: 9g;
Cholesterol: 149mg;
Carbohydrates: 40g;
Fiber: 3g; Protein: 28g;
Sodium: 1,127mg

FOR THE CHICKEN

8 (4- to 5-ounce) boneless, skinless chicken thighs

½ teaspoon sea salt

⅛ teaspoon freshly ground pepper

1 yellow onion, chopped

3 garlic cloves, minced

2 large carrots, sliced

1 cup sliced celery

1 teaspoon dried basil

4 cups Chicken Stock (page 263 or store-bought)

½ cup heavy (whipping) cream

3 tablespoons cornstarch

FOR THE DUMPLINGS

1¾ cups all-purpose flour

¼ cup yellow cornmeal

2 teaspoons baking powder

1 teaspoon baking soda

½ teaspoon sea salt

⅓ cup cold unsalted butter, cut into cubes

¾ cup buttermilk

TO MAKE THE CHICKEN

1. Sprinkle the chicken thighs with the salt and pepper.
2. Place the onion, garlic, carrots, celery, and basil in a 4-quart slow cooker. Stir to combine. Arrange the chicken on top of the vegetables. Pour the stock over.
3. Cover and cook on low for 7 hours, or until the chicken is very tender. Using tongs, remove the chicken from the slow cooker, shred the meat, and return it to the slow cooker.

CONTINUED

Chicken and Dumplings *CONTINUED*

4. In a small bowl, whisk together the cream and cornstarch. Pour the mixture into the slow cooker and stir well to combine.

TO MAKE THE DUMPLINGS

5. In a large bowl, combine the flour, cornmeal, baking powder, baking soda, and salt.
6. Cut in the butter until the mixture looks like coarse cornmeal.
7. Add the buttermilk and stir just until the dough forms.
8. Drop the dumplings into the simmering mixture in the slow cooker, making 12 dumplings.
9. Cover and cook on low for 1 hour, or until the dumplings are cooked through when you cut one open. Serve.

Mexican-Style Turkey and Cornbread Casserole

Tamales are a favorite Mexican food for many people, but they can be time-consuming and difficult to make for the inexperienced cook. This casserole is quick and easy, and it gives you all the flavors of freshly made tamales. You can make the topping with any of your favorite cornbread recipes or keep it easy with a mix from the store. Although this recipe calls for cooked ground turkey, you can use cooked shredded chicken, ground pork, ground beef, or a combination of these. In fact, you can even make it completely vegetarian by eliminating all meat and adding another can of beans.

PREP TIME:
25 MINUTES

COOK TIME:
6 HOURS ON LOW
OR
3 HOURS ON HIGH

SERVES 4

PER SERVING:
Calories: 846; Fat: 28g;
Saturated Fat: 11g;
Cholesterol: 128mg;
Carbohydrates: 99g;
Fiber: 13g;
Protein: 46g;
Sodium: 1,205mg

Nonstick cooking spray

1 pound lean ground turkey

1 poblano chile, seeded and chopped

4 scallions, chopped

2 (15-ounce) cans black beans, drained and rinsed

2 cups fresh or frozen corn

1 large tomato, diced

½ cup chopped fresh cilantro

¼ cup sliced black olives

1 (10-ounce) can enchilada sauce

1 teaspoon ground cumin

½ teaspoon chili powder

¼ teaspoon freshly ground black pepper

1 (8.5-ounce) package cornbread mix, plus ingredients required on package

1 cup grated Colby cheese

1. Spray a 4-quart slow cooker with nonstick cooking spray.
2. Place a medium skillet over medium heat. Add the ground turkey and cook, breaking up the meat with a wooden spoon, for 8 to 10 minutes, until cooked through. Drain if necessary.
3. Place the cooked turkey, poblano chile, scallions, black beans, corn, tomato, cilantro, olives, enchi-

EXTRA EASY: If you'd like to save time, you can buy ready-made polenta. It comes in tubes, and you can cut it into 1-inch slices and lay them over the filling instead of using cornbread. You can usually find the tubes in the baking section of your grocery store.

CONTINUED

Mexican-Style Turkey and Cornbread Casserole *CONTINUED*

lada sauce, cumin, chili powder, and black pepper in the slow cooker. Stir to combine.

4. Make the cornbread batter according to the package instructions. Spoon the batter over the meat and bean mixture in the slow cooker. Sprinkle the cheese on top.

5. Cover and cook on low for 6 hours or on high for 3 hours, until the cornbread springs back to the touch. Serve hot, dishing up both the turkey mixture and the cornbread topping in each serving.

Bacon Ranch Chicken Casserole

GLUTEN-FREE, WEEKNIGHT HERO

This decadent but easy recipe combines rich and satisfying ingredients, like bacon and cheese, into a comforting casserole the whole family will enjoy. Chicken thighs are ideal to cook in the slow cooker because they have more fat than breasts, so they stay juicy and tender even after hours of cooking.

3 pounds boneless, skinless chicken thighs

4 slices bacon, cooked and crumbled

8 ounces low-fat cream cheese, cubed

8 ounces low-fat sour cream

8 ounces Cheddar cheese, shredded

¼ cup diced yellow onion

1 teaspoon garlic powder

1 teaspoon dried parsley

½ teaspoon sea salt

¼ teaspoon freshly ground black pepper

PREP TIME:
15 MINUTES

COOK TIME:
6 TO 8 HOURS ON LOW OR 3 TO 4 HOURS ON HIGH

SERVES 6

PER SERVING:
Calories: 637; Fat: 46g; Saturated Fat: 22g; Cholesterol: 262mg; Carbohydrates: 7g; Fiber: <1g; Protein: 48g; Sodium: 1,037mg

1. Place all the ingredients a 4-quart slow cooker. Stir to mix well.
2. Cover and cook on low for 6 for 8 hours or on high for 3 to 4 hours, until the chicken reads 165°F on a food thermometer.
3. Stir and serve.

EXTRA EASY: You can buy precooked bacon in most grocery stores. Just heat it in the microwave for a couple of minutes so you don't have to fry it on the stovetop. You can also buy pre-shredded cheese, which will save you a few minutes of preparation.

Chicken Cacciatore

GLUTEN-FREE

PREP TIME:
15 MINUTES

COOK TIME:
6 HOURS ON LOW

SERVES 4

PER SERVING:
Calories: 452; Fat: 16g;
Saturated Fat: 5g;
Cholesterol: 240mg;
Carbohydrates: 16g;
Fiber: 5g; Protein: 48g;
Sodium: 920mg

Cacciatore is a traditional Italian preparation for meats and loosely translates to "in the hunter style." The type of wine, white or red, used to help tenderize the meat and create a flavorful sauce varies by region. This recipe calls for red wine, but you can use whatever you like.

1 cup dry red wine

1 cup Chicken Stock (page 263 or store-bought)

1 (28-ounce) can plum tomatoes, undrained

1 red bell pepper, seeded and sliced

1 yellow onion, sliced

1 cup sliced button or cremini mushrooms

4 garlic cloves, minced

½ teaspoon sea salt

⅛ teaspoon freshly ground black pepper

8 bone-in chicken thighs, skin removed

1. Place the wine, stock, tomatoes with their juices, bell pepper, onion, mushrooms, and garlic in a 3½-quart slow cooker. Stir well to combine.
2. Sprinkle the salt and pepper over the chicken. Arrange the thighs on top of the vegetables.
3. Cover and cook on low for 6 hours, or until the vegetables are tender and the chicken reads 165°F on a food thermometer.

INGREDIENT TIP: Always use good wine that you'd like to drink in the food you make. Never use cooking wine because it is loaded with salt and just not as flavorful as drinking wine.

Chicken Saltimbocca

GLUTEN-FREE, LOW-CALORIE

Saltimbocca means "jump in your mouth" in Italian and is traditionally a dish made with veal. This version uses chicken and a delicious combination of spinach and Parmesan cheese wrapped in prosciutto for extra flavor. Enjoy with a side salad and roasted potatoes.

4 (6-ounce) boneless, skinless chicken breasts

½ teaspoon sea salt

⅛ teaspoon freshly ground black pepper

4 slices prosciutto

1 cup frozen chopped spinach, thawed and squeezed of excess moisture

¼ cup grated Parmesan cheese

½ cup dry white wine

½ cup Chicken Stock (page 263 or store-bought)

1. Place the chicken breasts between two pieces of parchment paper and use a mallet to pound the chicken to about ⅓ inch thick.
2. Remove the top sheet of parchment paper and sprinkle the chicken with the salt and pepper.
3. Top each piece of chicken with a slice of prosciutto. Divide the spinach and Parmesan cheese over the prosciutto slices.
4. Using your fingers, gently roll up each piece of chicken around the prosciutto, spinach, and cheese, and secure each roll with a couple of toothpicks.
5. Place the stuffed chicken breasts in a 3-quart slow cooker. Pour the wine and stock over them.
6. Cover and cook on low for 4 hours or on high for 2 hours, until the chicken reads at least 165°F on a food thermometer. Remove the toothpicks before serving.

PREP TIME:
15 MINUTES

COOK TIME:
4 HOURS ON LOW
OR
2 HOURS ON HIGH

SERVES 4

PER SERVING:
Calories: 292; Fat: 11g;
Saturated Fat: 2g;
Cholesterol: 111mg;
Carbohydrates: 3g;
Fiber: 2g; Protein: 44g;
Sodium: 858mg

Mediterranean Stuffed Chicken Breasts

GLUTEN-FREE, WEEKNIGHT HERO

PREP TIME:
15 MINUTES

COOK TIME:
6 TO 8 HOURS
ON LOW OR
3 TO 4 HOURS
ON HIGH

SERVES 4

PER SERVING:
Calories: 435; Fat: 17g;
Saturated Fat: 6g;
Cholesterol: 123mg;
Carbohydrates: 32g;
Fiber: 5g; Protein: 42g;
Sodium: 853mg

EXTRA EASY: Instead of pounding out the chicken breasts, you can cut a pocket in the side of each breast and stuff it with the filling. Use a toothpick to close the pocket and remove it before serving.

Mediterranean ingredients like feta cheese, garlic, and sun-dried tomatoes are stuffed into chicken breasts and cooked low and slow until the flavors blend.

1½ pounds baby potatoes

4 ounces feta cheese, crumbled

⅓ cup chopped sun-dried tomatoes

4 garlic cloves, minced

2 teaspoons dried oregano

¼ teaspoon sea salt

⅛ teaspoon freshly ground black pepper

4 (6-ounce) boneless, skinless chicken breasts

2 tablespoons extra-virgin olive oil, divided

1. Wash and dry the potatoes and prick them with a fork. Place them in a 4-quart slow cooker.
2. In a small bowl, mix together the feta cheese, sun-dried tomatoes, garlic, oregano, salt, and pepper.
3. Place the chicken breasts between two pieces of plastic wrap and pound them with a meat mallet until they are about ¼ inch thick. Brush the chicken breasts with 1 tablespoon of olive oil. Divide the cheese mixture among the chicken breasts. Using your fingers, gently roll up each piece of chicken, starting from the short side, around the cheese mixture, and secure each roll with toothpicks.
4. Place each stuffed chicken breast, seam-side down, on top of the potatoes. Brush them with the remaining 1 tablespoon of olive oil.
5. Cover and cook on low for 6 to 8 hours or on high for 3 to 4 hours.
6. Discard the toothpicks before serving the chicken with the potatoes.

Tequila and Lime Chicken Tacos

GLUTEN-FREE, LOW-CALORIE, WEEKNIGHT HERO

This dish is made with chicken thighs, which have more flavor than chicken breasts and also stay tender even after 8 hours of cooking. Although the recipe calls for tequila, you can substitute beer, orange juice, or pineapple juice if you prefer. Serve with your favorite accompaniments, like chopped red onion, diced avocado, chopped cilantro, shredded pepper Jack cheese, sour cream, and lime wedges.

PREP TIME:
10 MINUTES

COOK TIME:
8 HOURS ON LOW
OR
4 HOURS ON HIGH

SERVES 6

PER SERVING:
Calories: 355; Fat: 12g;
Saturated Fat: 3g;
Cholesterol: 120mg;
Carbohydrates: 28g;
Fiber: 5g; Protein: 25g;
Sodium: 321mg

INGREDIENT TIP:
Liquid smoke really is smoke that has been condensed into a liquid. Many brands contain lots of additives, but what you want to see on the label is smoke and water.

2 pounds boneless, skinless chicken thighs

1 yellow onion, chopped

½ cup tequila

¼ cup freshly squeezed lime juice

2 garlic cloves

2 tablespoons chopped chipotle chiles in adobo sauce

1 tablespoon chili powder

2 teaspoons liquid smoke (optional)

1 teaspoon ground cumin

1 teaspoon dried oregano

1 teaspoon ancho chili powder

½ teaspoon smoked paprika

12 corn tortillas

1. Place the chicken thighs, onion, tequila, lime juice, garlic, chipotle chiles in adobo sauce, chili powder, liquid smoke (if using), cumin, oregano, ancho chili powder, and smoked paprika in a 3-quart slow cooker. Stir well to combine.
2. Cover and cook on low for 8 hours or on high for 4 hours.
3. Using tongs, remove the chicken and shred it using two forks. Return the shredded chicken to the slow cooker and stir to combine.
4. Warm the tortillas in a dry skillet over medium heat. Fill them with the chicken mixture.

French Chicken, Bean, and Bacon Casserole

GLUTEN-FREE, WEEKNIGHT HERO

PREP TIME:
15 MINUTES

COOK TIME:
8 HOURS ON LOW

SERVES 4

PER SERVING:
Calories: 627; Fat: 19g;
Saturated Fat: 7g;
Cholesterol: 244mg;
Carbohydrates: 49g;
Fiber: 19g;
Protein: 65g;
Sodium: 450mg

The slow cooker provides a nearly authentic cooking vessel for this delicious French dish of beans, pork, and meat, traditionally called cassoulet. This version gets a healthy upgrade by using bone-in chicken thighs instead of duck confit and just a hint of smoky flavor from the bacon.

2 slices applewood-smoked bacon

2 cups dried navy beans, rinsed and picked over

2 small yellow onions, halved and thinly sliced

6 garlic cloves, minced

2 teaspoons herbes de Provence

6 cups Chicken Stock (page 263 or store-bought)

4 (8-ounce) bone-in, skinless chicken thighs

¼ teaspoon sea salt

Freshly ground black pepper

1. Place the bacon slices in a medium skillet. Cook over medium heat until crispy; drain on paper towels and then crumble.
2. Place the beans, bacon, onions, garlic, herbes de Provence, and stock in a 4-quart slow cooker. Stir until thoroughly mixed.
3. Arrange the chicken on top of the beans. Season with the salt and a few grinds of black pepper.
4. Cover and cook on low for 8 hours, or until the chicken reads 165°F on a food thermometer and the beans are cooked and tender.

IF YOU HAVE A MINUTE: Using tongs, remove the chicken thighs from the slow cooker and pull the meat off the bones, discarding the bones. Chop or shred the chicken and stir it back into the slow cooker before serving.

Coq au Vin

GLUTEN-FREE, WEEKNIGHT HERO

Coq au vin is a classic French dish that combines chicken with wine, mushrooms, and garlic. You can omit the wine if you'd like and just use more chicken stock. Serve this dish in shallow bowls to make sure everyone gets lots of sauce and with plenty of crusty French bread to devour every drop.

PREP TIME:
15 MINUTES

COOK TIME:
6 TO 8 HOURS
ON LOW

SERVES 4

PER SERVING:
Calories: 524; Fat: 38g;
Saturated Fat: 13g;
Cholesterol: 131mg;
Carbohydrates: 9g;
Fiber: 2g; Protein: 21g;
Sodium: 476mg

2 tablespoons unsalted butter

2 tablespoons extra-virgin olive oil

4 bone-in, skin-on chicken leg quarters

½ teaspoon sea salt

⅛ teaspoon freshly ground black pepper

2 cups dry white wine

2 shallots, minced

2 large carrots, sliced

1 (8-ounce) package button or cremini mushrooms, halved

2 thyme sprigs

2 cups Chicken Stock (page 263 or store-bought)

Chopped fresh parsley, for garnish (optional)

1. In a large skillet over medium-high heat, heat the butter and olive oil.
2. Pat the chicken legs dry with a paper towel and season with the salt and pepper. Place the chicken, skin-side down, in the hot pan and brown for 3 to 5 minutes. You may have to do this in batches to avoid crowding the pan. Once browned, place the chicken, skin-side up, in a 4-quart slow cooker.
3. Add the wine to the skillet and bring it to a boil; stir with a spatula or wooden spoon to scrape any browned bits from the bottom of the pan. Pour this into the slow cooker, and then add the shallots, carrots, mushrooms, thyme, and stock.
4. Cover and cook on low for 6 to 8 hours, or until the chicken and vegetables are tender. Discard the thyme sprigs and serve garnished with the parsley, if desired.

Miso Chicken with Broccoli

LOW-CALORIE

PREP TIME:
15 MINUTES:

COOK TIME:
6 HOURS ON LOW

SERVES 4

PER SERVING:
Calories: 185; Fat: 2g;
Saturated Fat: <1g;
Cholesterol: 68mg;
Carbohydrates: 9g;
Fiber: 3g; Protein: 32g;
Sodium: 1,131mg

This is a delicious and super healthy dish that requires very little preparation. You can easily throw everything in the slow cooker before you leave for work in the morning and have a fully cooked meal when you get home. If you like your broccoli a little crisper, simply leave it out and, when you're ready to eat, add it to the slow cooker and cook it for about 15 minutes. Serve with steamed or Slow Cooker Rice (page 258) or udon noodles.

2 cups Chicken Stock
   (page 263 or store-bought)
¼ cup white miso paste
1 garlic clove, minced
2 quarter-size slices
   peeled fresh ginger

½ teaspoon sea salt
4 boneless, skinless
   chicken breast halves
1 pound broccoli florets

1. Place the stock, miso paste, garlic, ginger, and salt in a 3½-quart slow cooker. Add the chicken and broccoli and stir to combine.
2. Cover and cook on low for 6 hours, or until the chicken is tender and falling apart.

INGREDIENT TIP: Miso is a fermented paste made of soy, rice, barley, and wheat that is popular in Japan. It adds what is called "umami," the fifth taste in addition to sweet, sour, salty, and bitter. White miso is made with soy and a lot of rice, giving it a slightly sweet taste. If you can't find it, substitute ¼ cup of tahini (sesame paste) and add 1 tablespoon soy sauce.

Chicken Tikka Masala

GLUTEN-FREE, LOW-CALORIE

The slow cooker works beautifully for preparing both traditional foods and those with more complex flavors. This easy chicken tikka masala is brimming with the spices of India, such as cumin, coriander, and ginger. Serve it with naan, flatbread, or a simple salad.

2 pounds boneless, skinless chicken breast

2 cups diced yellow onion

2 cups diced fresh tomatoes

1 teaspoon ground coriander

1 teaspoon ground cumin

1 teaspoon smoked paprika

¼ teaspoon red pepper flakes

2 teaspoons minced fresh ginger

2 cups Chicken Stock (page 263 or store-bought)

¼ cup heavy (whipping) cream or coconut cream

½ cup minced fresh cilantro, for garnish

PREP TIME:
15 MINUTES

COOK TIME:
6 HOURS ON LOW

SERVES 4 TO 6

PER SERVING:
Calories: 335; Fat: 11g; Saturated Fat: 5g; Cholesterol: 150mg; Carbohydrates: 13g; Fiber: 3g; Protein: 49g; Sodium: 416mg

1. Place the chicken, onions, tomatoes, coriander, cumin, paprika, red pepper flakes, ginger, and stock in a 4-quart slow cooker. Stir to combine.

2. Cover and cook on low for 6 hours, until the chicken reads 165°F on a food thermometer and the tomatoes and onions are soft.

3. Uncover and let stand in the slow cooker for 10 minutes; then stir in the cream. Garnish each serving with the cilantro.

EXTRA EASY: Prepare the onions, tomatoes, and spices the night before and store them in the refrigerate. In the morning, all you have to do is combine the ingredients in the slow cooker and turn it on.

Tandoori Chicken

GLUTEN-FREE, LOW-CALORIE, WEEKNIGHT HERO

PREP TIME:
15 MINUTES

COOK TIME:
7 HOURS ON LOW

SERVES 6

PER SERVING:
Calories: 332; Fat: 24g;
Saturated Fat: 8g;
Cholesterol: 113mg;
Carbohydrates: 4g;
Fiber: <1g;
Protein: 27g;
Sodium: 506mg

Tandoori chicken is a classic Indian dish. The chicken is traditionally cooked in a tandoor oven, which is made of clay, but the slow cooker is a good substitute. The yogurt and lemon juice tenderize the chicken as it cooks, while the spices add wonderful flavor. Serve over steamed or Slow Cooker Rice (page 258).

1 cup plain Greek yogurt

1 tablespoon freshly
squeezed lemon juice

2 garlic cloves, chopped

1 teaspoon ground coriander

1 teaspoon paprika

1 teaspoon sea salt

1 teaspoon ground turmeric

½ teaspoon ground cumin

½ teaspoon ground cardamom

1 (2- to 3-pound) chicken, cut
into 8 pieces, skin removed

1. Place the yogurt, lemon juice, garlic, coriander, paprika, salt, turmeric, cumin, and cardamom in a 4-quart slow cooker. Stir to combine.
2. Add the chicken and stir to coat all of the meat.
3. Cover and cook on low for 7 hours, or until the chicken reads at least 165°F on a food thermometer.

IF YOU HAVE A MINUTE: For a more authentic flavor in this traditional Indian dish, you can toast the spices in a small, dry skillet. Simply add the spices to the skillet (you can add them all at once) and turn on the heat. Shake the pan and watch what you're doing as they can burn quickly. You'll know they are done when they smell aromatic.

Butter Chicken

GLUTEN-FREE

Butter chicken is an Indian recipe with lots of different spices that provide excellent flavor and tenderize the chicken at the same time. Serve this rich dish over steamed or Slow Cooker Rice (page 258) to soak up the wonderful sauce.

1 yellow onion, thinly sliced

3 garlic cloves, minced

2 pounds boneless, skinless chicken thighs, cut into 1-inch pieces

1 (15-ounce) can coconut milk

½ cup tomato paste

1 tablespoon minced fresh ginger

1 tablespoon curry powder

2 tablespoons red curry paste

¼ teaspoon sea salt

⅛ teaspoon cayenne pepper

4 tablespoons unsalted butter

PREP TIME:
15 MINUTES

COOK TIME:
6 HOURS ON LOW

SERVES 4

PER SERVING:
Calories: 592; Fat: 44g;
Saturated Fat: 27g;
Cholesterol: 211mg;
Carbohydrates: 15g;
Fiber: 3g; Protein: 36g;
Sodium: 1,028mg

1. Place the onion, garlic, and chicken in a 3½-quart slow cooker.
2. In a medium bowl, whisk together the coconut milk, tomato paste, ginger, curry powder, red curry paste, salt, and cayenne pepper. Pour the mixture over the chicken and onion.
3. Cut the butter into pieces and scatter them across the top of the chicken mixture.
4. Cover and cook on low for 6 hours, or until the chicken reads at least 165°F on a food thermometer. Stir well and serve.

INGREDIENT TIP: Curry paste is a spicy and pungent paste that comes in three different colors. Red is the hottest, followed by yellow and then green. Use the paste that aligns with your heat and spice preference.

Duck à l'Orange

GLUTEN-FREE

PREP TIME:
15 MINUTES

COOK TIME:
6 HOURS ON LOW,
PLUS BROILING TIME

SERVES 4

PER SERVING:
Calories: 405; Fat: 19g;
Saturated Fat: 5g;
Cholesterol: 232mg;
Carbohydrates: 11g;
Fiber: <1g;
Protein: 42g;
Sodium: 733mg

This classic recipe can be made in the slow cooker. Although this isn't a particularly French method for cooking duck, it does provide the gentle heat needed to yield a succulent, flavorful piece of meat. The duck is broiled after it finishes cooking in the slow cooker to make the skin really crisp and brown.

4 (6-ounce) duck breasts

1 teaspoon sea salt

Freshly ground black pepper

1 cup freshly squeezed orange juice

½ cup Chicken Stock (page 263 or store-bought)

2 tablespoons orange liqueur, such as Grand Marnier

1 teaspoon cornstarch

1. Using a sharp knife, score the duck breasts by cutting through the outer layer of skin in a diamond-like pattern. Be careful not to cut all the way through the fat. Season the duck with the salt and pepper.

2. Place a large skillet over medium heat. Once hot, place the duck, skin-side down, in the skillet and cook for about 5 minutes (it should render a significant amount of fat). Remove the pan from the heat. Spoon about 1 tablespoon of the rendered fat into a 4-quart slow cooker to thoroughly coat the crock. Reserve the remaining fat for another purpose (see the Game Plan tip).

3. If you have a rack that fits your slow cooker, place it in the insert. If not, tear off 8 pieces of aluminum foil about 18 inches long and crumple them into balls. Place the foil balls in the slow cooker; then balance the duck breasts, skin-side up, on the rack or foil balls. This helps keep the duck out of the fat it will render as it cooks.

4. In a measuring cup, whisk together the orange juice, stock, liqueur, and cornstarch. Pour this mixture around the duck.
5. Cover and cook on low for 6 hours, or until the duck reads at least 165°F on a food thermometer.
6. Preheat the broiler. Remove the duck from the slow cooker and place it, skin-side up, on a broiler pan. Broil for 4 to 6 minutes, watching carefully, until the skin is crisp.
7. If you want to serve the sauce in the slow cooker, first skim off the fat. Slice the duck breasts and set them on a plate; then spoon the sauce over the slices.

GAME PLAN: Don't throw away that duck fat! It's great for roasting potatoes. Preheat the oven to 425°F. Scrub 3 russet potatoes and cut them into 1-inch pieces. Simmer the potato pieces in boiling water for about 5 minutes and then drain. Combine a few tablespoons of duck fat with the potatoes in a large roasting pan. Roast the potatoes for 35 to 40 minutes, turning them once during roasting time for the crispiest potatoes ever.

INGREDIENT TIP: Many experts consider duck to be red meat, so they cook it to a safe temperature as they do for beef and pork: 145°F. But the USDA says that the safe final internal temperature for duck is 165°F. The choice is yours, but if you have a family member in a high-risk group for food poisoning complications, such as young children, the elderly, pregnant women, or anyone with a chronic health condition, cook it to 165°F.

Barbecue Pork Ribs, page 194

CHAPTER 8

PORK

Pulled Pork

WEEKNIGHT HERO

PREP TIME:
15 MINUTES

COOK TIME:
10 HOURS ON LOW

SERVES 8

PER SERVING:
Calories: 501; Fat: 18g;
Saturated Fat: 5g;
Cholesterol: 133mg;
Carbohydrates: 36g;
Fiber: <1g;
Protein: 52g;
Sodium: 1,058mg

GAME PLAN:
This pulled pork can be used in so many different ways. Use it as a taco filling, in a sandwich, or as an enchilada or burrito filling. Freeze the shredded pork in an airtight container for up to 3 months. Just thaw it in the refrigerator overnight, heat it up, and you're ready to go.

Barbecue sauce is a very personal thing. Depending on where you live, it can mean a sweet sauce, a white sauce, or a fiery one. One thing all barbecue fans can agree on is that if the meat's not tender, it doesn't matter what kind of sauce it's cooked in. Tough meat just isn't worth the trouble. A slow braise in a slow cooker eliminates that possibility and really tenderizes the flavorful pork in this dish.

Nonstick cooking spray
1½ cups ketchup
1 medium yellow onion, chopped
3 tablespoons vegetable oil
2 tablespoons red wine vinegar
½ packed cup dark brown sugar
¼ cup soy sauce
2 tablespoons Worcestershire sauce
1 teaspoon garlic powder
1 (3- to 4-pound) boneless pork shoulder, trimmed of visible fat and cut into 3 pieces

1. Spray a 4- to 5-quart slow cooker with nonstick cooking spray.
2. Place the ketchup, onion, oil, vinegar, brown sugar, soy sauce, Worcestershire sauce, and garlic powder in the slow cooker. Stir to mix.
3. Add the pork pieces to the slow cooker, making sure that all of the pork is coated with the sauce.
4. Cover and cook on low for 10 hours, or until the pork is tender.
5. Using tongs, remove the meat from the slow cooker and shred it with two forks. Return the shredded meat to the slow cooker and stir to coat the meat with the sauce. Serve hot directly from the slow cooker.

Pork Chops with Apples and Onions

GLUTEN-FREE, LOW-CALORIE, WEEKNIGHT HERO

The apples and onions in this recipe cook down into a flavorful, thick, comforting compote, which is served on top of the tender and moist pork chops. A simple green salad complements this dish well.

2 apples, cored, peeled, and cut into 8 wedges

2 sweet yellow onions, cut into thick rings

2 teaspoons fresh thyme

½ teaspoon ground cinnamon

½ cup apple cider

4 (8-ounce) bone-in pork chops, about 1-inch thick

¼ teaspoon sea salt

Freshly ground black pepper

PREP TIME:
15 MINUTES

COOK TIME:
6 TO 8 HOURS
ON LOW

SERVES 4

PER SERVING:
Calories: 347; Fat: 14g;
Saturated Fat: 5g;
Cholesterol: 97mg;
Carbohydrates: 20g;
Fiber: 3g; Protein: 34g;
Sodium: 966mg

1. Place the apples, onions, thyme, and cinnamon in a 3-quart slow cooker and stir to combine. Pour in the apple cider.

2. Season the pork chops with the salt and a few grinds of black pepper. Arrange the chops on top of the apple and onion mixture.

3. Cover and cook on low for 6 to 8 hours, until the apples and onions are very soft and the pork chops are tender.

INGREDIENT TIP: The best apples to use in the slow cooker are Braeburn, McIntosh, Golden Delicious, and Granny Smith. These apples keep their shape and don't become mushy when cooked for long periods of time.

Jalapeño-Bacon Mac and Cheese

Whole-wheat pasta adds fiber and flavor to this comfort food, and it also takes a longer time to cook, making it perfect for the slow cooker. If you're serving this to kids, consider omitting the jalapeño unless they like spicy food. This isn't really a recipe you can start to cook, and then leave the house; it has to be stirred after the first hour.

PREP TIME:
10 MINUTES

COOK TIME:
3 TO 4 HOURS
ON LOW

SERVES 4

PER SERVING:
Calories: 595; Fat: 28g;
Saturated Fat: 14g;
Cholesterol: 176mg;
Carbohydrates: 54g;
Fiber: 5g; Protein: 31g;
Sodium: 543mg

2 teaspoons unsalted butter, at room temperature

1 cup evaporated milk

1½ cups 2% milk

2 large eggs

1½ cups grated sharp Cheddar cheese

8 ounces whole-wheat elbow macaroni

3 slices bacon, cooked crisp and crumbled

¼ cup canned jalapeño peppers, chopped

1. Grease a 3-quart slow cooker with the butter.
2. In a large bowl, whisk together the evaporated milk, 2% milk, and eggs.
3. Add the cheese, macaroni, bacon, and jalapeños to the bowl, and stir until thoroughly combined.
4. Pour the mixture into the slow cooker.
5. Cover and cook on low for 1 hour; then remove the lid and stir. Cover and cook for 2 to 3 hours longer, or until the macaroni is tender.

Franks and Beans

LOW-CALORIE, WEEKNIGHT HERO

PREP TIME:
15 MINUTES

COOK TIME:
7 HOURS ON LOW

SERVES 8

PER SERVING:
Calories: 335; Fat: 15g;
Saturated Fat: 6g;
Cholesterol: 29mg;
Carbohydrates: 37g;
Fiber: 5g; Protein: 13g;
Sodium: 1,044mg

This classic recipe is super easy to make in a slow cooker, and it makes a great dish for kids if you're having a sleepover or birthday party. The flavorful sauce the franks are cooked in is a bit spicy but still mild enough for kids.

Nonstick cooking spray

2 (14-ounce) cans navy beans, drained and rinsed

4 slices bacon

2 cups Vegetable Broth (page 264 or store-bought)

1 medium yellow onion, chopped

1 garlic clove, minced

½ cup ketchup

¼ cup molasses

¼ cup yellow mustard

2 tablespoons brown sugar

Pinch ground ginger

8 hot dogs, cut into bite-size pieces

½ teaspoon sea salt

1. Grease a 4-quart slow cooker with nonstick cooking spray. Place the beans in the slow cooker.
2. Place the bacon in a medium skillet over medium heat. Cook for 5 to 7 minutes, turning often, until crispy. Drain the bacon on paper towels and then crumble it.
3. Add the broth to the skillet and scrape the brown bits from the bottom of the pan with a spatula or wooden spoon. Transfer the bacon and broth to the slow cooker. Stir in the onion, garlic, ketchup, molasses, mustard, brown sugar, ginger, hot dogs, and salt.
4. Cover and cook on low for 7 hours, or until the beans are tender and the sauce is thickened.
5. Serve hot in bowls.

Italian Sausage and Peppers

GLUTEN-FREE, LOW-CALORIE

Combining onions, sausage, and peppers in one savory dish is an Italian staple, and like most Italian foods, this meal is simply delicious. It's also a really easy recipe to scale up or down. Just plan on one to one and a half sausages per person and about one pepper per person.

1½ pounds Italian sausage

2 tablespoons water

1½ cups Bone Broth (page 262 or store-bought) or Chicken Stock (page 263 or store-bought)

2 red bell peppers, seeded and sliced

2 green bell peppers, seeded and sliced

2 orange bell peppers, seeded and sliced

1 yellow onion, chopped

2 tablespoons extra-virgin olive oil

1 teaspoon garlic powder

1 teaspoon dried oregano

½ teaspoon sea salt

¼ teaspoon freshly ground black pepper

Pinch red pepper flakes

PREP TIME:
20 MINUTES

COOK TIME:
8 HOURS ON LOW

SERVES 6

PER SERVING:
Calories: 376; Fat: 28g; Saturated Fat: 13g; Cholesterol: 86mg; Carbohydrates: 11g; Fiber: 3g; Protein: 19g; Sodium: 1,299mg

1. Place the sausages in a large cold skillet with the water. Turn the heat to medium. Cook the sausages on all sides, turning often, for 8 to 10 minutes, until they start to brown. Discard the fat.

2. Place the whole sausages and broth in a 3-quart slow cooker.

3. In a large bowl, combine the bell peppers, onion, olive oil, garlic powder, oregano, salt, pepper, and red pepper flakes. Toss to coat the peppers in the oil and seasonings. Add the pepper mixture to the slow cooker.

4. Cover and cook on low for 8 hours, until the vegetables are tender and the sausages are cooked through and read at least 160°F on a food thermometer.

Honey-Mustard Pork Sandwiches

PREP TIME:
30 MINUTES

COOK TIME:
8 HOURS ON LOW

SERVES 8

PER SERVING:
Calories: 576; Fat: 22g;
Saturated Fat: 5g;
Cholesterol: 90mg;
Carbohydrates: 52g;
Fiber: 5g;
Protein: 43g;
Sodium: 915mg

GAME PLAN: You'll probably have some slaw left over after you make the sandwiches. It will keep for up to 4 days when stored in the refrigerator. Just eat it plain or use it to top of any other type of sandwich.

The sweet honey and tangy mustard make these tender pork sandwiches really tasty. Pork shoulder braised low and slow shreds easily to make a nice filling. For a bit of crunchiness, you'll enjoy the tasty slaw that goes on top of the pork before you make the sandwiches with the toasted buns.

FOR THE PORK

2 pounds boneless
    pork shoulder
1 cup Bone Broth (page 262
    or store-bought) or
    Chicken Stock (page 263
    or store-bought)

¼ cup honey
¼ cup Dijon mustard
½ teaspoon sea salt
¼ teaspoon freshly
    ground black pepper

FOR THE SLAW

1 head cabbage, shredded
6 scallions, thinly sliced
¼ cup apple cider vinegar
Grated zest and juice
    of 1 orange
¼ cup extra-virgin olive oil

2 garlic cloves, finely minced
½ teaspoon sea salt
¼ teaspoon freshly
    ground black pepper
8 hoagie buns, split
    and toasted

TO MAKE THE PORK

1. Place the pork shoulder, broth, honey, mustard, salt, and pepper in a 4-quart slow cooker.
2. Cover and cook on low for 8 hours, or until the pork is very tender.
3. Using 2 forks, shred the pork and mix it with the sauce.

TO MAKE THE SLAW

4. In a large bowl, combine the cabbage and scallions.
5. In a small bowl, whisk together the vinegar, orange zest and juice, olive oil, garlic, salt, and pepper. Toss with the cabbage and scallions.
6. Make sandwiches with the toasted buns, pork, and slaw.

Jalapeño and Honey Pork Shoulder

GLUTEN-FREE, WEEKNIGHT HERO

The sweetness of honey blends beautifully with the heat of jalapeño peppers in this tasty recipe. You can adjust the number of jalapeños to make this dish spicier or milder. Including the seeds will add even more heat, so keep them if you dare. Serve with a side salad for a balanced meal.

2½ pounds pork shoulder, cut into 1-inch cubes

¼ cup honey

Grated zest and juice of 1 orange

4 jalapeño peppers, seeded and minced

1 teaspoon garlic powder

1 teaspoon sea salt

⅛ teaspoon freshly ground black pepper

Pinch cayenne pepper

PREP TIME:
15 MINUTES

COOK TIME:
8 HOURS ON LOW

SERVES 6

PER SERVING:
Calories: 432; Fat: 16g;
Saturated Fat: 4g;
Cholesterol: 149mg;
Carbohydrates: 14g;
Fiber: 1g; Protein: 56g;
Sodium: 492mg

1. Place all of the ingredients in a 3-quart slow cooker. Stir to combine.
2. Cover and cook on low for 8 hours, until the pork is very tender. You can shred the pork if you'd like to serve on sandwiches.

IF YOU HAVE A MINUTE: To add deeper flavor, brown the pork before adding it to the slow cooker. Melt 2 tablespoons of olive oil in a large skillet over medium-high heat. Working in batches, brown the pork cubes for about 3 minutes per side. Don't overcrowd the pan or you'll wind up steaming the pork and not getting the browned bits on the outside that create the deeper flavors.

Barbecue Pork Ribs

WEEKNIGHT HERO

PREP TIME:
10 MINUTES

COOK TIME:
8 HOURS ON LOW
OR
4 HOURS ON HIGH,
PLUS BROILING TIME

SERVES 6

PER SERVING:
Calories: 733; Fat: 56g;
Saturated Fat: 21g;
Cholesterol: 223mg;
Carbohydrates: 9g;
Fiber: 2g; Protein: 47g;
Sodium: 734mg

Want ribs so tender they fall off the bone? Put them in the slow cooker. Choose your favorite barbecue sauce or make your own for this super easy recipe. This is a fantastic dish to bring to a summer picnic or family reunion.

2½ pounds baby back ribs

1½ teaspoons garlic powder

1 teaspoon sea salt

1 teaspoon freshly ground black pepper

½ teaspoon paprika

2 yellow onions, chopped

1 cup Barbecue Sauce (page 271 or store-bought) divided

1. Season the ribs with the garlic powder, salt, pepper, and paprika; rub the spices into the meat.
2. Place the seasoned ribs in a 4- to 5-quart slow cooker, standing up around the sides.
3. Place the onions in the center of the slow cooker.
4. Cover and cook on low for 3 to 4 hours or on high for 1½ to 2 hours.
5. Brush the ribs with ¾ cup of barbecue sauce.
6. Cover and cook on low for an additional 4 hours or on high for 2 hours, until the ribs are tender.
7. Preheat the broiler.
8. Place the ribs on a baking sheet and discard any liquid that remains in the slow cooker. Brush the ribs with the remaining ¼ cup of barbecue sauce. Broil for 5 to 10 minutes, turning once, or until the outsides are crispy.

INGREDIENT TIP: Baby back ribs are quite lean and very tender when cooked in the slow cooker. Spareribs are cut from the end of the baby back ribs. You can use either type of rib in this recipe, but spareribs are longer than baby back ribs, and you'll need a larger slow cooker to cook them. Spareribs should cook for another hour or two on low.

Pork Tenderloin with Rosemary Peaches

GLUTEN-FREE, LOW-CALORIE, WEEKNIGHT HERO

Peaches and rosemary are two favorite summer flavors. But you can enjoy this dish year-round by using frozen peaches. Add the frozen fruit to the slow cooker without thawing them first so they keep their shape. If you aren't a rosemary fan, use 1 teaspoon dried thyme.

4 peaches, peeled, pitted, and cut into wedges

1 red onion, halved and thinly sliced

Leaves from 2 rosemary sprigs

1 (1¼-pound) pork tenderloin

¼ teaspoon sea salt

Freshly ground black pepper

PREP TIME:
15 MINUTES

COOK TIME:
6 TO 8 HOURS
ON LOW

SERVES 4

PER SERVING:
Calories: 338; Fat: 12g;
Saturated Fat: 3g;
Cholesterol: 112mg;
Carbohydrates: 13g;
Fiber: 3g; Protein: 43g;
Sodium: 224mg

1. Place the peaches, onion, and rosemary leaves in a 3-quart slow cooker. Stir to combine.
2. Season the pork tenderloin with the salt and a few grinds of black pepper. Place the tenderloin on top of the peach and onion mixture.
3. Cover and cook on low for 6 to 8 hours, until the onion and fruit have softened and the pork is tender. Let the meat rest for 3 minutes before slicing to serve.

INGREDIENT TIP: Pork no longer has to be cooked until well done, according to the USDA. The recommendation changed in 2011. Because of the way modern pork is raised, it can be cooked to medium—145°F on a food thermometer—with a 3-minute rest before serving.

Smoky Beer-Braised Pork Tacos

WEEKNIGHT HERO

PREP TIME:
15 MINUTES

COOK TIME:
8 TO 10 HOURS ON
LOW OR
4 TO 5 HOURS ON
HIGH

SERVES 6

PER SERVING:
Calories: 539; Fat: 14g;
Saturated Fat: 5g;
Cholesterol: 80mg;
Carbohydrates: 63g;
Fiber: 5g; Protein: 36g;
Sodium: 1,072mg

Soft flour tortillas are filled with seasoned tender pork to make these delicious tacos. It doesn't get much simpler than that, and when the ingredients are this flavorful, you don't need much more than a squeeze of fresh lime and a sprinkle of cheese.

Nonstick cooking spray

2 pounds lean, boneless pork roast

1 teaspoon ground cumin

½ teaspoon sea salt

½ teaspoon freshly ground black pepper

2 teaspoons liquid smoke (optional)

3 garlic cloves, minced

1 medium yellow onion, chopped

1 cup chopped fresh cilantro

1 cup Red Salsa (page 268 or store-bought) or green salsa

½ cup Chicken Stock (page 263 or store-bought)

½ cup beer or additional chicken stock

3 medium jalapeños, seeded and chopped

12 (8-inch) flour tortillas, warmed

1. Grease a 3½-quart slow cooker. Rub the meat with the cumin, salt, and pepper.
2. Place the pork, liquid smoke (if using), garlic, onion, cilantro, salsa, stock, beer, and jalapeños in the slow cooker.
3. Cover and cook on low for 8 to 10 hours or on high for 4 to 5 hours, until the meat is tender.
4. Warm the tortillas in a dry skillet over medium-high heat or according to package directions.
5. Using tongs, remove the pork from the slow cooker; shred the meat using two forks. Place it in a large bowl. Scoop out the onion and any solids in the slow cooker with a slotted spoon and mix with the pork. Spoon a generous amount onto each tortilla and serve with toppings.

Pork Chops with Mashed Sweet Potatoes

GLUTEN-FREE, WEEKNIGHT HERO

Sweet potatoes don't have to be cooked with sugar and topped with marshmallows; when flavored with orange and nutmeg, they are just as delicious. And they pair beautifully with tender and savory pork chops.

3 large sweet potatoes, peeled and diced

Grated zest of 1 orange

Pinch ground nutmeg

½ cup Chicken Stock (page 263 or store-bought)

4 bone-in pork chops, about 8 ounces each

Sea salt

Freshly ground black pepper

3 tablespoons unsalted butter, at room temperature

PREP TIME:
15 MINUTES

COOK TIME:
6 TO 8 HOURS
ON LOW

SERVES 4

PER SERVING:
Calories: 475; Fat: 22g;
Saturated Fat: 10g;
Cholesterol: 120mg;
Carbohydrates: 29g;
Fiber: 5g; Protein: 37;
Sodium: 912mg

1. Place the sweet potatoes, orange zest, nutmeg, and stock in a 4-quart slow cooker. Gently stir them together.
2. Season the pork chops with salt and black pepper. Then arrange them on top of the sweet potatoes.
3. Cover and cook on low for 6 to 8 hours, until the sweet potatoes are completely soft and the pork is cooked to at least 145°F on a food thermometer.
4. Remove the pork chops from the slow cooker; place them on a clean plate and cover.
5. Add the butter to the sweet potatoes in the slow cooker and mash with a potato masher or the back of a spoon. Serve the sweet potatoes with the pork chops.

INGREDIENT TIP: To zest an orange means to remove only the orange part of the skin. You can use a zester, a tool developed just for this task, or the small holes on a grater. Be sure to grate or zest only the orange part; the white pith beneath the skin is bitter.

Braised Pork Carnitas with Lime

GLUTEN-FREE, WEEKNIGHT HERO

The slow cooker does the heavy lifting for you in this flavorful, Mexico City–inspired pork recipe. Carnitas are usually baked in the oven and then fried until crisp; here, the meat is broiled after it's cooked in the slow cooker, but you can omit that step if you prefer.

1 teaspoon extra-virgin olive oil

1 teaspoon ground cumin

1 teaspoon ground coriander

2 teaspoons garlic powder

1 teaspoon sea salt

Freshly ground black pepper

2½ pounds boneless pork shoulder roast

1 cup Chicken Stock (page 263 or store-bought) or water

3 tablespoons freshly squeezed lime juice

1 cup diced red onions, for garnish

2 avocados, pitted, peeled, and thinly sliced, for garnish

1. Grease a 4-quart slow cooker with the oil.
2. In a small bowl, combine the cumin, coriander, garlic powder, salt, and pepper. Rub this seasoning mix all over the pork and then place the meat in the slow cooker. Pour the stock around the meat.
3. Cover and cook on low for 8 to 10 hours, until the meat is tender and reads at least 145°F on a food thermometer. Using two forks, shred the pork. Stir in the lime juice.
4. Spread the shredded meat in a 13-by-9-inch metal baking pan. Preheat the broiler.
5. Place the pan under the broiler about 4 inches from the heat source. Broil for 4 to 6 minutes, until the surface of the meat is crispy.
6. Use the meat in tacos or burritos or serve with rice, garnished with the onions and avocado.

PREP TIME:
15 MINUTES

COOK TIME:
8 TO 10 HOURS ON LOW, PLUS BROILING TIME

SERVES 6

PER SERVING:
Calories: 503; Fat: 25g; Saturated Fat: 5g; Cholesterol: 149mg; Carbohydrates: 8g; Fiber: 5g; Protein: 58g; Sodium: 510mg

GAME PLAN: Freeze leftovers in 2-cup portions in freezer bags or airtight containers. Thaw the bags overnight in the refrigerator and reheat the carnitas in a skillet with a bit of olive oil.

Sweet and Sour Country-Style Ribs

WEEKNIGHT HERO

PREP TIME:
10 MINUTES

COOK TIME:
8 HOURS ON LOW

SERVES 6

PER SERVING:
Calories: 707; Fat: 49g;
Saturated Fat: 18g;
Cholesterol: 197mg;
Carbohydrates: 8g;
Fiber: <1g;
Protein: 55g;
Sodium: 627mg

The glaze for these ribs has a mouthwatering sweet and sour flavor—a perfect balance between the two flavors—with a bit of savory thrown in as well. The ribs lend themselves well to slow cooking and come out moist and tender. Serve this dish with steamed vegetables for a complete meal.

3 pounds country-style spareribs

1 cup unsweetened pineapple juice

2 tablespoons low-sodium soy sauce

¼ cup apple cider vinegar

1 tablespoon chili garlic sauce

1 teaspoon grated orange zest

1 tablespoon cornstarch

1 teaspoon fish sauce

1 teaspoon garlic powder

1 teaspoon onion powder

½ teaspoon sea salt

1. Arrange the spareribs in a 4- to 5-quart slow cooker.
2. In a medium bowl, whisk together the pineapple juice, soy sauce, vinegar, chili garlic sauce, orange zest, cornstarch, fish sauce, garlic powder, onion powder, and salt.
3. Pour the sauce over the pork.
4. Cover and cook on low for 8 hours, or until the meat is very tender.

IF YOU HAVE A MINUTE: To add deeper flavor, brown the spareribs before adding them to the slow cooker. Place 2 tablespoons of olive oil in a large skillet over medium-high heat. Working in batches, brown the ribs for about 5 minutes per side. Transfer them to the slow cooker, discarding the fat, and proceed with the recipe.

Orange-Chipotle Country-Style Ribs

GLUTEN-FREE, WEEKNIGHT HERO

A little sweet and a little smoky heat makes these tender ribs flavorful and aromatic. Adding carrots makes it a one-pot meal that's quick and convenient. These ribs freeze well, so you can make big batches and enjoy them later when, instead of cooking, thawing and reheating is the order for the day.

3 pounds boneless country-style spareribs

1 pound baby carrots

1 yellow onion, chopped

1 cup Bone Broth (page 262 or store-bought) or Chicken Stock (page 263 or store-bought)

Juice of 2 oranges

2 tablespoons honey

1 teaspoon garlic powder

1 teaspoon chipotle chili powder

1 teaspoon sea salt

¼ teaspoon freshly ground black pepper

PREP TIME:
10 MINUTES

COOK TIME:
8 HOURS ON LOW

SERVES 6

PER SERVING:
Calories: 744; Fat: 49g; Saturated Fat: 18g; Cholesterol: 197mg; Carbohydrates: 18g; Fiber: 2g; Protein: 56g; Sodium: 790mg

1. Place the ribs, carrots, and onion in a 4- to 5-quart slow cooker.
2. In a medium bowl, mix the broth, orange juice, honey, garlic powder, chipotle chili powder, salt, and pepper. Pour the mix into the slow cooker.
3. Cover and cook on low for 8 hours, until the ribs are very tender.

IF YOU HAVE A MINUTE: To make the ribs glazed and browned with a crunchy crust, remove them from the slow cooker when they're done and put them on a broiler pan. Broil them for 3 to 5 minutes per side, turning once, until the ribs are browned and crunchy.

Pork and Paprika Meatballs

PREP TIME:
30 MINUTES

COOK TIME:
5 TO 6 HOURS
ON LOW

SERVES 8

PER SERVING:
Calories: 405; Fat: 31g;
Saturated Fat: 10g;
Cholesterol: 128mg;
Carbohydrates: 8g;
Fiber: 2g; Protein: 22g;
Sodium: 428mg

Slow cooking guarantees that these meatballs are extra juicy and tender. This recipe calls for hot smoked paprika, but you can use any type of paprika you like.

2 pounds ground pork

1 medium yellow onion, finely chopped, divided

1½ teaspoons ground cumin

1½ teaspoons hot smoked paprika, divided

5 tablespoons dried bread crumbs

2 large eggs, lightly beaten

3 tablespoons chopped fresh parsley

½ teaspoon sea salt, plus more for seasoning

¼ teaspoon freshly ground black pepper

3 tablespoons extra-virgin olive oil, divided

1 (28-ounce) can diced tomatoes, undrained

1. In a large bowl, combine the pork, ¼ cup of onion, the cumin, ½ teaspoon of paprika, the bread crumbs, the eggs, and the parsley. Season with the salt and pepper. Mix thoroughly to combine.

2. Roll the meat mixture into 25 meatballs (each about 1½ inches in diameter) and put on a plate.

3. In a large nonstick skillet, heat 1½ tablespoons of olive oil over medium-high heat. Once hot, add half the meatballs and brown on all sides, about 8 minutes. Transfer to a 4-quart slow cooker. Repeat with the remaining 1½ tablespoons of olive oil and remaining meatballs.

4. Add the remaining onion to the skillet and cook for about 2 minutes, stirring often, until fragrant. Transfer the cooked onion to the slow cooker, sprinkle in the remaining 1 teaspoon of paprika, and add the tomatoes with their juices. Season with salt and pepper.

5. Cover and cook on low for 5 to 6 hours, until the meatballs are cooked through and read at least 160°F on a food thermometer.

Mustard and Herb Pork Loin

GLUTEN-FREE

Mustard, rosemary, thyme, and garlic enhance the savory and mild flavor of a pork loins. Boneless pork loins can weigh up to 10 pounds. You can either cook the whole thing in a very large slow cooker or cut the loin into smaller portions, freezing the rest and just cooking what you need.

1 pound baby carrots

4 cups peeled and cubed celeriac

¼ cup chopped fresh parsley

3 tablespoons Dijon mustard

2 tablespoons extra-virgin olive oil

2 teaspoons dried thyme

2 teaspoons dried rosemary

1 teaspoon sea salt

½ teaspoon freshly ground black pepper

1 (4-pound) boneless pork loin

PREP TIME:
20 MINUTES

COOK TIME:
8 HOURS ON LOW

SERVES 8

PER SERVING:
Calories: 407; Fat: 20g;
Saturated Fat: 7g;
Cholesterol: 110mg;
Carbohydrates: 12g;
Fiber: 3g; Protein: 44g;
Sodium: 1,320mg

1. Place the carrots and celeriac in a 4- to 5-quart slow cooker.
2. In a small bowl, whisk together the parsley, mustard, olive oil, thyme, rosemary, salt, and pepper.
3. Rub the mustard and herb mixture all over the pork loin. Arrange the loin on top of the vegetables.
4. Cover and cook on low for 8 hours, until the pork reaches at least 145°F on a food thermometer. Slice the pork to serve along with the vegetables.

INGREDIENT TIP: Celeriac is also called celery root. It looks like a big, round, nubbly potato, but when cooked, it becomes sweet and tender with a mild celery flavor.

Pork Loin with Caramelized Onions and Chard

GLUTEN-FREE, LOW-CALORIE, WEEKNIGHT HERO

PREP TIME:
15 MINUTES

COOK TIME:
6 TO 8 HOURS
ON LOW

SERVES 8

PER SERVING:
Calories: 216; Fat: 11g;
Saturated Fat: 4g;
Cholesterol: 59mg;
Carbohydrates: 6g;
Fiber: 2g; Protein: 23g;
Sodium: 674mg

INGREDIENT TIP:
Chard is a dark
leafy green that
is full of fiber
and nutrients. It
is sturdier than
spinach but more
tender than kale.
These greens can
be cooked for long
or short times in
the slow cooker,
depending on if
you want really
tender greens or
something with
a bit of a bite.

Technique is everything when it comes to healthy cooking. When prepared properly, natural ingredients can bring so much flavor to a dish, reducing the amount of sugar, fat, or salt needed. Onions are a perfect example: long, slow cooking brings out their natural sugars and adds a rich, sweet, yet savory flavor to dishes. The sweet caramelized onions are the perfect complement to tender pork and bitter chard.

1 tablespoon unsalted butter, at room temperature

2 yellow onions, sliced into thin rings

1 tablespoon extra-virgin olive oil

½ teaspoon sea salt

Pinch sugar

⅛ teaspoon freshly ground black pepper

2 to 3 pounds boneless pork loin

1 cup Chicken Stock (page 263 or store-bought)

1 bunch Swiss chard, roughly chopped

1. Grease the bottom of a 4-quart slow cooker with the butter.
2. Place the onions in the slow cooker and drizzle them with the oil. Stir to coat the onions in the oil. Season with the salt, sugar, and pepper.
3. Arrange the pork loin on top of the onions. Pour in the stock.
4. Cover and cook on low for 6 to 8 hours, or until the onions are light golden brown and the pork is tender and cooked to at least 145°F on a food thermometer.
5. In the final 30 minutes of cooking, put the chard on top of the other ingredients and cook until tender and wilted. Stir and serve.

Balsamic-Glazed Pork Tenderloin and Carrots

GLUTEN-FREE, WEEKNIGHT HERO

The flavors of onion, carrots, and balsamic vinegar blend together beautifully in this recipe and really complement the pork. The long, slow cooking allows the sugars in the vegetables to intensify and caramelize. They're offset beautifully by the tangy balsamic vinegar and the richness of the pork tenderloin.

1 red onion, halved
  and thinly sliced

6 carrots, cut into 2-inch pieces

4 garlic cloves, minced

1 (1¼-pound) pork tenderloin

¼ teaspoon sea salt

Freshly ground black pepper

⅓ cup balsamic vinegar

¾ cup Chicken Stock (page 263
  or store-bought) or
  Vegetable Broth (page 264
  or store-bought)

1. Place the onion, carrots, and garlic in a 3- to 4-quart slow cooker. Stir to combine.
2. Season the pork tenderloin with the salt and a few grinds of black pepper. Arrange the tenderloin on top of the vegetables. Pour the vinegar and stock over the meat.
3. Cover and cook on low for 6 to 8 hours, until the vegetables and meat are tender.

EXTRA EASY: You can prepare, cover, and refrigerate the vegetables the night before. Then just assemble the food in the slow cooker in the morning, turn it on, and go about your day. Dinner will be ready when you are.

PREP TIME:
15 MINUTES

COOK TIME:
6 TO 8 HOURS
ON LOW

SERVES 4

PER SERVING:
Calories: 410; Fat: 14g;
Saturated Fat: 4g;
Cholesterol: 134mg;
Carbohydrates: 15g;
Fiber: 3g; Protein: 52g;
Sodium: 323mg

Cranberry-Glazed Pork Tenderloin

GLUTEN-FREE, WEEKNIGHT HERO

PREP TIME:
10 MINUTES

COOK TIME:
8 HOURS ON LOW

SERVES 4

PER SERVING:
Calories: 454; Fat: 14g;
Saturated Fat: 4g;
Cholesterol: 134mg;
Carbohydrates: 27g;
Fiber: 1g; Protein: 50g;
Sodium: 258mg

While cranberry sauce is usually considered a holiday condiment with turkey, it makes a simple and tasty glaze for meat any time of the year. It's especially delicious with pork since the mild white meat pairs well with just about any flavor or cuisine.

1 (1¼-pound) pork
 tenderloin
¼ teaspoon sea salt
Freshly ground
 black pepper

1 cup whole berry
 cranberry sauce
½ cup Chicken Stock (page 263
 or store-bought)

1. Season the pork with the salt and a few grinds of black pepper. Place it in a 3-quart slow cooker.
2. Pour the cranberry sauce and stock over the top of the tenderloin.
3. Cover and cook on low for 8 hours, or until the pork is tender. Slice to serve with the sauce in the slow cooker.

INGREDIENT TIP: There are two kinds of cranberry sauce on the market. One is solid, or jellied, and is usually served sliced. The other is called whole berry cranberry sauce, and it has whole cranberries in it; that's the kind to choose for this recipe.

Cuban Pork Tenderloin

GLUTEN-FREE

The bright flavor of coriander and citrus-infused pork, onion, and peppers provides the perfect entrée for any meal. Serve this mixture over steamed or Slow Cooker Rice (page 258) or Basic Quinoa (page 257). Add avocado and sour cream as garnishes to really complete this dish.

2 teaspoons extra-virgin olive oil

1 (1¼-pound) pork tenderloin

Grated zest and juice of 1 orange

Grated zest and juice of 1 lime

4 garlic cloves, minced

1 teaspoon ground cumin

1 teaspoon ground coriander

¼ teaspoon sea salt

Freshly ground black pepper

1 red onion, halved and thinly sliced

2 red bell peppers, seeded and thinly sliced

1 green bell pepper, seeded and thinly sliced

¼ cup chopped fresh cilantro, for garnish

PREP TIME:
20 MINUTES

COOK TIME:
8 HOURS ON LOW

SERVES 4

PER SERVING:
Calories: 415; Fat: 17g; Saturated Fat: 4g; Cholesterol: 134mg; Carbohydrates: 10g; Fiber: 3g; Protein: 52g; Sodium: 246mg

1. Grease a 3½-quart slow cooker with the olive oil.
2. Place the pork tenderloin in the slow cooker.
3. In a small measuring cup, whisk together the orange and lime zest and juice, garlic, cumin, coriander, salt, and a few grinds of black pepper. Pour this mixture over the pork.
4. Place the onion and bell peppers in the slow cooker, around and on top of the pork.
5. Cover and cook on low for 8 hours or until the pork is very tender.
6. Using tongs, remove the pork from the slow cooker and let it rest for 10 minutes. Shred the meat with a fork. Return it to the slow cooker and toss with the vegetables and juices. Garnish with the cilantro.

Pork Ragù

GLUTEN-FREE, LOW-CALORIE, WEEKNIGHT HERO

PREP TIME:
15 MINUTES

COOK TIME:
7 TO 8 HOURS
ON LOW

SERVES 4

PER SERVING:
Calories: 298; Fat: 10g;
Saturated Fat: 3g;
Cholesterol: 90mg;
Carbohydrates: 13g;
Fiber: 4g; Protein: 36g;
Sodium: 759mg

In Italian cooking, ragù is a sauce made from ground or shredded meat, onions, and tomato purée and served over pasta. If you're avoiding gluten, there are many gluten-free pastas available on the market—including rice pasta, chickpea pasta, and shirataki noodles—or consider serving it over polenta, which is naturally gluten-free.

1 medium yellow onion, diced

1 red bell pepper, seeded and diced

1 (28-ounce) can diced tomatoes, undrained

2 teaspoons chili powder

1 teaspoon garlic powder

½ teaspoon ground cumin

½ teaspoon smoked paprika

½ teaspoon sea salt

Pinch red pepper flakes

1 (1-pound) pork tenderloin

1. Place the onion, red bell pepper, and tomatoes with their juices in a 3½-quart slow cooker.
2. In a small bowl, combine the chili powder, garlic powder, cumin, paprika, salt, and red pepper flakes. Rub half of this mixture onto the pork. Stir the remaining chili powder mixture into the vegetable mixture in the slow cooker. Place the pork on top of the vegetables.
3. Cover and cook on low for 7 to 8 hours, or until the pork is very tender.
4. Using tongs, remove the pork loin and shred it with a fork. Return the shredded meat to the slow cooker and stir it into the sauce.

IF YOU HAVE A MINUTE: Brown the pork tenderloin before you add it to the slow cooker for more flavor and color. Rub the spices into the meat. Heat some olive oil in a medium skillet over medium heat. Once hot, add the tenderloin and sear the meat on all sides for about four minutes total. Add the pork to the slow cooker and continue with the recipe.

Pork Chops with Figs and Shallots

GLUTEN-FREE, WEEKNIGHT HERO

Figs are a classic pairing for pork because of their unctuous sweetness. Here, fresh whole figs are combined with fig butter for the ultimate effect. This recipe is special enough for company but easy enough to make any night of the week.

1 cup roughly chopped
 fresh figs

2 shallots, roughly chopped

½ cup dry white wine

4 (8-ounce) bone-in
 pork loin chops

½ teaspoon sea salt

Freshly ground black pepper

½ cup fig butter or jam

1. Place the figs, shallots, and wine in a 3½-quart slow cooker. Stir to mix well.
2. Season the pork chops with the salt and a few grinds of black pepper. Spread the top of each chop with the fig butter. Arrange the chops on top of the fig and shallot mixture.
3. Cover and cook on low for 8 hours, or until the chops are very tender.

PREP TIME:
15 MINUTES

COOK TIME:
8 HOURS ON LOW

SERVES 4

PER SERVING:
Calories: 442; Fat: 14g;
Saturated Fat: 5g;
Cholesterol: 97mg;
Carbohydrates: 38g;
Fiber: 4g; Protein: 34g;
Sodium: 1,106mg

Sausage Lasagna

PREP TIME:
20 MINUTES

COOK TIME:
4 TO 6 HOURS
ON LOW

SERVES 6 TO 8

PER SERVING:
Calories: 656; Fat: 30g;
Saturated Fat: 15g;
Cholesterol: 124mg;
Carbohydrates: 47g;
Fiber: 5g; Protein: 49g;
Sodium: 1,587mg

This hearty and classic recipe is delicious in the slow cooker. To fit lasagna noodles into a round slow cooker, just break them up into smaller pieces. There's no need to precook the noodles; when the rest of the lasagna is done, the noodles will also be ready.

1 pound Italian pork sausage, casings removed

1 pound ground beef sirloin

1 medium yellow onion, finely chopped

2 medium carrots, finely chopped

2 garlic cloves, minced

½ teaspoon sea salt

⅛ teaspoon freshly ground black pepper

1 (6-ounce) can tomato paste

1 (28-ounce) can crushed tomatoes

9 lasagna noodles

2 cups shredded part-skim mozzarella cheese (about 8 ounces), divided

1. Place a 5-quart Dutch oven or large heavy pot over medium-high heat. Once hot, add the sausage and beef and cook, stirring often and breaking up the meat with a wooden spoon, for 4 to 6 minutes, until no longer pink. Drain. Return the pot and meat to the stovetop.

2. Add the onion, carrots, and garlic and season with the salt and pepper. Cook for 3 to 5 minutes, until the onion has softened.

3. Stir in the tomato paste and then the crushed tomatoes. Bring to a boil, and then remove the pot from the heat.

4. Spoon 2 cups of the meat mixture into a 4-quart slow cooker. Layer 3 lasagna noodles (breaking them, as needed, to fit) over the mixture. Then spread 2 more of the cups meat mixture over the noodles, followed by ½ cup of mozzarella cheese. Repeat with two more layers. Refrigerate the remaining ½ cup of mozzarella cheese for topping.

5. Cover and cook on low for 4 to 6 hours. Sprinkle the lasagna with the remaining ½ cup of mozzarella cheese. Cover and cook for about 10 minutes, until the cheese has melted.
6. Serve hot.

EXTRA EASY: Since the meat is completely cooked in step 1, you can make the sauce the day before you cook and serve the lasagna. Cover and store it in the refrigerator. Layer the ingredients in the slow cooker and then cover and cook, adding about ½ hour cooking time because you started with cold ingredients.

Ginger Pork with Baby Bok Choy

LOW-CALORIE, WEEKNIGHT HERO

PREP TIME:
15 MINUTES

COOK TIME:
6 TO 8 HOURS
ON LOW

SERVES 4

PER SERVING:
Calories: 303; Fat: 15g;
Saturated Fat: 4g;
Cholesterol: 83mg;
Carbohydrates: 5g;
Fiber: 1g; Protein: 34g;
Sodium: 1,676mg

Bok choy, a type of cabbage, is a common ingredient in traditional Chinese cooking, and there are many reasons to love this leafy green. Its flavor is mild, the dark green leaves provide healthy nutrients, and thicker stems provide great texture. The combination of textures and flavors in this recipe is outstanding.

1 yellow onion, thinly sliced into rings

2 tablespoons toasted sesame oil, divided

4 (6-ounce) boneless loin pork chops

¼ teaspoon sea salt

⅛ teaspoon freshly ground black pepper

½ cup Chicken Stock (page 263 or store-bought)

¼ cup low-sodium soy sauce

2 tablespoons rice wine vinegar

1 tablespoon minced fresh ginger

4 baby bok choy, halved lengthwise

1. Place the onion in a 3-quart slow cooker and drizzle it with 1 tablespoon of sesame oil. Toss to coat the onion.
2. Season the pork chops with the salt and pepper. Arrange the chops on top of the onion.
3. In a small bowl, whisk together the stock, soy sauce, vinegar, and ginger. Pour the mixture over the pork chops.
4. Lay the bok choy, cut-side down, over the pork chops.
5. Cover and cook on low for 6 to 8 hours, or until the pork chops and bok choy are tender. Drizzle with the remaining 1 tablespoon of sesame oil and serve.

Pork and Pineapple Teriyaki

GLUTEN-FREE, LOW-CALORIE

If you like the sweet, tangy, slightly salty, and spicy flavor of teriyaki, then you'll love this pork recipe. Chunks of pineapple and broccoli make this a tasty one-dish meal. If you want, try serving it with some Slow Cooker Rice (page 258).

2 pounds pork shoulder, cut into 1-inch cubes

1 pound broccoli, cut into florets

2 cups fresh pineapple chunks

3 tablespoons tamari or low-sodium soy sauce

Grated zest and juice of 1 orange

3 tablespoons honey

2 tablespoons cornstarch

1 tablespoon chili garlic sauce

1 tablespoon grated fresh ginger

1 teaspoon garlic powder

2 tablespoons sesame seeds

3 scallions, thinly sliced on an angle

PREP TIME:
20 MINUTES

COOK TIME:
8 HOURS ON LOW

SERVES 12

PER SERVING:
Calories: 301; Fat: 19g;
Saturated Fat: 7g;
Cholesterol: 71mg;
Carbohydrates: 13g;
Fiber: 2g; Protein: 20g;
Sodium: 331mg

1. Place the pork shoulder, broccoli, and pineapple in a 4-quart slow cooker. Stir to combine.
2. In a small bowl, whisk together the tamari, orange zest and juice, honey, cornstarch, chili garlic sauce, ginger, and garlic powder. Pour the mixture over the pork and vegetables.
3. Cover and cook on low for 8 hours, or until the pork is very tender.
4. Sprinkle with the sesame seeds and scallions just before serving.

EXTRA EASY: You can find precut broccoli florets and pineapple in the produce aisle of most grocery stores. Using this shortcut would cut the preparation time by 10 minutes.

Chorizo, Sweet Potato, and Chile Stew

GLUTEN-FREE, WEEKNIGHT HERO

PREP TIME:
15 MINUTES

COOK TIME:
8 HOURS ON LOW

SERVES 6

PER SERVING:
Calories: 482; Fat: 29g;
Saturated Fat: 10g;
Cholesterol: 101mg;
Carbohydrates: 27g;
Fiber: 4g; Protein: 27g;
Sodium: 1,950mg

Chorizo is a spicy, flavorful sausage originally from Spain and Portugal. It can be a bit hot, but the sweetness and the starch in the sweet potatoes soak up some of the heat of the chorizo. Be sure to use dried chorizo, not fresh, as it isn't cooked before it's added to the slow cooker. Chile peppers add freshness, and a dash of cilantro added at the end brings a nice fresh, herbal quality to the dish.

1½ pounds dried chorizo, sliced

4 cups cubed sweet potatoes

3 poblano peppers, seeded and minced

1 yellow onion, chopped

1 teaspoon garlic powder

1 cup water

Juice of 1 orange

½ teaspoon sea salt

⅛ teaspoon freshly ground black pepper

¼ cup chopped fresh cilantro

Juice of 1 lime

1. Place the chorizo, sweet potatoes, poblano peppers, onion, garlic powder, water, orange juice, salt, and pepper in a 3½-quart slow cooker. Stir to combine.
2. Cover and cook on low for 8 hours, or until the potatoes are tender.
3. Stir in the cilantro and lime juice just before serving.

Glazed Ham

GLUTEN-FREE, LOW-CALORIE, WEEKNIGHT HERO

The slow cooker is the perfect way to cook ham, which can dry out so easily in the oven. The ham is glazed with a sweet and spicy mixture of mustard, maple syrup, and brown sugar. The maple syrup adds a smoky flavor that complements the savory ham. A spiral cut ham is called for in this recipe, but you can use an ordinary ham if you'd like.

1 (5- to 6-pound) spiral cut ham
⅓ cup Dijon mustard
½ cup pure maple syrup
⅓ cup brown sugar
4 garlic cloves, minced
½ teaspoon freshly ground black pepper

1. Remove the ham from its wrappings and discard the glaze packet. Place it, cut-side down, in a 5- to 6-quart slow cooker.
2. In a small saucepan over low heat, combine the mustard, maple syrup, brown sugar, garlic, and pepper and heat until melted, stirring to combine.
3. Pour the mustard mixture over the ham, covering it completely.
4. Cover and cook on low for 8 hours, or until the ham is hot and glazed. Carefully remove the ham from the slow cooker and slice to serve.

GAME PLAN: Leftover ham is a wonderful thing to have in the refrigerator. Leftovers can be placed in a zip-top bag or airtight container and refrigerated up to 4 days. After that, freeze the ham for up to 3 months. Use leftover ham in soups, sandwiches, pasta recipes, or scrambled eggs. Save the ham bone for the Split Pea Soup (page 80).

PREP TIME:
10 MINUTES

COOK TIME:
8 HOURS ON LOW

SERVES 12

PER SERVING:
Calories: 376; Fat: 18g;
Saturated Fat: 7g;
Cholesterol: 111mg;
Carbohydrates: 22g;
Fiber: 0g; Protein: 33g;
Sodium: 2,230mg

**Korean
Short Ribs
and Carrots,**
page 231

CHAPTER 9

BEEF AND LAMB

Meatloaf

LOW-CALORIE

PREP TIME:
20 MINUTES

COOK TIME:
8 HOURS ON LOW

SERVES 6

PER SERVING:
Calories: 329; Fat: 13g;
Saturated Fat: 5g;
Cholesterol: 154mg;
Carbohydrates: 22g;
Fiber: 1g; Protein: 30g;
Sodium: 641mg

Meatloaf is one of my favorite meals to make for winter evenings. Using a combination of ground beef and turkey lightens up this meatloaf, and the garlic and thyme add great flavor. Serve this dish with Slow Cooker Mashed Potatoes (page 64) and cooked carrots and peas for a classic American dinner.

1 cup dried bread crumbs	2 large eggs
1 yellow onion, minced	½ teaspoon sea salt
2 teaspoons minced garlic	⅛ teaspoon freshly
½ cup minced fresh parsley	ground black pepper
2 teaspoons dried thyme	1 pound lean ground beef
½ cup ketchup	¾ pound ground turkey
3 tablespoons yellow mustard	

GAME PLAN:
Leftover meatloaf makes fabulous sandwiches the next day. Refrigerate leftover meatloaf in an airtight container. The next day, make sandwiches with bread, meatloaf, some lettuce, and ketchup or mustard.

1. Tear off two long strips of aluminum foil, fold them in half lengthwise, and place them into an oval 5-quart slow cooker in a cross shape. This makes a sling so it will be easy to remove the meatloaf when it's done.
2. In a large bowl, combine the bread crumbs, onion, garlic, parsley, thyme, ketchup, mustard, eggs, salt, and pepper. Use your hands to mix all the ingredients together thoroughly.
3. Add the ground beef and turkey and mix gently but thoroughly with your hands.
4. Place the meatloaf mixture in the slow cooker and form it into a loaf shape.
5. Cover and cook on low for 8 hours, or until the meatloaf reads at least 165°F on a food thermometer.
6. Lift the meatloaf out of the slow cooker using the foil sling and place it on a serving plate. Cover with foil and let stand 10 minutes before slicing and serving.

Greek Meatballs

GLUTEN-FREE, LOW-CALORIE

Bring the flavors of the Mediterranean to your table with these simple, herb-infused Greek meatballs. Serve them with whole-grain pita bread and a cool tzatziki sauce made from Greek yogurt, garlic, and chopped cucumbers. Or, for a low-carb version, ditch the bread and wrap them in butter lettuce leaves.

PREP TIME:
15 MINUTES

COOK TIME:
6 HOURS ON LOW

SERVES 4

PER SERVING:
Calories: 368; Fat: 19g;
Saturated Fat: 5g;
Cholesterol: 120mg;
Carbohydrates: 17g;
Fiber: 3g; Protein: 29g;
Sodium: 856mg

½ cup cooked long-grain brown rice

1 yellow onion, finely chopped onion

3 garlic cloves, minced

2 tablespoons finely chopped fresh parsley

1 teaspoon finely chopped fresh mint

1 teaspoon finely chopped fresh oregano

¼ teaspoon sea salt

⅛ teaspoon freshly ground black pepper

1 large egg, whisked thoroughly

1 pound ground beef

2 tablespoons extra-virgin olive oil

3 cups beef broth

1 (15-ounce) can plum tomatoes, undrained

1. In a medium bowl, combine the rice, onion, garlic, parsley, mint, oregano, salt, pepper, and egg and mix well.
2. Add the ground beef and mix gently but thoroughly with your hands.
3. Form the mixture into 1½-inch round meatballs.
4. Place a large skillet over medium heat and add the olive oil. Once hot, add the meatballs, working in batches if needed to avoid crowding the pan, and brown them on all sides for about 5 minutes total.
5. Place the meatballs in a 3-quart slow cooker. Pour the broth and tomatoes with their juices over the meatballs.
6. Cover and cook on low for 6 hours, or until the meatballs read at least 160°F on a food thermometer.

INGREDIENT TIP:
All ground meats, including ground beef, pork, and veal, need to be cooked to at least 160°F for food safety reasons. Ground chicken and turkey should be cooked to 165°F.

Meatballs in Marinara Sauce

The best meatballs use a combination of ground meats for best flavor and perfect fat-to-protein ratio. Combining lean meat with bread crumbs soaked in milk, which is called a panade, keeps these meatballs moist and tender with less fat than traditional recipes.

½ cup dried bread crumbs

¼ cup 2% milk

2 large eggs, whisked thoroughly

1 teaspoon dried oregano

1 teaspoon sea salt

⅛ teaspoon freshly ground black pepper

1 pound lean ground beef

½ pound ground pork

½ pound ground veal

1 tablespoon extra-virgin olive oil

8 cups Basic Marinara Sauce (page 261 or store-bought)

1 cup shredded mozzarella cheese

PREP TIME:
20 MINUTES

COOK TIME:
2 HOURS ON HIGH

SERVES 6

PER SERVING:
Calories: 503; Fat: 25g; Saturated Fat: 10g; Cholesterol: 186mg; Carbohydrates: 23g; Fiber: 6g; Protein: 42g; Sodium: 1,197mg

1. In a large bowl, mix together the bread crumbs and milk. Add the eggs, oregano, salt, and pepper and mix well.

2. Add the ground beef, pork, and veal and mix gently but thoroughly with your hands until combined.

3. Using your hands, form the meat mixture into large balls, about 2 inches in diameter.

4. Place a large skillet over medium heat and add the oil. Once hot, add the meatballs and cook for 5 to 7 minutes, until browned on all sides (they will not be completely cooked through). Place the meatballs in a 4-quart slow cooker. Pour in the marinara sauce and top with the shredded cheese.

5. Cover and cook on high for 2 hours, or until the meatballs read at least 160°F on a food thermometer and the cheese is melted.

Sloppy Joes

LOW-CALORIE

PREP TIME:
15 MINUTES

COOK TIME:
4 HOURS ON LOW

SERVES 4

PER SERVING:
Calories: 284; Fat: 14g;
Saturated Fat: 5g;
Cholesterol: 70mg;
Carbohydrates: 16g;
Fiber: 3g; Protein: 25g;
Sodium: 1,093mg

A slow cooker is the perfect vessel for making sloppy joes. Simply brown the meat and onions first; then cook on low until ready to serve. Serve it on split and toasted hamburger buns with a generous sprinkle of grated sharp Cheddar cheese.

1 tablespoon extra-
   virgin olive oil
1 yellow onion, diced
1 pound ground beef
1 (15-ounce) can tomato sauce
1 tablespoon
   Worcestershire sauce

1 tablespoon brown sugar
1 tablespoon yellow mustard
½ teaspoon sea salt
⅛ teaspoon freshly
   ground black pepper

1. Place a large skillet over medium heat and add the olive oil. Once hot, add the onion and cook for about 10 minutes, until soft and golden. Transfer the cooked onion to a 3-quart slow cooker.
2. Raise the heat under the skillet to medium-high. Crumble the ground beef into the skillet and brown, stirring with a wooden spoon to break up the meat, for 7 to 8 minutes, until cooked through. Drain off any excess fat and transfer the cooked beef to the slow cooker.
3. Add the tomato sauce, Worcestershire sauce, brown sugar, mustard, salt, and pepper to the slow cooker and stir to combine.
4. Cover and cook on low for 4 hours.

INGREDIENT TIP: If you use ground turkey or chicken instead of ground beef, this recipe is called a sloppy jane (see Turkey Joes on page 154). Brown the chicken just as you did the beef before you add it to the slow cooker.

French Dip Sandwich

WEEKNIGHT HERO

A French dip sandwich is a roll stuffed with tender sliced beef and onions served with beef stock for dipping. The best beef for this recipe is a chuck roast. The long cooking time renders the beef so tender and juicy—perfect for this delicious sandwich.

3½ pounds beef chuck roast

1 teaspoon dried marjoram

1 teaspoon sea salt

¼ teaspoon freshly ground black pepper

2 yellow onions, chopped

4 garlic cloves, minced

3 cups beef broth

1 cup dry red wine or additional beef broth

1 bay leaf

6 to 8 large French bread rolls

2 tablespoons unsalted butter, at room temperature

6 to 8 slices Monterey Jack or Havarti cheese

1. Cut the roast into 2 pieces and sprinkle each with the marjoram, salt, and pepper.
2. Place the onions and garlic in a 4-quart slow cooker. Place the beef on top. Pour the broth and wine over the beef and add the bay leaf.
3. Cover and cook on low for 8 hours, or until the beef is very tender.
4. Using tongs, remove the beef and shred it with a fork. Place the beef in a large bowl. Remove and discard the bay leaf.
5. Using a slotted spoon, transfer the onions and garlic to the shredded beef. Mix well.
6. Preheat the broiler. Split the rolls and butter them. Place a slice of cheese on the bottom half of each roll. Place the rolls on a baking sheet and broil for 3 to 5 minutes, watching carefully, until the buns are toasted and the cheese melts.
7. Put the meat and onion mixture into the rolls. Pour the juices from the slow cooker into ramekins and serve it with each sandwich for dipping.

PREP TIME:
15 MINUTES

COOK TIME:
8 HOURS ON LOW, PLUS BROILING TIME

SERVES 6 TO 8

PER SERVING:
Calories: 855; Fat: 32g; Saturated Fat: 13g; Cholesterol: 200mg; Carbohydrates: 49g; Fiber: 3g; Protein: 82g; Sodium: 1,459mg

IF YOU HAVE A MINUTE: Brown the beef before you add it to the slow cooker for even more flavor. Sprinkle the beef with the marjoram, salt, and pepper. Heat 2 tablespoons of olive oil in a large skillet over medium heat. Brown the beef on all sides for about 10 minutes total. Then add the beef to the slow cooker and continue with the recipe.

Bolognese Sauce

GLUTEN-FREE, LOW-CALORIE

PREP TIME:
15 MINUTES

COOK TIME:
6 HOURS ON LOW

SERVES 6

PER SERVING:
Calories: 195; Fat: 8g;
Saturated Fat: 3g;
Cholesterol: 47mg;
Carbohydrates: 10g;
Fiber: 3g; Protein: 21g;
Sodium: 450mg

Serve this rich and meaty sauce over pasta and top it with some grated Parmesan cheese for a classic Italian dinner. You can also use it in recipes for lasagna, stuffed shells, and cannelloni.

1 teaspoon extra-virgin olive oil	1 cup diced celery
1 pound lean ground beef	2 garlic cloves, minced
1 (28-ounce) can crushed tomatoes	1 teaspoon dried Italian seasoning
½ cup dry white wine	½ teaspoon sea salt
1 cup diced carrots	¼ teaspoon freshly ground black pepper
1 cup diced yellow onion	

1. Place a large skillet over medium-high heat and add the oil. Once hot, add the ground beef and cook, stirring with a wooden spoon to break up the meat, for 8 to 10 minutes, until browned. Drain if necessary.

2. Place the cooked beef in a 3½-quart slow cooker. Add the tomatoes, wine, carrots, onion, celery, garlic, Italian seasoning, salt, and pepper. Stir to mix well.

3. Cover and cook on low for 6 hours, or until the sauce is blended and simmering. Stir well and serve.

A LITTLE LIGHTER: For a lower-fat sauce, use ground turkey instead of beef. Just be sure to purchase lean ground turkey; some ground turkey is a combination of light and dark meat and may contain as many calories as ground beef.

Ground Beef–Stuffed Bell Peppers

LOW-CALORIE

This recipe has many of the flavors you love in a lasagna but in a neat little package. Fennel is an unusual spice to use in stuffed bell peppers, but it adds a wonderful Italian flavor. Sprinkle the finished recipe with some chopped parsley for added color.

1 teaspoon extra-virgin olive oil

4 large red bell peppers, top ½ inch sliced off, seeded, and cored

1 pound lean ground beef

1 cup diced yellow onion

1 teaspoon ground fennel seed

2 teaspoons minced garlic

1 tablespoon dried Italian seasoning

¼ cup tomato paste

2 large eggs, beaten

¼ cup dried bread crumbs

½ cup grated Parmesan cheese

⅓ cup water

PREP TIME:
20 MINUTES

COOK TIME:
8 HOURS ON LOW

SERVES 4

PER SERVING:
Calories: 382; Fat: 18g;
Saturated Fat: 7g;
Cholesterol: 173mg;
Carbohydrates: 21g;
Fiber: 5g; Protein: 34g;
Sodium: 483mg

1. Grease a 3½-quart slow cooker with the olive oil. Arrange the bell peppers inside (you may need to slice a small portion off the bottom of each pepper to help them stand up, but be careful not to make a hole that would allow the filling to escape).

2. Place a large skillet over medium heat. Once hot, add the ground beef and cook, stirring to break up the meat, for 8 to 10 minutes, until browned and cooked through. Drain well.

3. In a large bowl, combine the ground beef, onion, fennel seed, garlic, Italian seasoning, tomato paste, eggs, bread crumbs, and Parmesan cheese. Use your hands to gently mix the ingredients together.

4. Spoon the mixture evenly into the peppers. Pour the water into the bottom of the slow cooker.

5. Cover and cook on low for 8 hours, or until the peppers are very tender.

Classic Pot Roast

GLUTEN-FREE, WEEKNIGHT HERO

PREP TIME:
15 MINUTES

COOK TIME:
8 TO 10 HOURS
ON LOW

SERVES 6

PER SERVING:
Calories: 650; Fat: 24g;
Saturated Fat: 7g;
Cholesterol: 188mg;
Carbohydrates: 33g;
Fiber: 4g; Protein: 73g;
Sodium: 703mg

No worries about what's for dinner! Tonight, your slow cooker will have it ready and waiting—meat, vegetables, and potatoes, all cooked to tender perfection. There's nothing better than coming home to a house that smells like pot roast.

1 (3- to 4-pound) beef chuck roast

1 teaspoon sea salt

¼ teaspoon freshly ground black pepper

2 tablespoons extra-virgin olive oil

⅓ cup dry red wine

4 large carrots

1 yellow onion, cut crosswise in rings

6 red potatoes, halved

1 rosemary sprig

1 cup beef broth

1. Pat the beef dry with paper towels. Season the beef on all sides with the salt and pepper.
2. Place a large skillet over medium-high heat and add the olive oil. Once hot, add the beef and brown the meat on all sides for about 10 minutes total. Remove the beef and set aside.
3. Add the wine to the skillet and bring to a simmer, using a spatula or wooden spoon to scrape the browned bits and drippings from the bottom of the pan.
4. Place the carrots, onion, potatoes, and rosemary in a 5-quart slow cooker. Pour in the wine and drippings from the skillet. Arrange the browned beef on top of the vegetables.
5. Cover and cook on low for 8 to 10 hours, or until the meat is very tender.
6. Discard the rosemary sprig. Slice the meat against the grain and serve alongside the cooked vegetables and potatoes.

INGREDIENT TIP:
Slicing meat "against the grain" is the best way to ensure a tender result. The "grain" in meat is just the way the fibers run, so cut perpendicular to the fibers.

Italian Pot Roast

GLUTEN-FREE, WEEKNIGHT HERO

The difference between this dish and American pot roast is the addition of tomatoes and dried Italian seasoning. You can serve this recipe as a stew in big bowls.

1 (3-pound) beef chuck roast, trimmed and halved crosswise

4 garlic cloves, cut into slivers (4 slivers per clove), divided

1 teaspoon coarse sea salt

1 teaspoon freshly ground black pepper

1 tablespoon extra-virgin olive oil

1½ pounds small white potatoes

1 large yellow onion, cut into 8 wedges

1 (28-ounce) can whole tomatoes in purée

2 teaspoons dried Italian seasoning

PREP TIME:
15 MINUTES

COOK TIME:
8 HOURS ON LOW

SERVES 8

PER SERVING:
Calories: 409; Fat: 14g;
Saturated Fat: 4g;
Cholesterol: 120mg;
Carbohydrates: 23g;
Fiber: 3g; Protein: 47g;
Sodium: 673mg

1. With a sharp paring knife, cut 4 slits in each of the beef roast halves. Stuff each slit with a garlic sliver. Season the beef with the salt and pepper.
2. Place a large skillet over medium-high heat and add the olive oil, swirling to coat the bottom of the pan. Once hot, add the beef and brown on all sides for about 10 minutes total.
3. Place the potatoes and onion in a 5-quart slow cooker. Place the beef, fat-side up, on the vegetables. Pour the tomatoes over all, and sprinkle with the Italian seasoning and the remaining 8 garlic slivers.
4. Cover and cook on low for 8 hours, until the meat is fork-tender.
5. Transfer the meat to a cutting board. Thinly slice and discard any fat or gristle.
6. Skim the fat from the top of the sauce remaining in the slow cooker.
7. Serve hot, dividing the beef and vegetables among 8 bowls and generously spooning the sauce over the top.

INGREDIENT TIP:
Small potatoes usually cook quickly in a slow cooker, but adding the tomatoes slows the cooking time down. Acid will prevent potatoes from cooking too quickly, so the little spuds are perfectly tender without being mushy even after this long cooking time.

Barbecue Beef Brisket

GLUTEN-FREE, WEEKNIGHT HERO

PREP TIME:
10 MINUTES

COOK TIME:
8 TO 10 HOURS
ON LOW

SERVES 8 TO 10

PER SERVING:
Calories: 515; Fat: 27g;
Saturated Fat: 9g;
Cholesterol: 185mg;
Carbohydrates: 5g;
Fiber: 1g; Protein: 60g;
Sodium: 695mg

This delicious slow-cooked beef can be served on sandwiches. For a healthier option, serve it atop a bed of steamed brown rice with a side of crisp coleslaw.

1 (3- to 4-pound) beef brisket
1 teaspoon sea salt
¼ teaspoon freshly ground black pepper
1 tablespoon extra-virgin olive oil
¼ cup water

1 teaspoon liquid smoke (optional)
¼ cup Sriracha
1 cup Barbecue Sauce (page 271 or store-bought gluten-free)

1. Sprinkle the brisket with the salt and pepper.
2. Place a large skillet over medium-high heat and add the olive oil. Once hot, add the brisket and brown on all sides, turning the beef frequently, for about 10 minutes total. Place the brisket in a 4-quart slow cooker.
3. Add the water to the skillet. Bring it to a boil, scraping any browned bits and drippings from the bottom of the pan with a spatula or wooden spoon. Pour this over the brisket.
4. In a small bowl, whisk together the liquid smoke (if using), Sriracha, and barbecue sauce. Pour the mixture over the beef.
5. Cover and cook on low for 8 to 10 hours, or until the beef is very tender. You can slice or shred this beef before serving. Store leftovers in an airtight container in the refrigerator up to 4 days.

INGREDIENT TIP: Brisket is a large cut of meat, often weighing between 8 and 10 pounds. It can be cut in half. The point cut is shaped like a triangle and is best for this recipe. The flat cut has less fat and is more expensive.

Beef Brisket with Onions

GLUTEN-FREE, LOW-CALORIE, WEEKNIGHT HERO

Slow cooking leads to fall-apart, tender brisket you'll enjoy serving to family and guests alike. A whole brisket comprises a first and second cut; for this recipe, if possible, opt for the leaner first cut, also called the "flat cut" (see Ingredient Tip on page 228), although either cut will work. The fat layer should be trimmed down to ¼ inch, which is plenty for keeping the meat moist as it cooks.

3 large yellow onions, thinly sliced

5 garlic cloves, minced

1 (4-pound) beef brisket

Coarse sea salt

Freshly ground black pepper

2 tablespoons extra-virgin olive oil

2 cups beef broth

2 tablespoons chopped fresh parsley, for serving

1. Place the onions and garlic in a 4- to 5-quart slow cooker. Stir to combine.
2. Season the brisket with salt and pepper.
3. Place a large skillet over medium heat and add the olive oil. Once hot, add the brisket, fat-side down, and brown it for 5 minutes. Then turn and brown on the second side for another 5 minutes. Place the brisket, fat-side up, in the slow cooker.
4. Add the broth to the slow cooker.
5. Cover and cook on low for 7 to 8 hours, or until the brisket is fork-tender.
6. Remove the brisket to a cutting board and thinly slice across the grain.
7. Skim the excess fat off the top of the liquid remaining in the slow cooker and discard it. Serve the sliced beef with the onion and some cooking liquid, and sprinkle with the parsley.

PREP TIME:
15 MINUTES

COOK TIME:
7 TO 8 HOURS
ON LOW

SERVES 8

PER SERVING:
Calories: 349; Fat: 13g;
Saturated Fat: 4g;
Cholesterol: 94mg;
Carbohydrates: 6g;
Fiber: 1g; Protein: 51g;
Sodium: 313mg

GAME PLAN:
This recipe should give you lots of leftovers, which are excellent for roast beef sandwiches. Pile the thinly sliced beef on toasted onion buns or hamburger buns and top them with mustard or horse-radish.

Tangy Beef Short Ribs

GLUTEN-FREE, WEEKNIGHT HERO

PREP TIME:
15 MINUTES

COOK TIME:
8 HOURS ON LOW

SERVES 4

PER SERVING:
Calories: 684; Fat: 36g;
Saturated Fat: 15g;
Cholesterol: 177mg;
Carbohydrates: 30g;
Fiber: 1g; Protein: 60g;
Sodium: 1,326mg

Short ribs are one of the easiest dishes you'll make in your slow cooker. The rich beef becomes meltingly tender after hours of cooking, and the mustard, ketchup, brown sugar, and vinegar create a wonderful sauce. Serve with Slow Cooker Rice (page 258) or Slow Cooker Mashed Potatoes (page 64) to soak up all the sauce.

1 yellow onion, cut crosswise into thick rings

4 pounds bone-in beef short ribs

1 cup beef broth

1 cup ketchup

¼ cup mustard

¼ cup apple cider vinegar

2 tablespoons brown sugar

1 teaspoon liquid smoke (optional)

1. Place the onion in a 4-quart slow cooker. Arrange the short ribs on top.
2. In a small bowl, whisk together the broth, ketchup, mustard, vinegar, brown sugar, and liquid smoke (if using). Pour the mixture over the ribs.
3. Cover and cook on low for 8 hours, or until the beef is very tender. Serve with the liquid in the slow cooker.

Korean Short Ribs and Carrots

WEEKNIGHT HERO

These short ribs are so tender and flavorful, seasoned with delicious Asian ingredients including fish sauce, which is salty, and Sriracha, which adds a spicy kick. Serve these succulent short ribs with Slow Cooker Rice (page 258) or sweet potatoes to soak up the wonderful sauce.

2 tablespoons low-sodium soy sauce

2 tablespoons fish sauce

2 tablespoons rice wine vinegar

1 to 2 teaspoons Sriracha

1 teaspoon toasted sesame oil

2 teaspoons minced garlic

2 teaspoons minced fresh ginger

2 pounds bone-in Korean-cut short ribs, trimmed of fat

4 carrots, cut into 2-inch pieces

3 cups low-sodium beef broth

2 tablespoons cornstarch

3 tablespoons water

1 scallion, white and green parts, thinly sliced, for garnish

PREP TIME:
15 MINUTES

COOK TIME:
8 HOURS ON LOW, PLUS 10 MINUTES ON HIGH

SERVES 4

PER SERVING:
Calories: 475; Fat: 25g; Saturated Fat: 10g; Cholesterol: 130mg; Carbohydrates: 12g; Fiber: 2g; Protein: 48g; Sodium: 1,530mg

1. In a small bowl, whisk together the soy sauce, fish sauce, vinegar, Sriracha, sesame oil, garlic, and ginger. Spread this mixture onto the short ribs to coat thoroughly.

2. Place the carrots into a 4-quart slow cooker. Arrange the short ribs on top. Pour in the beef broth.

3. Cover and cook on low for 8 hours, or until the ribs are very tender.

4. In a small bowl, combine the cornstarch and water and blend well. Stir this mixture into the slow cooker. Cover and cook on high for 10 minutes to thicken the sauce. To serve, garnish the short ribs with the scallions.

INGREDIENT TIP: If you can't find Korean-cut short ribs, you can use flanken-cut short ribs or regular bone-in short ribs instead. The cooking time will remain the same.

Horseradish-Braised Short Ribs

GLUTEN-FREE

PREP TIME:
25 MINUTES

COOK TIME:
8 HOURS ON LOW

SERVES 6

PER SERVING:
Calories: 913; Fat: 50g;
Saturated Fat: 20g;
Cholesterol: 263mg;
Carbohydrates: 15g;
Fiber: 3g; Protein: 97g;
Sodium: 672mg

INGREDIENT TIP:
Peeling pearl onions is very difficult unless you know this trick: Just cut off the root end from each little onion. Plunge the onions into boiling water for 1 minute; then remove the onions and put them into ice water. Let them stand for 5 minutes. The onion skins will just slip off.

Short ribs are delicious when you braise them in a slow cooker. This recipe makes liberal use of horseradish, which adds a peppery bite.

2 slices bacon

6 pounds bone-in beef short ribs

4 cups Bone Broth (page 262 or store-bought) or beef broth, divided

1 yellow onion, chopped

2 cups fresh or frozen pearl onions, peeled

3 cups baby carrots

1 (8-ounce) package button mushrooms, halved

3 tablespoons grated fresh horseradish

1 teaspoon chopped fresh thyme

½ teaspoon sea salt

½ teaspoon freshly ground black pepper

3 tablespoons cornstarch

1. In a large skillet over medium heat, cook the bacon, turning frequently, for 7 to 10 minutes, until brown and crispy. Drain the bacon on paper towels, leaving the bacon fat in the pan; then crumble it.
2. Place the short ribs in the skillet in batches; brown them on all sides, turning frequently, for 5 to 7 minutes. Drain the fat from the skillet.
3. Add 1 cup of broth to the skillet and bring to a boil, scraping the browned bits from the bottom of the pan. Transfer this to a large bowl.
4. Place the cooked bacon, browned short ribs, yellow onion, pearl onions, carrots, mushrooms, horseradish, thyme, salt, and pepper in a 4- to 5-quart slow cooker. Stir to combine.
5. Add the remaining 3 cups of broth and the cornstarch to the deglazing liquid in the large bowl. Whisk it together. Pour the broth mixture into the slow cooker.
6. Cover and cook on low for 8 hours, until the ribs are very tender. Serve the ribs with the vegetables.

Beef and Broccoli

LOW-CALORIE

This Chinese takeout–inspired recipe is healthy and delicious. The combination of beef and broccoli is classic. The flank steak is cooked whole in this recipe, so it stays tender and doesn't overcook. Serve this dish over Slow Cooker Rice (page 258) for a complete meal.

4 cups broccoli florets

1¼ pounds flank steak

1 cup beef broth

3 tablespoons low-sodium soy sauce

¼ cup honey or pure maple syrup

1 teaspoon toasted sesame oil

2 teaspoons minced garlic

2 tablespoons cornstarch

2 tablespoons water

PREP TIME:
10 MINUTES

COOK TIME:
6 HOURS ON LOW,
PLUS 10 MINUTES
ON HIGH

SERVES 4

PER SERVING:
Calories: 345; Fat: 10g;
Saturated Fat: <1g;
Cholesterol: 56mg;
Carbohydrates: 26g;
Fiber: 2g; Protein: 33g;
Sodium: 644mg

1. Place the broccoli in a 4-quart slow cooker. Top with the steak.
2. In a measuring cup or small bowl, whisk together the broth, soy sauce, honey, sesame oil, and garlic. Pour this mixture over the beef and broccoli.
3. Cover and cook on low for 6 hours, or until the beef is tender.
4. Remove the beef from the slow cooker and thinly slice it into strips.
5. In a measuring cup or small bowl, whisk together the cornstarch and water. Add the beef and cornstarch mixture to the slow cooker and stir well to combine. Cover and cook on high for 10 minutes, or until the sauce thickens.

INGREDIENT TIP: Tougher and cheaper cuts of meat, such as flank steak, cook very well in the slow cooker. The long and slow cooking time helps break down the connective tissue in the beef, so it's meltingly tender.

Beef Ragù

GLUTEN-FREE, WEEKNIGHT HERO

PREP TIME:
10 MINUTES

COOK TIME:
9 HOURS ON LOW

SERVES 6

PER SERVING:
Calories: 556; Fat: 22g;
Saturated Fat: 7g;
Cholesterol: 215mg;
Carbohydrates: 6g;
Fiber: 1g; Protein: 80g;
Sodium: 921mg

Traditional ragù is a sauce of braised meat that may be flavored with tomato—not tomato sauce with meat in it. In parts of Southern Italy, especially Campania, substantial quantities of large, whole cuts of beef and pork are often the basis for ragùs. Serve hot over pasta, hot mashed potatoes, or rice for a gluten-free option. If you have time, brown the beef to add extra flavor.

1 medium yellow onion, diced

3 garlic cloves, minced

6 tablespoons tomato paste

3 tablespoons chopped fresh oregano or 1 tablespoon dried oregano

1 (4-pound) beef chuck roast, halved

1 teaspoon coarse sea salt

½ teaspoon freshly ground black pepper

2 cups beef broth

2 tablespoons red wine vinegar

1. Place the onion, garlic, tomato paste, and oregano in a 5-quart slow cooker. Stir well to combine.
2. Season the roast halves with the salt and pepper. Arrange the beef on top of the onion mixture in the slow cooker. Add the beef broth.
3. Cover and cook on low for 9 hours, until the meat is tender and can easily be pulled apart with a fork. Let cool, covered, for 10 minutes.
4. Using two forks, shred the meat in the slow cooker. Stir the vinegar into the sauce.

IF YOU HAVE A MINUTE: Brown the two halves of the chuck roast in a skillet for richer color and flavor in the finished recipe. Sprinkle the beef with salt and pepper. Heat 2 tablespoons of olive oil in a large skillet over medium heat and brown the beef halves, one at a time, for 5 to 6 minutes on each side until brown. Place the beef in the slow cooker. Add 1 cup of the beef broth to the skillet and scrape up the browned bits drippings from the bottom of the pan. Add this stock to the skillet along with the remaining 1 cup of beef broth and proceed with the recipe.

INGREDIENT TIP: Lean and expensive cuts of beef such as prime rib and ribeye do not do well in the slow cooker; they cook best when cooked quickly over high heat. The long, slow cooking time in a slow cooker melts the connective tissue in cheaper cuts of meat, making them tender and succulent.

Beef Stroganoff

LOW-CALORIE, WEEKNIGHT HERO

PREP TIME:
15 MINUTES

COOK TIME:
8 HOURS ON LOW,
PLUS 10 TO 15 MIN-
UTES ON HIGH

SERVES 6

PER SERVING:
Calories: 397; Fat: 19g;
Saturated Fat: 10g;
Cholesterol: 125mg;
Carbohydrates: 9g;
Fiber: 1g; Protein: 44g;
Sodium: 635mg

This one-dish meal is a classic in American cooking. The fresh herbs and Dijon mustard add wonderful flavor to this recipe. Serve it over cooked egg noodles or Slow Cooker Mashed Potatoes (page 64) for true comfort food.

2 pounds beef chuck steak or roast, cut into 1-inch chunks

2 cups beef broth

1 (8-ounce) package sliced mushrooms

¼ cup roughly chopped fresh parsley, plus more for garnish

2 garlic cloves, minced

1 yellow onion, diced

2 thyme sprigs

1 bay leaf

2 tablespoons Dijon mustard

½ teaspoon sea salt

⅛ teaspoon freshly ground black pepper

1 cup full-fat sour cream

2 tablespoons all-purpose flour

1. Place the beef, broth, mushrooms, parsley, garlic, onion, thyme, bay leaf, mustard, salt, and pepper in a 3½-quart slow cooker. Stir well to mix.

2. Cover and cook on low for 8 hours, or until the beef and mushrooms are very tender. Remove and discard the thyme stems and bay leaf.

3. In a medium bowl, combine the sour cream with the flour and mix well. Whisk in ½ cup of the liquid from the slow cooker until thoroughly blended.

4. Stir the sour cream mixture into the slow cooker. Cover and cook on high for another 10 to 15 minutes, or until the sauce has thickened. Sprinkle with the parsley and serve.

Beer-Braised Beef

WEEKNIGHT HERO

While the French are famous for cooking meat in wine, Americans have perfected cooking with beer. Although it may not enjoy the same highbrow reputation, this beef stew is just as tender and flavorful as the classic French version. You can substitute additional beef broth for the beer if you'd like.

PREP TIME:
15 MINUTES

COOK TIME:
8 HOURS ON LOW

SERVES 6

PER SERVING:
Calories: 484; Fat: 31g;
Saturated Fat: 14g;
Cholesterol: 128mg;
Carbohydrates: 13g;
Fiber: 1g; Protein: 34g;
Sodium: 656mg

3 yellow onions, sliced

5 garlic cloves, minced

¼ cup all-purpose flour

½ teaspoon sea salt

¼ teaspoon freshly ground black pepper

2 pounds beef chuck, cut into 1-inch pieces

20 ounces dark beer, such as stout or porter

4 cups beef broth

2 thyme sprigs

1. Place the onions and garlic in a 4-quart slow cooker. Stir to mix.
2. Place the flour in a shallow dish or plate and stir in the salt and pepper. Dredge the beef in the flour and arrange on top of the onions and garlic.
3. Pour in the beer and broth. Add the thyme.
4. Cover and cook on low for 8 hours, or until the beef is very tender.

IF YOU HAVE A MINUTE: For even more flavor, brown the beef on the stove top before putting it in the slow cooker: In a medium skillet over medium-high heat, add 2 tablespoons of oil. Once hot, add the flour-dredged beef and cook it until browned on all sides. Place the flour-dredged beef in the slow cooker. Stir about 1 cup of the beer into the skillet, scraping any browned bits on the bottom of the pan. Pour this into the slow cooker; add the remaining beer, broth, and thyme and continue with the recipe.

Balsamic-Glazed Beef with Red Cabbage

GLUTEN-FREE, LOW-CALORIE, WEEKNIGHT HERO

PREP TIME:
15 MINUTES

COOK TIME:
8 HOURS ON LOW

SERVES 4

PER SERVING:
Calories: 336; Fat: 9g;
Saturated Fat: 3g;
Cholesterol: 113mg;
Carbohydrates: 13g;
Fiber: 2g; Protein: 39g;
Sodium: 602mg

Stewed beef and cabbage with mustard has a gratifying "old country" taste to it. Make sure to layer the ingredients into the slow cooker as indicated, so the cabbage gets tender. This spicy dish is delicious served over Slow Cooker Rice (page 258) or Slow Cooker Mashed Potatoes (page 64).

4 cups chopped red cabbage

1 cup thinly sliced red onion

1½ pounds beef stew meat, trimmed of excess fat and cut into 1-inch pieces

¾ cup dry red wine or beef broth

⅓ cup balsamic vinegar

2 tablespoons Dijon mustard

1 teaspoon ground cumin

½ teaspoon sea salt

Freshly ground black pepper

1. Place the cabbage and onion in a 4-quart slow cooker. Arrange the beef on top of the vegetables.
2. In a large measuring cup or small bowl, whisk together the wine, vinegar, mustard, cumin, salt, and a few grinds of black pepper. Pour this mixture into the slow cooker.
3. Cover and cook on low for 8 hours, or until the cabbage and beef are very tender.

IF YOU HAVE A MINUTE: Brown the beef in a skillet (over medium heat in 1 tablespoon of olive oil) before adding it to the slow cooker for more flavor. Add the browned beef to the slow cooker. Pour ¼ cup of the wine or beef broth into the skillet and bring it to a boil, scraping the browned bits and drippings from the bottom of the pan. Add that to the slow cooker and continue with the recipe.

Beef Goulash with Pumpkin, Mushrooms, and Pumpkin Seeds

GLUTEN-FREE, LOW-CALORIE

This hearty beef stew is perfect for fall. It combines the sweet spices of cinnamon and allspice with savory flavors of bay leaf and thyme. The pumpkin seeds (also called pepitas) add a slight crunch.

PREP TIME:
25 MINUTES

COOK TIME:
8 HOURS ON LOW

SERVES 4

PER SERVING:
Calories: 373; Fat: 13g;
Saturated Fat: 4g;
Cholesterol: 113mg;
Carbohydrates: 22g;
Fiber: 6g; Protein: 44g;
Sodium: 441mg

1½ pounds beef stew meat, trimmed of excess fat and cut into 1-inch cubes

1 small pie pumpkin or butternut squash, peeled, seeded, and cut into 1-inch cubes

2 cups quartered button mushrooms

1 yellow onion, halved and thinly sliced

3 garlic cloves, minced

½ teaspoon ground cinnamon

¼ teaspoon ground allspice

1 bay leaf

2 thyme sprigs

½ teaspoon sea salt

3 cups Chicken Stock (page 263 or store-bought)

¼ cup pumpkin seeds, for garnish

1. Place the beef, pumpkin, mushrooms, onion, garlic, cinnamon, allspice, bay leaf, thyme, salt, and stock in a 4-quart slow cooker. Stir gently to mix.

2. Cover and cook on low for 8 hours, or until the beef and pumpkin are tender. Remove and discard the thyme sprigs and bay leaf.

3. Garnish with the pumpkin seeds.

IF YOU HAVE A MINUTE: For a richer beef flavor and a deeper color, brown the beef before you add it to the slow cooker. Sprinkle the beef with a bit of flour to thicken the stew if you'd like; then brown it in a tablespoon of olive oil for 2 to 3 minutes. Put the beef in the slow cooker. Pour 1 cup of the broth into the skillet and bring it to a boil, scraping the browned bits and drippings from the bottom of the pan. Add this to the slow cooker and continue with the recipe.

Smoky Chipotle and Beef Tacos

WEEKNIGHT HERO

PREP TIME:
15 MINUTES

COOK TIME:
8 HOURS ON LOW
OR
4 HOURS ON HIGH

SERVES 6

PER SERVING:
Calories: 570; Fat: 19g;
Saturated Fat: 7g;
Cholesterol: 108mg;
Carbohydrates: 53g;
Fiber: 3g; Protein: 48g;
Sodium: 1,704mg

IF YOU HAVE A MINUTE: Brown the spice-rubbed meat on all sides in a large skillet with 2 tablespoons of olive oil and deglaze with beef stock before continuing with the recipe.

Beef tacos are a classic Mexican street food. The long, slow cooking time called for in this recipe results in tender meat, spicy with chipotle and ancho chile flavors. The cinnamon adds a bit of warm spice.

1 tablespoon chili powder

1½ teaspoons sea salt

1 teaspoon ground cumin

1 teaspoon ancho chili powder

½ teaspoon smoked paprika

½ teaspoon ground cinnamon

2 pounds lean boneless
   beef chuck roast

1 medium yellow onion, diced

6 garlic cloves, minced

1 cup beef broth

2 chipotle chiles in adobo
   sauce, minced, plus 2
   tablespoons adobo sauce

12 flour tortillas

1. In a small bowl, combine the chili powder, salt, cumin, ancho chili powder, smoked paprika, and cinnamon. Rub this mixture all over the beef. Place the beef in a 3½- to 4-quart slow cooker and top it with the onion and garlic.
2. In a medium bowl, whisk together the broth, chipotle chiles, and adobo sauce, and pour over the beef.
3. Cover and cook on low for 8 hours or on high for 4 hours, until the beef is very tender
4. Carefully transfer the beef to a cutting board. Shred the meat using two forks.
5. Using a slotted spoon, remove the onion and garlic from the slow cooker and mix them with the beef. Serve the meat in the flour tortillas with your favorite toppings. Discard the liquid left in the slow cooker.

Osso Buco

The slow cooker is the perfect vessel to cook osso buco. If you can't find veal shanks or prefer not to eat veal, you can also use lamb or beef shanks for this recipe. It's a wonderful meal for a special occasion or when you're craving something really rich. Serve with Mashed Sweet Potatoes (page 65) or Slow Cooker Polenta (page 259).

PREP TIME:
25 MINUTES

COOK TIME:
8 HOURS ON LOW

SERVES 4

PER SERVING:
Calories: 689; Fat: 20g; Saturated Fat: 4g; Cholesterol: 357mg; Carbohydrates: 19g; Fiber: 3g; Protein: 94g; Sodium: 665mg

4 veal shanks, about 2½ pounds

¼ cup all-purpose flour

2 tablespoons extra-virgin olive oil

1 cup dry red wine or beef broth

2 teaspoons fresh rosemary

2 teaspoons fresh thyme

2 teaspoons minced garlic

1 tablespoon tomato paste

½ teaspoon sea salt

Freshly ground black pepper

1 cup diced yellow onion

2 cups sliced carrots

½ cup diced celery

1 teaspoon grated orange zest

1 cup Chicken Stock (page 263 or store-bought) or beef broth

1. Coat the veal shanks with the flour.
2. Place a large skillet over medium-high heat and add the olive oil. Once hot, add the shanks and brown them on all sides for 6 to 8 minutes in total. Place the shanks in a 4- to 5-quart slow cooker.
3. Pour the wine into the skillet and bring it to a boil, scraping the browned bits and drippings from the bottom of the pan. Set aside.
4. In a small bowl, combine the rosemary, thyme, garlic, tomato paste, salt, and a few grinds of black pepper. Sprinkle the veal shanks with this mixture.
5. Place the onion, carrots, celery, and orange zest in the slow cooker over and around the shanks. Pour in the red wine from the skillet and the chicken stock.
6. Cover and cook on low for 8 hours, or until the meat is very tender.

INGREDIENT TIP:
Shanks are part of the leg bone. The marrow in the center of the bone melts during the long cooking time, making the sauce velvety and silky.

Lamb Tagine

GLUTEN-FREE, LOW-CALORIE, WEEKNIGHT HERO

PREP TIME:
15 MINUTES

COOK TIME:
8 HOURS ON LOW

SERVES 8

PER SERVING:
Calories: 255; Fat: 10g;
Saturated Fat: 3g;
Cholesterol: 70mg;
Carbohydrates: 18g;
Fiber: 2g; Protein: 24g;
Sodium: 390mg

The dish is named after the Moroccan earthenware vessel it is traditionally cooked in. Fortunately, the slow cooker mimics the effects of cooking in a tagine—both are designed to capture condensation and retain moisture within the dish. The spices flavor the lamb deeply, and the onions and raisins add texture and flavor to the dish.

1 teaspoon ground turmeric
1 teaspoon ground ginger
1 teaspoon ground cinnamon
1 teaspoon smoked paprika
1 teaspoon sea salt
⅛ teaspoon freshly ground black pepper

2 pounds lamb shoulder, cut into 1-inch chunks
2 tablespoons extra-virgin olive oil, divided
2 yellow onions, diced
1 cup raisins
½ cup fresh cilantro leaves, for serving

1. In a small bowl, mix together the turmeric, ginger, cinnamon, paprika, salt, and pepper.
2. In a large bowl, toss the lamb with 1 tablespoon of olive oil. Add the spice mixture and toss again to coat.
3. Place the lamb in a 4-quart slow cooker. Stir in the onions, raisins, and remaining 1 tablespoon of olive oil.
4. Cover and cook on low for 8 hours, or until the lamb is very tender. Serve garnished with the cilantro leaves.

Honey-Soy Lamb and Rice

WEEKNIGHT HERO

Honey and soy make a delicious sweet-and-sour combination, which perfectly complements rich and tender lamb. Because lamb has such unctuous fat, it needs something sharp to cut through the flavor. This recipe is fabulous served with a tangy cucumber salad.

1 teaspoon extra-virgin olive oil

1¼ cups long-grain brown rice

2½ cups Chicken Stock (page 263 or store-bought) or water

3 scallions, white and green parts, thinly sliced on an angle

¼ cup low-sodium soy sauce

¼ cup honey

2 tablespoons freshly squeezed lime juice

Pinch red pepper flakes

1¼ pounds boneless lamb shoulder, cut into 1-inch cubes

PREP TIME:
15 MINUTES

COOK TIME:
8 HOURS ON LOW

SERVES 4

PER SERVING:
Calories: 508; Fat: 11g;
Saturated Fat: 4g;
Cholesterol: 88mg;
Carbohydrates: 65g;
Fiber: 2g; Protein: 35g;
Sodium: 1,146mg

1. Grease a 3-quart slow cooker with the olive oil.
2. Place the brown rice, stock, and scallions in the slow cooker. Stir to mix well, making sure the rice is completely submerged in the liquid.
3. In a large bowl, whisk together the soy sauce, honey, lime juice, and red pepper flakes. Add the lamb cubes and toss to coat.
4. Place the lamb over the rice in the slow cooker.
5. Cover and cook on low for 8 hours, or until the lamb and rice are tender.

INGREDIENT TIP: You can substitute beef or pork for the lamb in this recipe. Use the same amount and cut the meat into 1-inch cubes.

GAME PLAN: You can marinate the lamb the day before cooking it. Just follow step 3 of this recipe. Cover the bowl and refrigerate it overnight. Continue with step 1 of the recipe the next day.

Braised Lamb Shanks

GLUTEN-FREE, WEEKNIGHT HERO

PREP TIME:
15 MINUTES

COOK TIME:
8 TO 10 HOURS
ON LOW

SERVES 4

PER SERVING:
Calories: 460; Fat: 13g;
Saturated Fat: 4g;
Cholesterol: 152mg;
Carbohydrates: 12g;
Fiber: 2g; Protein: 50g;
Sodium: 1,215mg

Serve these lamb shanks with egg noodles or Slow Cooker Mashed Potatoes (page 64). They make an especially delicious holiday dinner.

4 (8- to 10-ounce) lamb shanks
2 cups full-bodied red wine
2 cups beef broth
2 tablespoons tomato paste
1 tablespoon extra-virgin olive oil
2 carrots, diced
2 celery stalks, diced

1 yellow onion, diced
4 garlic cloves, mashed
4 thyme sprigs
2 rosemary sprigs
1 teaspoon sea salt
¼ teaspoon freshly ground black pepper

1. Place all the ingredients in a 4- to 5-quart slow cooker. Stir to combine.
2. Cover and cook on low for 8 to 10 hours, or until the lamb is very tender. Remove the thyme and rosemary stems and serve.

GAME PLAN: To serve the wonderful sauce with the lamb, take the shanks out of the slow cooker, put them on a serving plate, and cover them with aluminum foil. Skim the fat off the surface of the liquid and transfer 3 cups of the liquid and solids to a saucepan. In a measuring cup, mix 2 tablespoons of all-purpose flour or cornstarch with ¼ cup of the cooking liquid. Stir this into the liquid in the pan. Boil it for 10 to 15 minutes or until thickened; then purée using an immersion blender. Serve the sauce with the lamb.

Lamb Vindaloo

GLUTEN-FREE, LOW-CALORIE, WEEKNIGHT HERO

Experiment with global flavors in this traditional Indian dish. Lamb shanks are the perfect choice for slow cooking since they become velvety and tender when cooked for a long period of time. This spicy dish should be served with Slow Cooker Rice (page 258) to help tame the heat.

1 yellow onion, thinly sliced

½ teaspoon cayenne pepper

1 teaspoon paprika

1 teaspoon ground cumin

1 teaspoon mustard powder

1 tablespoon garam masala

½ teaspoon sea salt

4 (8- to 10-ounce) lamb shanks

1 cup water

2 tablespoons apple cider vinegar

1 tablespoon tamarind paste

2 tablespoons tomato paste

4 garlic cloves, minced

1 tablespoon minced fresh ginger

PREP TIME:
15 MINUTES

COOK TIME:
9 HOURS ON LOW

SERVES 4

PER SERVING:
Calories: 316; Fat: 9g;
Saturated Fat: 3g;
Cholesterol: 150mg;
Carbohydrates: 8g;
Fiber: 2g; Protein: 48g;
Sodium: 600mg

1. Place the onion in a 4-quart slow cooker.
2. In a small bowl, combine the cayenne pepper, paprika, cumin, mustard powder, garam masala, and salt. Rub this mixture into the lamb shanks. Arrange the shanks on top of the onion slices.
3. In a separate small bowl, whisk together the water, vinegar, tamarind paste, tomato paste, garlic, and ginger. Pour the mixture into the slow cooker.
4. Cover and cook on low for 9 hours, or until the lamb is very tender.

INGREDIENT TIP: Tamarind paste is made from the tamarind fruit and is used a lot in Thai and Indian cooking. The paste is sweet and sour. If you can't find it, substitute an equal amount of lime juice and brown sugar or honey.

Roasted Garlic-Rosemary Lamb with Lemon Potatoes

GLUTEN-FREE, LOW-CALORIE, WEEKNIGHT HERO

PREP TIME:
10 MINUTES

COOK TIME:
8 HOURS ON LOW

SERVES 8

PER SERVING:
Calories: 379; Fat: 17g;
Saturated Fat: 10g;
Cholesterol: 83mg;
Carbohydrates: 24g;
Fiber: 3g; Protein: 32g;
Sodium: 872mg

Garlic and rosemary are classically paired with lamb in this easy one-dish meal. The lamb becomes meltingly tender when cooked in the slow cooker. A simple side salad or some steamed vegetables are all you need to complete this dish.

6 garlic cloves, minced

1 tablespoon minced fresh rosemary

¼ teaspoon kosher salt

¼ teaspoon freshly ground black pepper

3 pounds boneless leg of lamb, trimmed and cut into 2-inch pieces

2 pounds small yellow potatoes

2 tablespoons extra-virgin olive oil

Grated zest and juice of 1 lemon

½ cup dry white wine or Chicken Stock (page 263 or store-bought)

1. Using a mortar and pestle or a food processor, grind the garlic, rosemary, salt, and pepper to a rough paste.
2. In a large bowl, rub the lamb pieces with the rosemary mixture.
3. Place the potatoes, olive oil, and lemon zest and juice in a 4-quart slow cooker. Mix until the potatoes are thoroughly coated. Pour in the wine. Arrange the rosemary-coated lamb pieces on top.
4. Cover and cook on low for 8 hours, or until the lamb is very tender and the potatoes are done.

GAME PLAN: You can prepare the rosemary mixture the night before. Add it to the lamb pieces and rub it into the meat. Cover and refrigerate the seasoned lamb overnight; then continue with the recipe in the morning.

Roasted Lamb with Mustard and Fennel

GLUTEN-FREE, WEEKNIGHT HERO

The sweet flavor of fennel intensifies with long, slow cooking in wine and oil and is the perfect accompaniment to the tender lamb. Serve this dish with crusty bread to sop up all the delicious broth.

2 tablespoons extra-virgin olive oil, divided

1 teaspoon grainy Dijon mustard

1 teaspoon fennel seeds, crushed

1 teaspoon sea salt

⅛ teaspoon freshly ground black pepper

1 (3-pound) boneless leg of lamb

1 fennel bulb, peeled and thinly sliced

2 garlic cloves, minced

½ cup dry white wine

PREP TIME:
15 MINUTES

COOK TIME:
8 HOURS ON LOW

SERVES 6

PER SERVING:
Calories: 409; Fat: 23g;
Saturated Fat: 6g;
Cholesterol: 110mg;
Carbohydrates: 10g;
Fiber: 1g; Protein: 41g;
Sodium: 1,469mg

1. In a small bowl, mix together 1 tablespoon of olive oil, the mustard, the fennel seeds, the salt, and the pepper. Rub this mixture all over the lamb.

2. Place the fennel, garlic, remaining 1 tablespoon of olive oil, and wine in a 4-quart slow cooker. Stir to mix well. Arrange the lamb on top.

3. Cover and cook on low for 8 hours, or until the lamb is tender.

INGREDIENT TIP: You can easily crush fennel seeds by putting them on the counter and crushing them with the little bottle they come in. Or you can put them into a small plastic bag and crush them with a rolling pin.

Rosemary Lamb Chops

GLUTEN-FREE

Lamb chops are tender and flavorful when cooked in the slow cooker. They are seasoned with onion, garlic, and herbs in this delicious recipe. The balsamic vinegar cuts through the unctuous lamb fat for a burst of flavor. Serve this dish with steamed broccoli and crusty bread for a delicious dinner.

1 medium yellow onion, sliced

1 teaspoon garlic powder

2 teaspoons chopped fresh rosemary

½ teaspoon sea salt

½ teaspoon dried thyme

⅛ teaspoon freshly ground black pepper

8 bone-in loin lamb chops (about 3 pounds)

2 tablespoons balsamic vinegar

PREP TIME:
15 MINUTES

COOK TIME:
4 TO 6 HOURS
ON LOW

SERVES 4

PER SERVING:
Calories: 467; Fat: 17g;
Saturated Fat: 7g;
Cholesterol: 218mg;
Carbohydrates: 4g;
Fiber: 1g; Protein: 70g;
Sodium: 512mg

1. Line the bottom of a 3-quart slow cooker with the onion.
2. In a small bowl, stir together the garlic powder, rosemary, salt, thyme, and pepper. Rub the chops evenly with the spice mixture and place them in the slow cooker.
3. Drizzle the vinegar over the top.
4. Cover and cook on low for 4 to 6 hours, until the lamb and onions are tender.

Corned Beef and Cabbage

GLUTEN-FREE, LOW-CALORIE

PREP TIME:
10 MINUTES

COOK TIME:
4 HOURS ON LOW

SERVES 6

PER SERVING:
Calories: 226; Fat: 6g;
Saturated Fat: 2g;
Cholesterol: 60mg;
Carbohydrates: 13g;
Fiber: 5g; Protein: 33g;
Sodium: 1,161mg

Don't wait until St. Patrick's Day to enjoy this hearty meal. Salty and meaty corned beef is delicious when cooked with cabbage, which becomes sweet and mellow during the low, slow cooking time. Serve this dish with roasted potatoes for a great dinner.

1 large head green or red cabbage, cored and sliced

1 small yellow onion, finely chopped

4 cups Chicken Stock (page 263 or store-bought)

1½ pounds cooked corned beef, sliced ½-inch thick against the grain

¼ teaspoon sea salt

⅛ teaspoon freshly ground black pepper

1. Place the cabbage and onion in a 4-quart slow cooker. Stir to mix. Pour the stock over the vegetables. Add the beef, salt, and pepper.

2. Cover and cook on low for 4 hours, or until the cabbage is very tender.

Shepherd's Pie

GLUTEN-FREE

Shepherd's pie is a hearty and comforting dish that is easy to make in the slow cooker. Ground beef is cooked with peas, carrots, and onions and then topped with mashed potatoes, which serve as the "crust." It's a one-dish meal that everyone will love.

1 pound lean ground beef or ground lamb

2 cups frozen peas

2 cups sliced carrots

1 cup diced yellow onion

1 teaspoon dried marjoram

¼ teaspoon sea salt

Freshly ground black pepper

3 cups Slow Cooker Mashed Potatoes (page 64)

½ cup shredded sharp Cheddar cheese

PREP TIME:
20 MINUTES

COOK TIME:
8 HOURS ON LOW

SERVES 4

PER SERVING:
Calories: 506; Fat: 22g; Saturated Fat: 12g; Cholesterol: 98mg; Carbohydrates: 45g; Fiber: 9g; Protein: 35g; Sodium: 595mg

1. Place a large skillet over medium heat. Add the ground beef and cook, stirring with a wooden spoon to break up the meat, for 8 to 10 minutes, until it is cooked through. Drain if necessary.

2. Place the cooked beef, peas, carrots, and onion in a 3½-quart slow cooker. Stir together thoroughly. Season the mixture with the marjoram, salt, and a few grinds of black pepper.

3. Spread the prepared mashed potatoes over the meat and vegetable mixture in an even layer.

4. Cover and cook on low for 8 hours, or until the meat mixture is bubbling around the edges.

5. Sprinkle the top of the shepherd's pie with the Cheddar cheese just before serving.

EXTRA EASY: If you have leftover homemade mashed potatoes from another meal, that's a good excuse for making shepherd's pie. It's easy to make mashed potatoes with refrigerated products available in most grocery stores. You can also rehydrate instant potato flakes—they are made from real potatoes! Follow the directions on the box to make 3 cups.

Beef and Poblano Tamale Pie

GLUTEN-FREE

PREP TIME:
20 MINUTES

COOK TIME:
5 HOURS ON LOW

SERVES 6

PER SERVING:
Calories: 456; Fat: 22g;
Saturated Fat: 10g;
Cholesterol: 95mg;
Carbohydrates: 33g;
Fiber: 5g; Protein: 33g;
Sodium: 597mg

Tamale pie gives you the flavor of tamales without the work. While most tamale pies have a cornmeal topping, this one is made in layers with corn tortillas. As they cook, the tortillas get soft, and everything combines to make a kid-friendly, comfort-food dinner that is deceptively easy. If you'd like to cut back on the meat, use half the amount and add a can of drained and rinsed kidney beans, black beans, or pinto beans.

Nonstick cooking spray

1½ pounds lean ground beef

1 medium yellow onion, chopped

½ medium poblano chile, seeded and chopped

2 cups fresh or frozen corn

1 (10-ounce) can enchilada sauce

9 corn tortillas, divided

1½ cups grated Colby cheese, divided

1. Spray a 3- to 4-quart slow cooker with nonstick cooking spray.
2. Place a large skillet over medium-high heat. Add the ground beef, onion, and poblano chile and cook, stirring with a wooden spoon to break up the meat, for 4 to 6 minutes, until the meat is no longer pink. Drain off the fat.
3. Add the corn and enchilada sauce to the skillet and mix well.
4. Place 3 tortillas, overlapping, in the bottom of the slow cooker. Layer one-third of the meat over the tortillas and top with ½ cup of Colby cheese. Repeat the layers twice more, leaving off the last ½ cup of cheese on the last layer.
5. Cover and cook on low for 5 hours, or until the casserole is bubbling.
6. Top with the remaining ½ cup of cheese, cover the slow cooker, and turn off the heat. Serve when the cheese is melted.

Cuban Picadillo

GLUTEN-FREE, LOW-CALORIE, WEEKNIGHT HERO

Picadillo is a hash-like dish that is very popular in Latin American countries and in the Philippines. It's a nice recipe to make for breakfast, lunch, or dinner. Serve it with a side of cauliflower rice or Slow Cooker Mashed Potatoes (page 64) to soak up the wonderful sauce.

PREP TIME:
15 MINUTES

COOK TIME:
6 TO 8 HOURS
ON LOW OR
3 TO 4 HOURS
ON HIGH

SERVES 4

PER SERVING:
Calories: 203; Fat: 10g;
Saturated Fat: 3g;
Cholesterol: 70mg;
Carbohydrates: 6g;
Fiber: 2g; Protein: 23g;
Sodium: 796mg

1 pound lean ground beef

1 cup low-sodium or no-salt-added diced tomatoes, drained

½ cup pimento-stuffed green olives

2 teaspoons capers

1 small yellow onion, diced

1 tablespoon tomato paste

½ teaspoon ground cumin

¼ teaspoon sea salt

⅛ teaspoon freshly ground black pepper

1. Place a large skillet over medium heat. Add the ground beef and cook, stirring with a spoon to break up the meat, for 6 to 8 minutes, until the beef is browned. Drain off any fat.
2. Place the cooked ground beef, tomatoes, olives, capers, onion, tomato paste, cumin, salt, and pepper in a 3-quart slow cooker. Stir to mix well.
3. Cover and cook on low for 6 to 8 hours or on high for 3 to 4 hours.

GAME PLAN: You can serve this picadillo over rice or potatoes or make sandwiches using pita breads or sliced, toasted potato rolls. Double the recipe and freeze half of it for another meal.

Bone Broth,
page 262, and
Chicken Stock,
page 263

CHAPTER 10

Basic Beans

GLUTEN-FREE, LOW-CALORIE, VEGAN

PREP TIME:
8 HOURS TO SOAK

COOK TIME:
7 TO 8 HOURS
ON LOW

SERVES 6

PER SERVING:
Calories: 195; Fat: 0g;
Saturated Fat: 0g;
Cholesterol: 0mg;
Carbohydrates: 43g;
Fiber: 11g; Protein: 15g;
Sodium: 11mg

Sure, you can buy canned beans, but cooking them from dry is cheaper, you know exactly how much salt is in them, and this hands-off method is basically as easy as popping open a can. Keep a batch of cooked ones in your freezer for a head-start on healthy meals anytime.

1 pound dried beans, any kind	**10 cups cool water**

1. Rinse the beans and pick out any broken ones or possible rocks, twigs, or dirt particles.
2. Put the beans in a large bowl or in your slow cooker and cover with water by at least 2 inches. Let them soak for a minimum of 8 hours or overnight at room temperature.
3. Drain and rinse the beans well, discarding the soaking liquid. Put them in a 3-quart slow cooker and cover with 10 cups of fresh water.
4. Cover and cook on low for 7 to 8 hours, or until the beans are soft and cooked through. Drain and serve.

INGREDIENT TIP: Dried bean varieties include pinto, black, kidney, adzuki, cranberry, butter, pink, navy, white, and cannellini beans. They all cook for the same amount of time and are delicious stirred into soups and stews.

Basic Quinoa

GLUTEN-FREE, LOW-CALORIE, VEGAN

Keeping a container of cooked quinoa in your refrigerator for the week ahead gives you a ready-made creative base for quick or on-the-go meals in a pinch. It's an extremely versatile seed (although it's often treated as a grain) that is not only full of fiber but is also considered a complete protein as it has a full amino acid profile. Be sure you rinse the quinoa before you cook with it to remove the bitter coating.

2 cups quinoa, rinsed well

4 cups Vegetable Broth (page 264 or store-bought)

1. In a 3-quart slow cooker, combine the quinoa and broth.
2. Cover and cook on low for 4 to 6 hours, until the quinoa has absorbed the broth. Fluff with a fork, cool, and serve.

PREP TIME:
15 MINUTES

COOK TIME:
4 TO 6 HOURS
ON LOW

SERVES 8

PER SERVING:
Calories: 181; Fat: 3g;
Saturated Fat: 0g;
Cholesterol: 0mg;
Carbohydrates: 33g;
Fiber: 3g; Protein: 7g;
Sodium: 115mg

Slow Cooker Rice

GLUTEN-FREE, LOW-CALORIE, VEGETARIAN

PREP TIME:
5 MINUTES

COOK TIME:
2 HOURS ON HIGH

SERVES 6

PER SERVING:
Calories: 118; Fat: 1g;
Saturated Fat: <1g;
Cholesterol: 2mg;
Carbohydrates: 25g;
Fiber: <1g; Protein: 2g;
Sodium: 2mg

Does the list of tasks a slow cooker can achieve ever end? Not any time soon! This versatile appliance can also double as a rice cooker. Bonus: no rice water boiling over onto your stovetop. And you don't have to babysit it; the rice will be tender and perfectly cooked.

1 teaspoon unsalted butter, at room temperature

1 cup white rice

Pinch sea salt

2 cups water

1. Coat the interior bottom and just a bit up the sides of a 2-quart slow cooker with the butter. Add the rice, salt, and water.

2. Cover and cook on high for 2 hours, occasionally stirring to prevent the rice from sticking or clumping.

INGREDIENT TIP: You should use long-grain white rice in this recipe. Plain American long-grain rice works well, while basmati rice is fluffy and smells like popcorn as it cooks, and Jasmine rice has a floral scent and slightly buttery taste. If you want to use brown rice, increase the cooking time to 3 hours.

Slow Cooker Polenta

GLUTEN-FREE, LOW-CALORIE, VEGAN

Polenta is simply cooked cornmeal. You can find it premade in the refrigerated section of the grocery store, but precooked polenta doesn't come close to replicating the delicious flavor and creamy texture of homemade polenta. You can use it as a substitute for potatoes or rice as a side dish for grilled chicken or pork chops.

3½ cups hot water
1 tablespoon extra-virgin olive oil

½ teaspoon sea salt
1 cup polenta (not quick-cooking)

1. Place the water, olive oil, and salt in a 2-quart slow cooker. Pour the polenta into the water in a thin, steady stream, whisking continuously to ensure that no lumps form.
2. Cover and cook on low for 2 hours, or until the cornmeal has absorbed all the water and is tender.

PREP TIME:
5 MINUTES

COOK TIME:
2 HOURS ON LOW

SERVES 6

PER SERVING:
Calories: 107; Fat: 3g;
Saturated Fat: <1g;
Cholesterol: 0mg;
Carbohydrates: 18g;
Fiber: 1g; Protein: 2g;
Sodium: 194mg

Basic Marinara Sauce

GLUTEN-FREE, LOW-CALORIE, VEGAN

Use this tomato sauce as a base for lasagna or simply slather it over pizza or pasta for a quick weeknight meal. Unlike store-bought versions, this tomato sauce contains no added sugar or, worse yet, high-fructose corn syrup. When you start with good-quality ingredients, you just need to step aside and let them shine.

2 (28-ounce) cans whole plum tomatoes, undrained

¼ cup roughly chopped fresh basil

2 garlic cloves, minced

1 large yellow onion, diced

1 teaspoon sea salt

¼ teaspoon freshly ground black pepper

PREP TIME:
10 MINUTES

COOK TIME:
6 HOURS ON LOW

SERVES 8

PER SERVING:
Calories: 61; Fat: 0g;
Saturated Fat: 0g;
Cholesterol: 0g;
Carbohydrates: 11g;
Fiber: 4g; Protein: 2g;
Sodium: 677mg

1. Place the tomatoes with their juices, basil, garlic, and onion in a 3-quart slow cooker. Use the back of a spoon to break up the tomatoes. Season with the salt and pepper.
2. Cover and cook on low for 6 hours, or until the sauce is blended.
3. If desired, you can use an immersion blender or a potato masher to purée the sauce.
4. Cool, uncovered, for 1 hour. The sauce can be refrigerated in an airtight container for up to 4 days. You can freeze this sauce in 1-cup portions for up to 5 months.

Bone Broth

GLUTEN-FREE, LOW-CALORIE

PREP TIME:
10 MINUTES

COOK TIME:
20 TO 24 HOURS
ON LOW OR
10 TO 12 HOURS
ON HIGH

SERVES 16

PER SERVING:
Calories: 41; Fat: 1g;
Saturated Fat: 0g;
Cholesterol: 0g;
Carbohydrates: 3g;
Fiber: 0g; Protein: 5g;
Sodium: 98mg

Bone broth can be used in soups and stews, or you can just drink it straight. It's a good source of calcium, magnesium, potassium, and vitamins and minerals, and it's rich in protein. The very long cooking time gives this wonderful broth the hours it needs to extract every drop of nutritional value from the bones. You can use two different types of bones from any type of animal here: jointy bones, which are cartilage-rich, like wings and necks, or meaty bones, like ribs or marrow bones.

4 pounds bones, including beef, chicken, and pork

8 cups water

4 celery stalks, halved crosswise

4 carrots, halved crosswise

2 yellow onions, quartered

5 garlic cloves, minced

¼ cup white vinegar

½ teaspoon salt

½ teaspoon freshly ground black pepper

1 bay leaf

1. Place the bones, water, celery, carrots, onions, garlic, vinegar, salt, pepper, and bay leaf in a 5- to 6-quart slow cooker.
2. Cover and cook on low for 20 to 24 hours or on high for 10 to 12 hours.
3. Strain the broth using a fine-mesh strainer over a large bowl. Cool and refrigerate in an airtight container for up to 3 days. Alternatively, portion into 1-cup freezer bags or airtight containers and freeze for up to 6 months. To thaw, place it in the refrigerator overnight.

INGREDIENT TIP: If you use bones with lots of cartilage or connective tissue, which is rich in collagen, your broth will start to gel as it cools. But if your bone broth doesn't gel, that's okay. It's still full of important minerals and amino acids, though it might be a bit lower in protein. Heat it on the stovetop or in the microwave if you want to drink it.

Chicken Stock

GLUTEN-FREE, LOW-CALORIE, WEEKNIGHT HERO

Whenever you roast a chicken or cook bone-in thighs or breasts, save the bones to make this rich, flavorful stock. It's perfect as a base for soups or risotto. You can add other herbs and spices to change the character of the stock; for instance, use lemongrass and ginger to make an Asian-inspired stock. Or add some dried basil and oregano along with a Parmesan cheese rind for an Italian version.

2 whole cooked chicken carcasses, stripped of most of the meat

1 cup diced yellow onion

1 cup diced carrots

1 cup diced celery

2 thyme sprigs

¼ teaspoon sea salt

12 cups cold water

PREP TIME:
10 MINUTES

COOK TIME:
8 HOURS ON LOW

SERVES 16

PER SERVING:
Calories: 29; Fat: 1g; Saturated Fat: 0g; Cholesterol: 0g; Carbohydrates: 3g; Fiber: 0g; Protein: 2g; Sodium: 54mg

1. Place the chicken carcasses, onion, carrots, celery, and thyme in a 5-quart slow cooker. Sprinkle with the salt and pour in the cold water.
2. Cover and cook on low for 8 hours.
3. Let cool for about 1 hour, until safe to handle; then pour the stock through a fine-mesh strainer into a bowl. Discard the solids in the strainer.
4. Use immediately or refrigerate in an airtight container for up to 3 days. You can also freeze this stock; pour 2 cups into an airtight freezer container, label it, and freeze it for up to 1 year. To thaw, add the frozen stock right to a soup, or thaw it in the refrigerator overnight.

GAME PLAN: One whole chicken carcass is about equivalent to the bones from 2 breasts, 2 thighs, and 2 wings.

INGREDIENT TIP: You can make this recipe using a 10- to 12-pound cooked turkey carcass as well. You may need a 6-quart slow cooker to hold the bird.

Vegetable Broth

GLUTEN-FREE, LOW-CALORIE, VEGAN, WEEKNIGHT HERO

PREP TIME:
15 MINUTES

COOK TIME:
8 TO 10 HOURS
ON LOW

SERVES 24

PER SERVING:
Calories: 9; Fat: 0g;
Saturated Fat: 0g;
Cholesterol: 0g;
Carbohydrates: 2g;
Fiber: 0g; Protein: 0g;
Sodium: 114mg

This broth can be used in many recipes in this book. A good broth should be deeply flavored and rich, and a good vegetable broth uses ingredients such as celery, onions, and mushrooms to build that great depth of flavor. While you can buy some fairly good boxed broths, the canned ones are usually tinny-tasting and too salty.

4 carrots, chopped

5 celery stalks, chopped

3 yellow onions,
   unpeeled, sliced

4 large tomatoes, chopped

2 cups sliced cremini
   mushrooms

6 garlic cloves, sliced

1 teaspoon sea salt

1 teaspoon black peppercorns

½ teaspoon green peppercorns

1 thyme sprig

1 bay leaf

10 cups water

1. Place all the ingredients in a 5-quart slow cooker. Stir well to combine.
2. Cover and cook on low for 8 to 10 hours, or until the broth tastes rich and well seasoned. Add more salt or thyme to taste.
3. Strain the broth through a fine-mesh strainer into a large container, discarding the solids. Let the broth cool for 20 minutes and refrigerate it in an airtight container.
4. To freeze, portion the cooled broth into 1-cup containers, labeled with the name of the recipe and the date it was made, and freeze them up to 4 months. To use, thaw it in the refrigerator overnight or put the broth straight into a slow cooker to use in a recipe.

Applesauce

GLUTEN-FREE, LOW-CALORIE, VEGAN

Applesauce can serve as a substitute for oil in many baked goods to reduce fat, or it can be used to add flavor to meat dishes. But the best way to enjoy applesauce is when it's slightly chunky and still warm from the slow cooker. Mix it with yogurt and sprinkle it with some granola for a hearty breakfast.

10 tart apples, peeled, cored, and diced

Juice of 1 lemon

1 teaspoon ground cinnamon

⅓ cup water

Pinch sea salt

1. Place all the ingredients in a 4-quart slow cooker and stir to combine.
2. Cover and cook on low for 8 hours, or until the apples are very tender. You can mash them right in the slow cooker or stir them vigorously with a spoon for a chunkier version.
3. Cool and refrigerate the applesauce in an airtight container for up to 4 days. You can freeze the applesauce for up to 5 months.

INGREDIENT TIP: The best tart apples for cooking include Granny Smith, McIntosh, Braeburn, Winesap, and Jonagold. If this sauce is too tart for your family's taste, sweeten it with a spoonful of honey or maple syrup.

PREP TIME:
20 MINUTES

COOK TIME:
8 HOURS ON LOW

SERVES 8

PER SERVING:
Calories: 92; Fat: <1g;
Saturated Fat: 0g;
Cholesterol: 0mg;
Carbohydrates: 25g;
Fiber: 4g; Protein: 1g;
Sodium: <1mg

Apple Butter

GLUTEN-FREE, LOW-CALORIE, VEGAN, WEEKNIGHT HERO

PREP TIME:
5 MINUTES

COOK TIME:
10 HOURS ON LOW

MAKES 5 CUPS

PER 2-TABLESPOON
SERVING:
Calories: 31; Fat: 0g;
Saturated Fat: 0g;
Cholesterol: 0mg;
Carbohydrates: 10g;
Fiber: 1g; Protein: <1g;
Sodium: 3mg

Applesauce can be enjoyed by the bowlful, but apple butter is a concentrated condiment, perfect for adding to appetizer platters along with crisp crackers. The flavors are much sweeter and stronger because of the added sugar as well as the apples' own sugar, which breaks down and caramelizes beautifully during the long, slow cooking time.

6 cups Applesauce (page 265) or store-bought unsweetened applesauce

1 tablespoon ground cinnamon

½ teaspoon ground cloves

¼ teaspoon ground allspice

¾ packed cup brown sugar

1. Place all the ingredients in a 3-quart slow cooker and stir well to combine.
2. Cover and cook on low for 10 hours. If you're home while the apple butter cooks, stir it occasionally, scraping the sides of the slow cooker. This prevents burning and allows steam to escape, which will help the apple flavor condense.
3. The apple butter is done when it is a deep brown color and thick. Let it cool before storing.
4. Refrigerate the apple butter in an airtight container for up to 2 weeks. Freeze it in 1-cup containers for up to 6 months. Thaw it overnight in the refrigerator before serving.

Caramelized Onions

GLUTEN-FREE, LOW-CALORIE, VEGETARIAN, WEEKNIGHT HERO

Caramelized onions are an essential ingredient in many recipes, and the slow cooker is the perfect way to make them! These onions are cooked until they are deep golden brown and are falling apart. They add a rich and slightly sweet taste to recipes and are delicious served on their own.

4 onions, chopped

4 onions, sliced

¼ cup unsalted butter or extra-virgin olive oil

1 teaspoon granulated sugar

1½ teaspoons sea salt

PREP TIME:
15 MINUTES

COOK TIME:
12 HOURS ON LOW

MAKES 8 CUPS

PER ¼-CUP SERVING:
Calories: 24; Fat: 2g;
Saturated Fat: 1g;
Cholesterol: 4mg;
Carbohydrates: 3g;
Fiber: 1g; Protein: <1g;
Sodium: 120mg

1. Place the chopped and sliced onions, butter, sugar, and salt in a 3-quart slow cooker and stir well to combine.
2. Cover and cook on low for 10 hours, or until the onions are soft and brown.
3. Stir the onions, partially cover the slow cooker by adding the lid but leaving it ajar, and cook on low for another 2 hours.
4. Stir the onions again.
5. Let the onions cool; then refrigerate them in an air-tight container for up to 1 week or freeze for up to 3 months.

INGREDIENT TIP: You can use any color of onions in this excellent recipe. Try a combination of yellow, white, and red onions for real depth of flavor.

Red Salsa

GLUTEN-FREE, LOW-CALORIE, VEGAN

PREP TIME:
10 MINUTES

COOK TIME:
6 HOURS ON LOW
OR
3 HOURS ON HIGH

MAKES 3 CUPS

PER ½-CUP SERVING:
Calories: 64; Fat: 1g;
Saturated Fat: <1g;
Cholesterol: 0mg;
Carbohydrates: 14g;
Fiber: 3g; Protein: 3g;
Sodium: 27mg

Fresh raw salsas are delicious, but they can't be made ahead and frozen for later use without losing their bright flavors and crisp textures. This red salsa is cooked, so it freezes well. The recipe can be doubled or tripled, and you can freeze it for up to 3 months without any change in flavor or texture.

3 pounds Roma tomatoes, halved

1 yellow onion, cut into quarters

3 jalapeños, stems removed

2 garlic cloves

1 bunch fresh cilantro, stems removed, divided

Juice of 1 lime

Sea salt

1. Place the tomatoes, onion, jalapeños, and garlic in a 3-quart slow cooker and stir to combine.
2. Cover and cook on low for 6 hours or on high for 3 hours.
3. Pour 2 cups of the salsa into a food processor or blender, add one-third of the cilantro, and pulse the mixture a few times to combine. Pour the salsa into a large bowl and repeat until all the tomato mixture and all the cilantro has been used.
4. Squeeze the lime juice over the salsa and stir gently with a wooden spoon to blend. Season with salt to taste.
5. Refrigerate the salsa in an airtight, nonreactive container for up to 1 week, or freeze it for up to 3 months.

INGREDIENT TIP: Most of the heat in jalapeño peppers is in the seeds and white ribs. If you love spicy food, leave them in. If you like milder salsas, just cut the peppers in half and remove and discard the ribs and seeds. Be sure to wash your hands well after this task because the capsaicin in the peppers can really burn your eyes if you touch them.

Orange-Cranberry Sauce

GLUTEN-FREE, LOW-CALORIE, VEGETARIAN, WEEKNIGHT HERO

Tangy cranberries and sweet citrus blend beautifully in this delicious sauce that's perfect for the holidays. Mixing in chopped nuts adds a little bit of crunch. This recipe makes a good side dish or a tasty dessert or breakfast. It freezes well in single-serving containers, or you can refrigerate it for up to 5 days.

1 pound fresh or frozen whole cranberries

Grated zest of 1 orange

Juice of 2 oranges

½ cup honey

1 teaspoon ground cinnamon

Pinch sea salt

¼ cup chopped walnuts

1. Place the cranberries, orange zest and juice, honey, cinnamon, and salt in a 2-quart slow cooker and stir to combine.
2. Cover and cook on low for 8 hours, or until the cranberries have popped and the sauce is slightly thickened.
3. Stir in the walnuts, transfer the sauce to a bowl, and let it cool for 2 hours. Serve, or refrigerate in an airtight container up to a week. Freeze for longer storage.

PREP TIME:
10 MINUTES

COOK TIME:
8 HOURS ON LOW

SERVES 6

PER SERVING:
Calories: 165; Fat: 3g;
Saturated Fat: <1g;
Cholesterol: 0mg;
Carbohydrates: 36g;
Fiber: 5g; Protein: 1g;
Sodium: 3mg

Barbecue Sauce

GLUTEN-FREE, LOW-CALORIE, VEGAN

Slather this sweet and savory homemade barbecue sauce on burgers or grilled tofu, dip fries in it, or use it for cooking beef or pork ribs. It's convenient to have on hand, and it will taste better than any commercial barbecue sauce. You can add more herbs and spices to this recipe if you'd like; a teaspoon each of dried basil and thyme would be delicious. It's a great one to play with and make it your own.

2 (15-ounce) cans tomato sauce

½ cup apple cider vinegar

2 cups water

¼ packed cup vegan dark brown sugar

1 teaspoon ground mustard

1 teaspoon onion powder

1 teaspoon garlic powder

2 tablespoons vegan Worcestershire sauce

1. Place the tomato sauce, vinegar, and water in a 3-quart slow cooker and stir well to combine.

2. In a medium bowl, whisk together the brown sugar, mustard, onion powder, and garlic powder. Whisk in the Worcestershire sauce and a tablespoon or two of the tomato mixture from the slow cooker until there are no lumps. Stir the brown sugar mixture into the tomato mixture in the slow cooker.

3. Cover and cook on low for 6 hours, stirring occasionally if you are home.

INGREDIENT TIP: Most barbecue sauces are spicier than this recipe, which is quite mild. If you like a spicy barbecue sauce, add 1 or 2 minced jalapeño peppers and ⅛ to ¼ teaspoon of cayenne pepper.

PREP TIME:
10 MINUTES

COOK TIME:
6 HOURS ON LOW

MAKES 6 CUPS

PER ¼-CUP SERVING:
Calories: 24; Fat: <1g; Saturated Fat: 0g; Cholesterol: 0mg; Carbohydrates: 7g; Fiber: 1g; Protein: 1g; Sodium: 231mg

**Dark Chocolate
Brownies,** page 278

CHAPTER 11

DESSERTS

Almond Blueberry-Peach Cobbler

GLUTEN-FREE, VEGAN

A vegan dessert that is also gluten-free is not easy to come by. But no one will miss the butter (or gluten, for that matter) in this delicious recipe. Serve this dessert with a scoop of lemon gelato for a perfect end to the meal.

5 tablespoons coconut oil, divided

3 large fresh peaches, peeled and sliced

2 cups frozen blueberries

1 cup almond flour

1 cup rolled oats

1 tablespoon pure maple syrup

1 tablespoon coconut sugar

1 teaspoon ground cinnamon

½ teaspoon pure vanilla extract

Pinch ground nutmeg

PREP TIME:
15 MINUTES

COOK TIME:
2 HOURS ON HIGH

SERVES 4

PER SERVING:
Calories: 515; Fat: 34g;
Saturated Fat: 17g;
Cholesterol: 0mg;
Carbohydrates: 49g;
Fiber: 10g; Protein: 10g;
Sodium: 1mg

1. Grease the bottom of a 3-quart slow cooker with 1 tablespoon of coconut oil.
2. Arrange the peaches and blueberries in the bottom of the slow cooker.
3. In a small bowl, stir together the almond flour, oats, remaining 4 tablespoons of coconut oil, maple syrup, coconut sugar, cinnamon, vanilla extract, and nutmeg until crumbly. Gently crumble the topping over the fruit in the slow cooker.
4. Place 3 paper towels on the top of the slow cooker to absorb moisture, and cover. Cook on high for 2 hours, until the fruits are bubbly. Serve.

INGREDIENT TIP: Not all oats are gluten-free. Although the oat grain itself doesn't contain gluten, some oats are processed on the same equipment as wheat. Make sure to read the labels so you know that the oats you buy are gluten-free.

Rice Pudding

GLUTEN-FREE

PREP TIME:
10 MINUTES

COOK TIME:
1 HOUR ON HIGH

SERVES 4

PER SERVING:
Calories: 542; Fat: 20g;
Saturated Fat: 12g;
Cholesterol: 149mg;
Carbohydrates: 79g;
Fiber: 2g; Protein: 12g;
Sodium: 129mg

Tender and sweet rice pudding is an old-fashioned treat. The slow cooker is the absolute best cooking method for making rice pudding. The even and low heating allows the starches in the rice to thicken the half-and-half to the perfect consistency.

1 tablespoon unsalted butter, at room temperature

4 cups cooked long-grain white rice

2 large eggs, whisked

2 cups half-and-half

1 tablespoon pure vanilla extract

½ teaspoon ground cinnamon

Pinch sea salt

1 cup raisins

1. Grease the bottom and partially up the sides of a 3-quart slow cooker with the butter.
2. In a large bowl, combine the rice, eggs, half-and-half, vanilla extract, cinnamon, salt, and raisins. Mix well. Pour this mixture into the slow cooker.
3. Cover and cook on high for 1 hour, or until the rice is tender and the liquid is absorbed.
4. Remove the lid and let cool for at least 30 minutes before serving.

Cinnamon-Pecan Stuffed Apples

GLUTEN-FREE, LOW-CALORIE, VEGETARIAN

This recipe resembles an inside-out apple pie, but it is much lower in carbs and saturated fat given that the "crust" is made of walnuts, cinnamon, and just a hint of brown sugar. The aroma this recipe produces is just intoxicating and will remind you of the holiday season.

½ cup chopped pecans

2 tablespoons vegan
   brown sugar

1 teaspoon ground cinnamon

¼ teaspoon ground nutmeg

Pinch sea salt

4 apples

2 teaspoons unsalted butter

½ cup apple cider

PREP TIME:
15 MINUTES

COOK TIME:
5 HOURS ON LOW

SERVES 4

PER SERVING:
Calories: 226; Fat: 13g;
Saturated Fat: 2g;
Cholesterol: 5mg;
Carbohydrates: 31g;
Fiber: 5g; Protein: 2g;
Sodium: 62mg

1. In a small bowl, combine the pecans, brown sugar, cinnamon, nutmeg, and salt.
2. Peel a strip around the top of each apple to prevent them from splitting as they cook. Using an apple corer, remove the core from the top and discard.
3. In a 3-quart slow cooker, place the apples upright. (You may need to slice a little off the base to help them stand up straight.) Gently stuff the apples with the sugar mixture. Dot the tops with ½ teaspoon of butter each.
4. Gently pour the apple cider around the bottom of the apples.
5. Cover and cook on low for 5 hours, or until the apples are tender and fragrant.

Dark Chocolate Brownies

LOW-CALORIE, VEGETARIAN

PREP TIME:
20 MINUTES

COOK TIME:
4 HOURS ON LOW,
PLUS 3 HOURS
COOLING TIME

SERVES 16

PER SERVING:
Calories: 291; Fat: 17g;
Saturated Fat: 10g;
Cholesterol: 50mg;
Carbohydrates: 37g;
Fiber: 3g; Protein: 3g;
Sodium: 131mg

When the cooking time is up, these brownies will still look pretty raw. Don't worry, they'll continue to cook in the retained heat of the slow cooker. Let them cool for at least 3 hours before serving, no matter how tempted you are to eat one.

Nonstick cooking spray

1¼ cups all-purpose flour

¼ cup unsweetened extra-dark cocoa powder

¾ teaspoon baking powder

½ teaspoon sea salt

8 ounces bittersweet chocolate, chopped

½ cup unsalted butter, cut into small pieces

1 cup granulated sugar

3 large eggs, beaten

1 cup dark chocolate chips

1. Spray a 3-quart slow cooker with nonstick cooking spray, line the bottom with parchment paper, and then spray the parchment paper.
2. In a medium bowl, whisk together the flour, cocoa powder, baking powder, and salt. Set aside.
3. In a large microwave-safe bowl, microwave the bittersweet chocolate and butter until the mixture is melted, stirring every 30 seconds.
4. Stir the sugar into the melted chocolate mixture and then mix in the beaten eggs.
5. Add the dry ingredients and chocolate chips to the wet ingredients and fold them in just until moistened. Do not overmix. Spoon the batter into the slow cooker.

6. Cover and cook on low for 3½ hours; then remove the lid and cook for another 30 minutes.
7. Remove the crock insert from the base. Run a knife around the edge of the brownies to loosen them. Let them cool in the crock for about 3 hours. The brownies won't look done at first, but they will be perfect after 3 hours of cooling.

Pears Poached in Spiced Wine

GLUTEN-FREE, LOW-CALORIE, VEGAN

PREP TIME:
10 MINUTES

COOK TIME:
4 HOURS ON LOW

SERVES 6

PER SERVING:
Calories: 222; Fat: <1g;
Saturated Fat: 0g;
Cholesterol: 0mg;
Carbohydrates: 35g;
Fiber: 5g; Protein: 1g;
Sodium: 7mg

During the holiday season, instead of serving a heavy, high-carb dessert after dinner, try these spiced poached pears, perhaps with some gelato or sorbet for a cooling contrast. They're warming, sophisticated, and oh-so-easy in the slow cooker.

1 (750-ml) bottle dry red wine, such as pinot noir or Shiraz
¼ cup brown sugar
1 orange, thinly sliced

4 (3-inch) cinnamon sticks
2 whole star anise pods
6 ripe pears, peeled and left whole with the stem on

1. Place the wine, brown sugar, orange slices, cinnamon sticks, and star anise in a 4-quart slow cooker. Stir well to combine.
2. Using a paring knife, slice the bottom off each pear to create a flat surface so they can stand upright. Place the pears in the slow cooker.
3. Cover and cook on low for 4 hours, or until the pears are tender, fragrant, and a brilliant dark red.

GAME PLAN: Don't discard the cooking liquid in this recipe. Remove and discard the orange slices and star anise. You can freeze this liquid to make this recipe again or use it to poach other fruits.

Bananas Foster

LOW-CALORIE, VEGETARIAN

Bananas Foster is an old-fashioned, spectacular dish that is popular in many classic restaurants. The recipe is typically set aflame tableside, but you don't have to do that. Serve this rich recipe, sauce and all, over vanilla ice cream and top with toasted pecans for a bit of crunch.

½ cup (1 stick) unsalted butter, melted

¼ packed cup brown sugar

½ teaspoon ground cinnamon

¼ teaspoon ground nutmeg

4 nearly ripe but firm bananas, peeled and halved lengthwise

¼ cup dark rum

PREP TIME:
10 MINUTES

COOK TIME:
2 HOURS ON LOW,
PLUS 15 MINUTES

SERVES 4

PER SERVING:
Calories: 394; Fat: 23g;
Saturated Fat: 15g;
Cholesterol: 62mg;
Carbohydrates: 46g;
Fiber: 3g; Protein: 2g;
Sodium: 171mg

1. Pour the melted butter into a 3-quart slow cooker and whisk in the brown sugar, cinnamon, and nutmeg.
2. Place the bananas in the slow cooker in a single layer. Turn to coat them evenly in the butter and spice mixture.
3. Cover and cook on low for 2 hours, or until the bananas are very tender and the sauce is slightly thickened.
4. Pour in the rum and stir to combine. Some of the bananas may break up and that's okay. Cover and cook for 15 minutes more; then serve.

Salted Almond-Caramel Sauce

GLUTEN-FREE, LOW-CALORIE, VEGETARIAN, WEEKNIGHT HERO

PREP TIME:
10 MINUTES

COOK TIME:
8 TO 9 HOURS
ON LOW

SERVES 16

PER SERVING:
Calories: 214; Fat: 8g;
Saturated Fat: 3g;
Cholesterol: 13mg;
Carbohydrates: 31g;
Fiber: 1g; Protein: 5g;
Sodium: 199mg

INGREDIENT TIP:
If you don't like
the flavor of
almonds, you can
still make this
recipe. Use dairy
butter in place of
the almond butter
and use whole
milk in place of
the almond milk.

Salted caramel sauce is a trendy flavor—but the best kind of trend. It's delicious on everything from ice cream to pound cake to rice pudding. Some people even eat it straight from the refrigerator with a spoon! But did you know you can make this sweet sauce in the slow cooker? You can, and you won't be sorry about it—not one bit.

2 (14-ounce) cans sweetened condensed milk

¼ cup almond butter

¼ cup almond milk

1 teaspoon sea salt

¼ cup amaretto liqueur (optional) or more almond milk

4 teaspoons pure vanilla extract, divided

1. In a large bowl, whisk together the condensed milk, almond butter, almond milk, salt, and amaretto liqueur (if using) until smooth.
2. Divide the mixture between 2 pint-size heatproof canning jars with lids. Make sure there is at least ½ inch of headspace in the jars. Seal them tightly.
3. Place the jars in a 4-quart slow cooker and pour in enough water so the jars are completely covered by 1 inch over the top.
4. Cover and cook on low for 8 to 9 hours.
5. Turn off the slow cooker and, using tongs and hot pads, carefully remove the hot jars from the water. Set them on a wire rack to cool. Once they are cool enough to remove the lids, stir 2 teaspoons of the vanilla extract into each jar.
6. Cover tightly again and refrigerate for up to 3 months. Use some sauce in a recipe, or heat it in the microwave and drizzle over your favorite dessert.

Pumpkin Bread Pudding

VEGETARIAN

It's all about the pumpkin in this bread pudding—
pumpkin bread, puréed pumpkin, and pumpkin butter.
Serve it for Thanksgiving for an excellent dessert and a
nice change from pumpkin pie.

1 loaf store-bought
  pumpkin bread, cubed

1 cup dried cranberries

1 cup canned solid-pack
  pumpkin purée (not
  pumpkin pie filling)

1 cup half-and-half

¼ cup pumpkin butter

½ cup brown sugar

2 large eggs

2 large egg yolks

⅓ cup unsalted butter, melted

2 teaspoons ground cinnamon

⅛ teaspoon ground nutmeg

⅛ teaspoon sea salt

1 cup Salted Almond-Caramel
  Sauce (page 282, optional)

Ice cream, for serving (optional)

PREP TIME:
25 MINUTES

COOK TIME:
4 TO 6 HOURS
ON LOW

SERVES 8

PER SERVING:
Calories: 506; Fat: 16g;
Saturated Fat: 9g;
Cholesterol: 125mg;
Carbohydrates: 74g;
Fiber: 4g; Protein: 7g;
Sodium: 394mg

1. Place the pumpkin bread and dried cranberries in a
   3½-quart slow cooker.

2. In a large bowl, mix the pumpkin purée with
   the half-and-half until smooth.

3. Stir in the pumpkin butter, brown sugar, eggs,
   egg yolks, butter, cinnamon, nutmeg, and salt
   and mix until smooth. Pour the mixture into the
   slow cooker, making sure all the bread cubes are
   covered.

4. Cover and cook on low for 4 to 6 hours, or until a
   food thermometer registers 160°F.

5. Serve the pudding warm with the caramel sauce
   and ice cream, if you like.

Chocolate Hazelnut Bread Pudding

VEGETARIAN

PREP TIME:
30 MINUTES

COOK TIME:
40 MINUTES IN
THE OVEN, PLUS 4
HOURS ON LOW,
PLUS 35 MINUTES
COOLING TIME

SERVES 8 TO 10

PER SERVING:
Calories: 933; Fat: 50g;
Saturated Fat: 25g;
Cholesterol: 314mg;
Carbohydrates: 113g;
Fiber: 4g; Protein: 15g;
Sodium: 496mg

The addition of chocolate chips gives this recipe an extra flavor boost along with the rich, creamy chocolate-hazelnut spread. Once cooked, the chocolate chips melt and become gooey. If you cannot find challah bread, use any other firm, high-quality sandwich bread instead. If your bread is stale, that's better still because you can skip toasting the bread.

Nonstick baking spray with flour

14 ounces challah bread, cut into 1-inch cubes (about 12 cups)

1 cup semisweet chocolate chips

2 cups heavy (whipping) cream

2 cups whole milk

9 large egg yolks

1 cup chocolate-hazelnut spread (like Nutella)

¾ cup plus 1 tablespoon granulated sugar, divided

1 tablespoon pure vanilla extract

¾ teaspoon sea salt

2 tablespoons light brown sugar

1. Line a 4-quart slow cooker with aluminum foil; then coat the foil with the baking spray.
2. Adjust the oven rack to the middle position. Preheat the oven to 225°F.
3. Spread the bread cubes over a baking sheet and bake, shaking the pan occasionally, until dry and crisp, about 40 minutes. Let the bread cool for 5 minutes; then place the bread cubes in the slow cooker.
4. Mix the chocolate chips into the dried bread cubes.
5. In a large bowl, whisk together the cream, milk, egg yolks, chocolate hazelnut spread, ¾ cup of granulated sugar, vanilla extract, and salt. Pour the mixture evenly over the bread cubes. Press gently on the bread cubes to submerge them in the cream mixture.

6. Mix the remaining 1 tablespoon of granulated sugar with the brown sugar in a small bowl; then sprinkle it over the top of the bread cube mixture.
7. Cover and cook on low for about 4 hours, until the center is set and reads at least 160°F on a food thermometer.
8. Uncover and let cool for 30 minutes. You can remove the bread pudding from the slow cooker by pulling it up by the foil edges and then placing it in a large shallow bowl or serving it straight from the slow cooker, warm or chilled. Refrigerate the leftovers in an airtight container for up to 4 days.

GAME PLAN: If you have leftovers of this wonderful bread pudding, you can reheat individual servings in the microwave oven. Place the bread pudding in a bowl and microwave on 50 percent power for 3 to 5 minutes, until the pudding is steaming hot.

Sour Cream Amaretti Cheesecake

GLUTEN-FREE, VEGETARIAN

PREP TIME:
20 MINUTES

COOK TIME:
3 HOURS ON HIGH,
PLUS 3 HOURS TO
CHILL

SERVES 6

PER SERVING:
Calories: 520; Fat: 35g;
Saturated Fat: 21g;
Cholesterol: 154mg;
Carbohydrates: 43g;
Fiber: 1g; Protein: 9g;
Sodium: 411mg

Cheesecake is wonderful cooked in a slow cooker because the cooker steams it throughout the cooking process, keeping the texture velvety. This recipe is particularly delicious and rich thanks to the presence of sour cream and amaretti cookies in place of the standard graham cracker crust. You'll need a slow cooker that has a steaming rack and will accommodate a 6-inch springform pan.

¾ cup amaretti cookie crumbs (around 3 ounces or 20 cookies, crushed)

2½ tablespoons unsalted butter, melted

½ teaspoon sea salt, divided

¼ teaspoon ground cinnamon

⅔ cup plus 1 tablespoon granulated sugar, divided

1½ (8-ounce) packages cream cheese, at room temperature

1 tablespoon cornstarch

2 large eggs

1 teaspoon almond or pure vanilla extract

1 cup sour cream

1. In a medium bowl, mix together the cookie crumbs, melted butter, ¼ teaspoon of salt, cinnamon, and 1 tablespoon of sugar. Press the crumb mixture into a 6-inch springform pan, covering the bottom of the pan and going about 1 inch up the side of the pan.
2. In a medium bowl, combine the cream cheese, cornstarch, the remaining ⅔ cup of sugar, and the remaining ¼ teaspoon of salt. Using an electric mixer, beat at medium-high speed until smooth.
3. Scrape down the sides of bowl. Add the eggs and the almond extract. Beat until blended.
4. Add the sour cream and beat until smooth.
5. Pour the batter into the cookie crumb crust in the springform pan.
6. Fill a 5-quart slow cooker with ½ inch of water and place the steaming rack in the bottom, making sure

the top of the rack is above the water. Set the spring-form pan on the rack. Cover the slow cooker with a triple layer of paper towels, and then cover with the lid. Cook on high for 2 hours without opening the slow cooker even once.

7. Turn off the heat and let stand until the cooker has cooled, again without opening lid, for at least 1 additional hour.

8. Remove the cheesecake and chill in the refrigerator for about 3 hours before slicing and serving.

INGREDIENT TIP: To make sure this recipe is gluten-free, use traditional amaretti cookies, which are made without flour. Be sure to read the label carefully before buying the cookies. If you don't mind gluten in this recipe, you can use the same amount of crushed graham crackers or vanilla wafers.

Key Lime Pots de Crème

GLUTEN-FREE, LOW-CALORIE, VEGETARIAN

PREP TIME:
10 MINUTES

COOK TIME:
2 HOURS ON HIGH,
PLUS 3 HOURS
COOLING TIME

SERVES 6

PER SERVING:
Calories: 293; Fat: 12g;
Saturated Fat: 7g;
Cholesterol: 150mg;
Carbohydrates: 39g;
Fiber: 0g; Protein: 7g;
Sodium: 79mg

Key lime pie is a delicious finish to almost any Mexican meal, but when you don't have the time to make a pie from scratch, give this recipe a try. The flavor is very much like Key lime pie, but there is a little kick of tequila that is unmistakable. The slow cooker creates a texture that is so silky and creamy that everyone will wonder how you did it.

2 tablespoons unsalted butter

4 large egg yolks

1 (14-ounce) can sweetened condensed milk

½ cup Key lime juice

2 teaspoons grated lime zest, plus more for serving

1 tablespoon tequila

Whipped cream, for serving

1. Grease 6 (4-ounce) ramekins or pots de crème cups with the butter.
2. In a medium bowl, whisk together the egg yolks and the condensed milk until well blended. Add the lime juice, lime zest, and tequila, and stir until smooth and well blended.
3. Place a folded tea towel on the bottom of a 4-quart slow cooker.
4. Pour the lime mixture into the ramekins and arrange them on the towel in the slow cooker.
5. Carefully pour warm water around the ramekins in the slow cooker until it reaches halfway up the sides of the ramekins. (Make sure the water reaches no more than halfway up the sides; it will ruin the pots de crème if it splashes into the ramekins.) Lay a clean kitchen towel over the top of the slow cooker and secure the lid on top of the towel.
6. Cook on high for 2 hours, or until a food thermometer registers at least 160°F.

7. Remove the ramekins using tongs or hot pads. Let them cool on a wire rack at room temperature for 1 hour, and then refrigerate them for at least 3 hours.
8. Top with a dollop of whipped cream and a sprinkling of lime zest before serving.

INGREDIENT TIP: Key lime juice is more floral than regular lime juice. You can sometimes find fresh ones in the produce section or bottled juice in the refrigerated section. If you can't find either, substitute ⅓ cup of regular fresh lime juice and 2½ tablespoons of orange juice.

Crème Brûlée

VEGETARIAN

Crème brûlée is the ultimate pudding. The texture is rich and velvety, topped with a thin crackling sugar crust. The slow cooker provides a perfect environment for this dish with low and even heat.

1 cup heavy (whipping) cream

1 cup half-and-half

4 large egg yolks

½ packed cup brown sugar

1 teaspoon pure vanilla extract

4 tablespoons granulated sugar

1. In a bowl, whisk the heavy cream, half-and-half, egg yolks, brown sugar, and vanilla extract. Divide the mixture among 4 (8-ounce) ramekins.

2. Pour 2 cups of hot water into the bottom of a 3½-quart slow cooker. Gently set the ramekins in the water. If the water doesn't come halfway up the sides of the ramekins, carefully add up to a cup more, making sure no water gets into the ramekins. Lay three paper towels over the top of the slow cooker and secure the lid on top of the towels.

3. Cover and cook on high for 2 hours. Test for doneness by jiggling one of the ramekins with a spoon. The top should be nearly set. If it is not, cover and cook for 15 minutes before checking again.

4. Using sturdy tongs, with a kitchen mitt on your other hand, carefully transfer the ramekins to a wire rack to cool for 1 hour; then transfer to the refrigerator to cool and set completely.

PREP TIME:
15 MINUTES

COOK TIME:
2¼ HOURS ON HIGH, PLUS COOLING TIME

SERVES 4

PER SERVING:
Calories: 521; Fat: 33g; Saturated Fat: 20g; Cholesterol: 290mg; Carbohydrates: 57g; Fiber: 0g; Protein: 6g; Sodium: 66mg

CONTINUED

Crème Brûlée CONTINUED

5. Just before serving, sprinkle the top of each of the custards evenly with 1 tablespoon sugar. Use a kitchen torch to caramelize the sugar, or you can place the ramekins on a baking sheet and broil them on high for a minute or two until the sugar browns and melts. Serve immediately.

Butterscotch-Chocolate Fondue

GLUTEN-FREE, VEGETARIAN

Fondue is a fun recipe to make for entertaining, and the slow cooker is the perfect appliance to use. Everyone gathers around the table and spears cookies, fruit chunks, waffle sticks, and pieces of cake to dip into this rich sauce.

½ cup unsalted butter, at room temperature

2 cups brown sugar

⅓ cup cocoa powder

1 cup semisweet chocolate chips

1 (14-ounce) can sweetened condensed milk

1 cup butterscotch ice cream sauce

2 teaspoons pure vanilla extract

¼ teaspoon sea salt

½ cup water

PREP TIME:
15 MINUTES

COOK TIME:
2 TO 3 HOURS
ON LOW

SERVES 8 TO 10

PER SERVING:
Calories: 670; Fat: 24g;
Saturated Fat: 15g;
Cholesterol: 50mg;
Carbohydrates: 127g;
Fiber: 3g; Protein: 6g;
Sodium: 395mg

1. In an 8-cup bowl that will fit inside a 4- to 5-quart slow cooker, combine the butter, brown sugar, cocoa powder, chocolate chips, condensed milk, butterscotch sauce, vanilla extract, and salt.
2. Place the bowl in the slow cooker and add the water to the bottom of the slow cooker, creating a bath around the bowl.
3. Cover and cook on low for 2 to 3 hours, stirring the mixture occasionally, until the sauce is smooth.

GAME PLAN: If you have any of this fondue left over, refrigerate it in an airtight container for up to one week. Heat some sauce in the microwave and pour it over ice cream, sorbet, or fresh fruit, or drizzle it over a piece of toast spread with cream cheese.

MEASUREMENT CONVERSIONS

	US STANDARD	US STANDARD (OUNCES)	METRIC (APPROXIMATE)
VOLUME EQUIVALENTS (LIQUID)	2 tablespoons	1 fl. oz.	30 mL
	¼ cup	2 fl. oz.	60 mL
	½ cup	4 fl. oz.	120 mL
	1 cup	8 fl. oz.	240 mL
	1½ cups	12 fl. oz.	355 mL
	2 cups or 1 pint	16 fl. oz.	475 mL
	4 cups or 1 quart	32 fl. oz.	1 L
	1 gallon	128 fl. oz.	4 L
VOLUME EQUIVALENTS (DRY)	⅛ teaspoon	——	0.5 mL
	¼ teaspoon	——	1 mL
	½ teaspoon	——	2 mL
	¾ teaspoon	——	4 mL
	1 teaspoon	——	5 mL
	1 tablespoon	——	15 mL
	¼ cup	——	59 mL
	⅓ cup	——	79 mL
	½ cup	——	118 mL
	⅔ cup	——	156 mL
	¾ cup	——	177 mL
	1 cup	——	235 mL
	2 cups or 1 pint	——	475 mL
	3 cups	——	700 mL
	4 cups or 1 quart	——	1 L
	½ gallon	——	2 L
	1 gallon	——	4 L
WEIGHT EQUIVALENTS	½ ounce	——	15 g
	1 ounce	——	30 g
	2 ounces	——	60 g
	4 ounces	——	115 g
	8 ounces	——	225 g
	12 ounces	——	340 g
	16 ounces or 1 pound	——	455 g

	FAHRENHEIT (F)	CELSIUS (C) (APPROXIMATE)
OVEN TEMPERATURES	250°F	120°C
	300°F	150°C
	325°F	180°C
	375°F	190°C
	400°F	200°C
	425°F	220°C
	450°F	230°C

INDEX

ABOUT THE EDITOR

 **Linda Larsen** is an author and home economist who has been developing recipes for years. She was the Busy Cooks Guide for About.com for 15 years, writing about how to cook, food safety, and quick cooking. She has written 43 cookbooks since 2005, including *The Complete Air Fryer Cookbook, The Complete Slow Cooking for Two Cookbook*, and *Eating Clean for Dummies*. Linda has worked for the Pillsbury Company since 1988, creating and testing recipes and working for the Pillsbury Bake-Off. She holds a BA in biology from St. Olaf College and a BS with High Distinction in food science and nutrition from the University of Minnesota. She lives in Minnesota with her husband.

CPSIA information can be obtained
at www.ICGtesting.com
Printed in the USA
JSHW041027010520
5444JS00005B/6

9 781646 117413